EDUCATION in America

OPPOSING VIEWPOINTS®

Other Books of Related Interest in the Opposing Viewpoints Series:

EDUCATION in America

OPPOSING
VIEWPOINTS®

David L. Bender & Bruno Leone, *Series Editors*

Charles P. Cozic, *Book Editor*

OPPOSING VIEWPOINTS SERIES ®

Greenhaven Press, Inc.   PO Box 289009   San Diego, CA 92198-0009

Library of Congress Cataloging-in-Publication Data

Education in America : opposing viewpoints / Charles P. Cozic,
book editor.
    p.   cm. — (Opposing viewpoints series)
  Includes bibliographical references and index.
  ISBN 0-89908-188-6 (lib.) . —ISBN 0-89908-163-0 (pbk.)
    1. Education—United States—Philosophy. 2. Education—
United States—Aims and objectives. I. Cozic, Charles P.,
1957- . II. Series.
LA217.2.E36 1992
370'.973—dc20   91-42495

"Congress shall make no law . . . abridging the freedom of speech, or of the press."

First Amendment to the U.S. Constitution

The basic foundation of our democracy is the first amendment guarantee of freedom of expression. The Opposing Viewpoints Series is dedicated to the concept of this basic freedom and the idea that it is more important to practice it than to enshrine it.

Contents

Why Consider Opposing Viewpoints?

"It is better to debate a question without settling it than to settle a question without debating it."

Joseph Joubert (1754-1824)

The Importance of Examining Opposing Viewpoints

The purpose of the Opposing Viewpoints Series, and this book in particular, is to present balanced, and often difficult to find, opposing points of view on complex and sensitive issues.

Probably the best way to become informed is to analyze the positions of those who are regarded as experts and well studied on issues. It is important to consider every variety of opinion in an attempt to determine the truth. Opinions from the mainstream of society should be examined. But also important are opinions that are considered radical, reactionary, or minority as well as those stigmatized by some other uncomplimentary label. An important lesson of history is the eventual acceptance of many unpopular and even despised opinions. The ideas of Socrates, Jesus, and Galileo are good examples of this.

Readers will approach this book with their own opinions on the issues debated within it. However, to have a good grasp of one's own viewpoint, it is necessary to understand the arguments of those with whom one disagrees. It can be said that those who do not completely understand their adversary's point of view do not fully understand their own.

A persuasive case for considering opposing viewpoints has been presented by John Stuart Mill in his work *On Liberty*. When examining controversial issues it may be helpful to reflect on this suggestion:

The only way in which a human being can make some approach to knowing the whole of a subject, is by hearing what can be said about it by persons of every variety of opinion, and studying all modes in which it can be looked at by every character of mind. No wise man ever acquired his wisdom in any mode but this.

Analyzing Sources of Information

The Opposing Viewpoints Series includes diverse materials taken from magazines, journals, books, and newspapers, as well as statements and position papers from a wide range of individuals, organizations, and governments. This broad spectrum of sources helps to develop patterns of thinking which are open to the consideration of a variety of opinions.

Pitfalls to Avoid

A pitfall to avoid in considering opposing points of view is that of regarding one's own opinion as being common sense and the most rational stance, and the point of view of others as being only opinion and naturally wrong. It may be that another's opinion is correct and one's own is in error.

Another pitfall to avoid is that of closing one's mind to the opinions of those with whom one disagrees. The best way to approach a dialogue is to make one's primary purpose that of understanding the mind and arguments of the other person and not that of enlightening him or her with one's own solutions. More can be learned by listening than speaking.

It is my hope that after reading this book the reader will have a deeper understanding of the issues debated and will appreciate the complexity of even seemingly simple issues on which good and honest people disagree. This awareness is particularly important in a democratic society such as ours where people enter into public debate to determine the common good. Those with whom one disagrees should not necessarily be regarded as enemies, but perhaps simply as people who suggest different paths to a common goal.

Developing Basic Reading and Thinking Skills

In this book, carefully edited opposing viewpoints are purposely placed back to back to create a running debate; each viewpoint is preceded by a short quotation that best expresses the author's main argument. This format instantly plunges the reader into the midst of a controversial issue and greatly aids that reader in mastering the basic skill of recognizing an author's point of view.

A number of basic skills for critical thinking are practiced in the activities that appear throughout the books in the series. Some of the skills are:

Evaluating Sources of Information. The ability to choose from among alternative sources the most reliable and accurate source in relation to a given subject.

Separating Fact from Opinion. The ability to make the basic distinction between factual statements (those that can be demonstrated or verified empirically) and statements of opinion (those that are beliefs or attitudes that cannot be proved).

Identifying Stereotypes. The ability to identify oversimplified, exaggerated descriptions (favorable or unfavorable) about people and insulting statements about racial, religious, or national groups, based upon misinformation or lack of information.

Recognizing Ethnocentrism. The ability to recognize attitudes or opinions that express the view that one's own race, culture, or group is inherently superior, or those attitudes that judge another culture or group in terms of one's own.

It is important to consider opposing viewpoints and equally important to be able to critically analyze those viewpoints. The activities in this book are designed to help the reader master these thinking skills. Statements are taken from the book's viewpoints and the reader is asked to analyze them. This technique aids the reader in developing skills that not only can be applied to the viewpoints in this book, but also to situations where opinionated spokespersons comment on controversial issues. Although the activities are helpful to the solitary reader, they are most useful when the reader can benefit from the interaction of group discussion.

Using this book and others in the series should help readers develop basic reading and thinking skills. These skills should improve the reader's ability to understand what is read. Readers should be better able to separate fact from opinion, substance from rhetoric, and become better consumers of information in our media-centered culture.

This volume of the Opposing Viewpoints Series does not advocate a particular point of view. Quite the contrary! The very nature of the book leaves it to the reader to formulate the opinions he or she finds most suitable. My purpose as publisher is to see that this is made possible by offering a wide range of viewpoints that are fairly presented.

David L. Bender
Publisher

Introduction

"The educational foundations of our society are presently being eroded by a rising tide of mediocrity that threatens our very future as a Nation and a people."

National Commission on Excellence in
Education, *A Nation at Risk*, 1983.

American education is in crisis. According to most critics—from the 1983 government report *A Nation at Risk*, to the analyses of scholars, to the commonly heard complaints of parents—the quality of education has deteriorated in the past twenty-five years. From 1965 to 1985, average SAT scores of college-bound seniors fell sixteen points on the math portion of the test and thirty points on the verbal. In addition, the number of high school drop-outs has increased dramatically: In 1987, more than one-fourth of American high school students did not graduate. As former secretary of education Lauro F. Cavazos states, "By any measure one wishes to apply, we are failing or not making progress" in education.

Debates concerning the reasons for the failure of education run the gamut. Many believe it is the educational system itself that is to blame. While some critics believe schools need more money, others believe that teachers are not doing their jobs. Still others, like Albert Shanker, president of the American Federation of Teachers, believe that reforms must go even further than addressing funding and teacher quality. Shanker argues for vast reforms to the entire structure of the public education system, including reorganizing school management, decreasing the government's involvement in schools, and increasing involvement of parents and communities. As Shanker asserts, "We can't fix the system. We need radical change."

Others argue that it is the quality of students, and not the system, that has deteriorated. These critics believe that changes in the family and society, such as the increase in divorce, in poverty, and in the number of children with two working parents, have caused children's lives to become increasingly unstable and insecure. This in turn has made it more difficult for

13

children to learn. These problems affect millions of American schoolchildren. In addition, some children face monumental problems such as physical abuse and neglect, substance abuse, and crime. A student from a poverty-stricken, abusive, single-parent home who arrives at school inadequately dressed and underfed will have difficulty concentrating on his or her studies, regardless of the caliber of the teacher, the school, or the curriculum. As Ann Reilly Dowd, associate editor for *Fortune*, explains, "An epidemic of social ills from drug abuse to homelessness continues to distract youngsters from the business of learning."

This broad range of concerns reveals that there is no quick solution to the nation's educational problems. Perhaps this is why the crisis in education continues to seem insurmountable, despite the number of studies written, speeches made, and programs created to address it. But while the crisis may seem overwhelming, it must be addressed. The United States already has twenty-seven million illiterate adults. Most analysts agree that if something is not done, the number of unskilled workers will climb and eventually will threaten the nation's prosperity. As Massachusetts governor John Silber states, "Our public schools are in terrible trouble, and their disarray threatens our nation's ability to compete economically just as it hinders our students' ability to achieve personal fulfillment."

Education in America: Opposing Viewpoints examines how education can be improved for this and future generations of America's youth. The authors debate many of the most discussed issues in education: How Can Public Education Be Improved? How Can the Teaching Profession Be Improved? Should Parents Be Allowed to Choose Their Children's Schools? Should Education for Minority Students Emphasize Ethnicity? What Role Should Religion Play in Public Education? What Is the State of Higher Education? The viewpoints presented should give readers added insight into the complexity of the educational crisis and into the necessity to find remedies for it.

1

How Can Public Education Be Improved?

EDUCATION in America

Chapter Preface

In 1991, the average SAT verbal score of American students was 422 out of a possible 800 points, the lowest since the test was introduced in 1926, according to the College Board, producers of the SAT. Also, the U.S. government reports that half of the nation's eighth graders now perform at a fifth-grade level in math. Statistics such as these have led many people to conclude that public schools are faltering, perhaps even failing.

As experts try to find ways to improve school performance, a common proposal is to increase funding. Many educators believe that these monies could be used to raise teacher salaries, hire more teachers, and buy much-needed classroom materials, such as books and charts.

While it is clear that schools need more teachers and materials, however, many Americans question whether money alone can solve the complex problems faced by the educational system. These people argue that an important first step in reform is to decrease government authority over public schools. This would allow local schools to gain more control over decisions involving curriculum, personnel, and purchasing. Schools would be able to target specific problems with specific solutions, rather than waiting for the government to act.

Still others believe the solution lies in improving communication between teachers, administrators, and parents, allowing these parties to work together in the best interests of students. These tasks, however, are not easily accomplished.

Clearly, the educational system must manage a host of complex problems. How well it does so will have important consequences for the education of young people and their future.

"The school institution 'schools' very well, but it does not 'educate'."

Public Education Needs Extensive Reform

John Taylor Gatto

Many Americans are dissatisfied with the education system in the U.S. They cite high dropout rates, poor grades, and indifference to learning among children as reasons to reassess current school programs. One of the most ardent advocates of school reform is the author of the following viewpoint, John Taylor Gatto. In this excerpt from his January 1990 acceptance speech as New York City Teacher of the Year, Gatto argues that the nation's schools are failing both children and society. Gatto maintains that schools should be revamped to involve children's families and communities. Most importantly, he contends, children need time alone, away from the class setting, to develop self-knowledge. Gatto resigned as a junior high school teacher in 1991.

As you read, consider the following questions:

1. According to Gatto, why is it important for schools to involve children in community affairs?
2. How does the present school system restrict a student's education, in the author's opinion?
3. How are students' families important to their education, according to Gatto?

Excerpted, with permission, from *Dumbing Us Down: The Hidden Curriculum of Compulsory Schooling* by John Taylor Gatto, published in 1992 by New Society Publishers, 4527 Springfield Ave., Philadelphia, PA 19143.

We live in a time of great school crisis. We rank at the bottom of 19 industrial nations in reading, writing, and arithmetic. At the very bottom. The world's narcotic economy is based upon our consumption of this commodity; if we didn't buy so many powdered dreams the business would collapse—and schools are an important sales outlet. Our teenage suicide rate is the highest in the world and suicidal kids are rich kids for the most part, not the poor. In Manhattan, 70% of all new marriages last less than five years. So something is wrong for sure.

Great Crisis

This great school crisis is interlinked with a greater social crisis in the community. We seem to have lost our identity. Children and old people are penned up and locked away from the business of the world to a degree without precedent—nobody talks to them anymore, and without children and old people mixing in daily life a community has no future and no past, only a continuous present. In fact the name "community" hardly applies to the way we interact with each other. We live in networks, not communities, and everyone I know is lonely because of that. School is a major actor in this tragedy as it is a major actor in the widening gulf among social classes. Using school as a sorting mechanism, we appear to be on the way to creating a caste system, complete with untouchables who wander through subway trains begging and sleeping upon the streets.

I've noticed a fascinating phenomenon in my 25 years of teaching—that schools and schooling are increasingly irrelevant to the great enterprises of the planet. No one believes anymore that scientists are trained in science classes or politicians in civics classes or poets in English classes. The truth is that schools don't really teach anything except how to obey orders. This is a great mystery to me because thousands of humane, caring people work in schools as teachers and aides and administrators but the abstract logic of the institution overwhelms their individual contributions. Although teachers do care and do work very, very hard, the institution is psychopathic, it has no conscience. It rings a bell and the young man in the middle of writing a poem must close his notebook and move to a different cell where he must memorize that man and monkeys derive from a common ancestor.

Our form of compulsory schooling is an invention of the State of Massachusetts around 1850. It was resisted—sometimes with guns—by an estimated 60% of the Massachusetts population, the last outpost in Barnstable on Cape Cod not surrendering its children until the 1880s when the area was seized by militia and children marched to school under guard.

18

Now here is a curious idea to ponder. Senator Ted Kennedy's office released a paper not too long ago claiming that prior to compulsory education the state literacy rate was 98% and after it the figure never again reached above 91%.

Steve Kelley. Reprinted with permission.

Here is another curiosity to think about. The homeschooling movement has quietly grown to a size where one and a half million young people are being educated entirely by their own parents; in December 1989, the education press reported the amazing news that children schooled at home seemed to be five or even ten years ahead of their formally trained peers in their ability to think.

I don't think we'll get rid of schools anytime soon, certainly not in my lifetime, but if we're going to change what's rapidly becoming a disaster of ignorance we need to realize that the school institution "schools" very well, but it does not "educate"—that's inherent in the design of the thing. It's not the fault of bad teachers or too little money spent. It's just impossible for education and schooling ever to be the same thing.

Schools were designed by Horace Mann and by Sears and Harper of the University of Chicago and Thorndyke of Columbia Teachers College and some other men to be instruments of the scientific management of a mass population. Schools are intended to produce through the application of formulae, formulaic human beings whose behavior can be predicted and controlled.

To a very great extent schools succeed in doing this, but in a national order increasingly disintegrated, in a national order in which the only "successful" people are independent, self-reliant, confident, and individualistic (because community life which protects the dependent and the weak is dead and only networks remain), the products of schooling are, as I've said, irrelevant. Well-schooled people are irrelevant. They can sell film and razor blades, push paper and talk on telephones, or sit mindlessly before a flickering computer terminal, but as human beings they are useless. Useless to others and useless to themselves.

Absurd Children

The daily misery around us is, I think, in large measure caused by the fact that, as Paul Goodman put it thirty years ago, we force children to grow up absurd. Any reform in schooling has to deal with its absurdities.

It is absurd and anti-life to be a part of a system that compels you to sit in confinement with people of exactly the same age and social class. That system effectively cuts you off from the immense diversity of life and the synergy of variety; indeed it cuts you off from your own past and future, sealing you in a continuous present much the same way television does.

It is absurd and anti-life to move from cell to cell at the sound of a gong for every day of your natural youth in an institution that allows you no privacy and even follows you into the sanctuary of your home demanding that you do its "homework."

"How will they learn to read?!" you say and my answer is "Remember the lessons of Massachusetts." When children are given whole lives instead of age-graded ones in cellblocks they learn to read, write, and do arithmetic with ease if those things make sense in the kind of life that unfolds around them.

But keep in mind that in the United States almost nobody who reads, writes or does arithmetic gets much respect. We are a land of talkers, we pay talkers the most and admire talkers the most and so our children talk constantly, following the public models of television and schoolteachers. It is very difficult to teach the "basics" anymore because they really aren't basic to the society we've made.

Two institutions at present control our children's lives—television and schooling, in that order. Both of these reduce the real world of wisdom, fortitude, temperance, and justice to a never-ending, non-stop abstraction. In centuries past the time of a child and adolescent would be occupied in real work, real charity, real adventures, and the realistic search for mentors who might teach what you really wanted to learn. A great deal of time was spent in community pursuits, practicing affection, meeting and studying every level of the community, learning how to make a home, and dozens of other tasks necessary to become a whole man or woman.

But here is the calculus of time the children I teach must deal with:

Out of the 169 hours in each week my children sleep 56. That leaves them 112 hours a week out of which to fashion a self.

My children watch 55 hours of television a week according to recent reports. That leaves them 57 hours a week in which to grow up.

My children attend school 30 hours a week, use about 8 hours getting ready, going and coming home, and spend an average of 7 hours a week in homework—a total of 45 hours. During that time they are under constant surveillance. They have no private time or private space, and are disciplined if they try to assert individuality in the use of time or space. That leaves them 12 hours a week out of which to create a unique consciousness. Of course my kids eat, too, and that takes some time—not much because they've lost the tradition of family dining, but if we allot 3 hours a week to evening meals we arrive at a net amount of private time for each child of 9 hours.

It's not enough, is it? The richer the kid, of course, the less television he watches, but the rich kid's time is just as narrowly proscribed by a somewhat broader catalogue of commercial entertainments and his inevitable assignment to a series of private lessons in areas seldom of his own choice.

A National Disease

But these things are just a more cosmetic way to create dependent human beings unable to fill their own hours, unable to initiate lines of meaning to give substance and pleasure to their existence. It's a national disease, this dependency and aimlessness, and I think schooling and television and lessons have a lot to do with it.

Think of the things which are killing us as a nation—narcotic drugs, brainless competition, recreational sex, the pornography of violence, gambling, alcohol, and the worst pornography of all, lives devoted to buying things, accumulation as a philosophy— all of them are addictions of dependent personalities and this is what our brand of schooling must inevitably produce.

I want to tell you what the effect is on our children of taking all their time from them—time they need to grow up—and forcing them to spend it on abstractions. You need to hear this because no reform that doesn't attack these specific pathologies will be anything more than a facade.

21

The children I teach are indifferent to the adult world. This defies the experience of thousands of years. A close study of what big people were up to was always the most exciting occupation of youth, but nobody wants us to grow up these days and who can blame them? Toys are us.

The children I teach have almost no curiosity and what they do have is transitory. They cannot concentrate for very long, even on things they choose to do. Can you see a connection between the bells ringing again and again to change classes and this phenomenon of evanescent attention?

The children I teach have a poor sense of the future, of how tomorrow is inextricably linked to today. As I said before, they live in a continuous present, the exact moment they are in is the boundary of their consciousness.

The children I teach are ahistorical, they have no sense of how past has predestined their own present, limiting their choices, shaping their values and lives.

The children I teach are cruel to each other, they lack compassion for misfortune, they laugh at weakness, they have contempt for people whose need for help shows too plainly.

Personality Disguise

The children I teach are uneasy with intimacy or candor. My guess is that they are like many adopted people I've known in this respect: they cannot deal with genuine intimacy because of a lifelong habit of preserving a secret inner self inside a larger outer personality made up of artificial bits and pieces of behavior borrowed from television or acquired to manipulate teachers. Because they are not who they represent themselves to be the disguise wears thin in the presence of intimacy so intimate relationships have to be avoided.

The children I teach are materialistic, following the lead of schoolteachers who materialistically "grade everything"— and television mentors who offer everything in the world for sale.

The children I teach are dependent, passive and timid in the presence of new challenges. This timidity is frequently masked by surface bravado, or by anger or aggressiveness, but underneath is a vacuum without fortitude.

I could name a few other conditions that school reform will have to tackle if our rational decline is to be arrested, but by now you will have grasped my thesis, whether you agree with it or not. Either schools have caused these pathologies or television or both. It's a simple matter of arithmetic—between schooling and television, all the time the children have is eaten up. There simply isn't enough other time in the experience of our kids for there to be other significant causes. . . .

It's high time we looked backwards to regain an educational

philosophy that works. One I like particularly well has been a favorite of the ruling classes of Europe for thousands of years. I use as much of it as I can manage in my own teaching, as much, that is, as I can get away with given the present institution of compulsory schooling. I think it works just as well for poor children as for rich ones.

New Educational Order

As the nation struggles to find cures for its ailing public schools, a consensus is emerging among leading educators that the answer lies not in any of the currently popular reforms but in the creation of a new American public school.

Instead of adhering to the decades-old notion of asking students to regurgitate information in rote fashion on standardized exams, some educational reformers are saying, the new educational order must focus on the ability to solve problems, think creatively and learn through doing rather than sitting passively while teachers lecture.

San Diego Union, November 17, 1990.

At the core of this elite system of education is the belief that self-knowledge is the only basis of true knowledge. Everywhere in this system, at every age, you will find arrangements that work to place the child alone in an unguided setting with a problem to solve. Sometimes the problem is fraught with great risks, such as the problem of galloping a horse or making it jump, but that, of course, is a problem successfully solved by thousands of elite children before the age of ten. Can you imagine anyone who had mastered such a challenge ever lacking confidence in his ability to do anything? Sometimes the problem is the problem of mastering solitude, as Thoreau did at Walden Pond, or Einstein did in the Swiss customs house.

Right now we are taking all the time from our children that they need to develop self-knowledge. That has to stop. We have to invent school experiences that give a lot of that time back. We need to trust children from a very early age with independent study, perhaps arranged in school but which takes place away from the institutional setting. We need to invent curricula where each kid has a chance to develop private uniqueness and self-reliance. . . .

Community Service

What else does a restructured school system need? It needs to stop being a parasite on the working community. Of all the pages in the human ledger, only our tortured country has warehoused children and asked nothing of them in service to the general good. For a while I think we need to make community service a required part of schooling. Besides the experience in acting unselfishly that it will teach, it is the quickest way to give young children real responsibility in the mainstream of life.

For five years I ran a guerrilla school program where I had every kid, rich and poor, smart and dipsy, give 320 hours a year of hard community service. Dozens of those kids came back to me years later, grown up, and told that one experience of helping someone else changed their lives. Taught them to see in new ways, to rethink goals and values. It happened when they were 13, in my Lab School program, and only made possible because my rich school district was in chaos. When "stability" returned the Lab closed. It was too successful with a widely mixed group of kids, at too small a cost, to be allowed to continue.

Independent study, community service, adventures and experience, large doses of privacy and solitude, a thousand different apprenticeships, the one-day variety or longer—these are all powerful, cheap and effective ways to start a real reform of schooling. But no large-scale reform is ever going to work to repair our damaged children and our damaged society until we force the idea of "school" open to include family as the main engine of education. . . .

Family and Education

I have many ideas to make a family curriculum and my guess is that a lot of you have many ideas, too. Our greatest problem in getting the kind of grassroots thinking going that could reform schooling is that we have large, vested interests pre-empting all the air time and profiting from schooling as it is despite rhetoric to the contrary.

We have to demand that new voices and new ideas get a hearing, my ideas and yours. We've all had a bellyful of authorized voices mediated by television and the press; a decade-long free-for-all debate is what is called for now, not any more "expert" opinions. Experts in education have never been right, their "solutions" are expensive, self-serving, and always involve further centralization. We've seen the results.

It's time for a return to Democracy, Individuality, and Family.

"There is no evidence that our educational system has ever worked any better than it works today."

Public Education Does Not Need Extensive Reform

Gerald Bracey

While education in America has many critics, it also has many supporters. In the following viewpoint, Gerald Bracey argues that the quality of lower education in the U.S. is currently at its highest level. Bracey maintains that the high school graduation rate is at an all-time high and that math scores and reading performance levels are higher than they have been for more than twenty years. Bracey also contends that the U.S. has achieved these results despite the fact that, compared to other nations, it allots relatively fewer resources to education and requires students to attend school for fewer days per year. Bracey is a policy analyst for the National Education Association, a leading educational organization in Washington, D.C.

As you read, consider the following questions:

1. Why is it important to consider differences in test scores between today's average students and those in 1941, according to Bracey?
2. According to the author, how are students exposed to a wider variety of education today than in the past?

Gerald Bracey, "The Greatly Exaggerated Death of Our Schools," *The Washington Post*, May 5, 1991. Reprinted with permission.

When George Bush announced his "Education 2000" programs in April 1991, he observed that we've "moved beyond the days of issuing report after report about the dismal state of our schools. We don't need any more of those." His comment reflects the common perception that the educational system has fallen into decline. But had Bush actually read the reports, he might have started from a more cheerful premise.

In fact, there is no evidence that our educational system has ever worked any better than it works today. This is not the same thing as saying the system works well. Nor to deny that it could—and should—work better. But it is to deny that American schools are in "dismal" shape.

The data supporting this conclusion are easily available in publications of the U.S. Department of Education such as "The Condition of Education 1990." A closer look at high school completion rates, dropout rates, college attendance, various test scores, expenditures and other indicators shows that, far from deteriorating, American schools continue to provide a high quality—in many ways vastly more sophisticated—education to the type of student they have traditionally served, while greatly expanding their service to larger numbers of students previously excluded from the system.

Dropout Rates

Let's look at some of the most commonly misinterpreted statistics:

Contrary to most perceptions, high school completion rates are at an all-time high. The number of 17-year-olds completing high school rose from 10 percent in 1910 to about 75 percent in 1965 and has remained constant since. Adding in General Equivalency Diplomas bumps the rate up to 83 percent. Unlike many countries, the United States operates a flexible re-entry system that allows people to return to finish their high school careers. And return they do. The U.S. Department of Education reports that by 1986, 91 percent of the class of 1980 had obtained a high school diploma.

In recent years the specter of the high school dropout as a threat to society has loomed large in portraits of a sick system. But if completion rates are high, the dropout rate must be low. And it is. Moreover the rate is declining for all ethnic groups except Hispanics, for whom it is stable. Although our stereotype of dropouts is that of a low-achieving inner-city minority youth, 66 percent of dropouts are white, 42 percent come from suburban high schools, 71 percent never repeated a grade.

Some would argue, of course, that higher high school completion rates don't prove much if we are simply handing diplomas to functionally illiterate know-nothings whom we have passed

26

through the system by grade inflation and social promotion. But scores on achievement tests, on the National Assessment of Educational Progress and on the Scholastic Aptitude Test (yes, on the SAT!) don't support this view either.

Test Scores

After falling in the late '60s and early '70s, scores on standardized achievement tests began to rise. By 1986, some had attained 30-year highs and scores have continued to rise since then. Nor can this improvement be explained away by charges that schools are aligning their curricula with tests or even cheating.

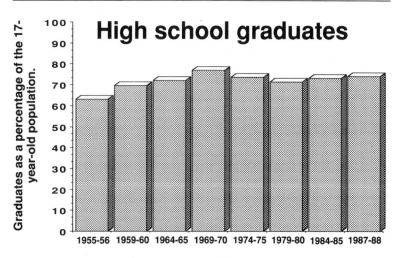

Source: National Center for Education Statistics.

Most striking in this regard is the fact that when students in a particular grade, say the third grade, are found to have scored better than earlier third-graders, they carry their relative success with them as they move into higher grades. Upturns in scores thus tend to ripple through schools like a wave at approximately one grade per year: If third-grade scores are observed to have risen in, say 1975, sixth-grade scores will show a rise three years later. This effect would not be observed if schools were implementing across-the-board changes in, for example, test-taking or scoring procedures.

Results from the National Assessment of Educational Progress (NAEP) similarly rebut the notion of national educational decline. Except for the scores of 17-year-olds on the science assessments, these scores have remained remarkably stable since

NAEP's inception in 1969. The science scores for the older students declined from 1969 to 1982 and have recovered about half their fall since.

As for reading and math, the 1990 NAEP publication "Accelerating Academic Achievement" puts it this way: "Across all three ages assessed (9, 13 and 17) overall reading performance in 1988 was as good if not slightly better than it was nearly two decades earlier. . . . In 1986, mathematics had changed very little from the levels achieved in 1973."

This picture of stable or improving average test scores becomes still brighter when we take into account the far broader range of students who now take these tests compared to earlier decades.

Shifting Demographics

None of the tests that "prove" we are failing academically is relied on more heavily than the "decline" of scores on the SATs taken by college-bound high school students. To understand the importance of changes in the American school population, we have to keep in mind that the standards for the SAT were set in 1941. A score of 500 (the number assigned to the average score in 1941) on the SAT-verbal in 1991 means the same thing in terms of scholastic aptitude as it did in 1941. Thus, if the students taking the test in 1991 have the same demographic characteristics as those of 1941, any changes may well be due to educational factors. But are they similar? Hardly.

In 1941, 10,654 students, a tiny fraction of the total population, showed up to take the test. They were mostly male, almost entirely white, mostly in the Northeast, mostly headed for Ivy League and other private colleges in northeastern states. They constituted, by any measure, an elite.

And in 1990? Some 1,025,523 seniors, about 42 percent of all seniors in the country, huddled in angst on a Saturday morning to hand in their answer sheets for the College Board. Twenty-seven percent of these students came from minority groups; 17 percent reported family income of less than $20,000; 52 percent were women (for reasons still in dispute, women SAT-takers have not scored as well as men SAT-takers). And 18 percent reported average high school grades of C or worse.

Obviously students of whatever background with mediocre or poor high school records will not do as well on the SAT as the academic elite who alone took the test in the old days. And minority and low-income children have added disadvantages to be overcome (though it should be noted that on almost all indicators, blacks and Hispanics have gained in recent years—on NAEP, on the SAT, in the number of engineering degrees received, etc.). Certainly schools should try still harder to overcome those disadvantages. But ignoring the effect that an expanded pool of test-takers has on reducing average scores produces a distorted picture of how well our schools are performing.

We cannot make a perfect comparison from the present to 1941 because we do not have precise information about the 1941 group. But if we look at the scores of white students who come from homes where at least one parent has attained a bachelor's degree—a group that reasonably approximates the 1941 elite (though now a majority are female)—we find a decline of about 30 points in SAT-verbal scores since the SAT began its celebrated fall in 1963 and 7 points on the SAT-math. On a scale of 800 points, these declines are trivial. Moreover, data from studies of the PSAT (the shortened version of the SAT that students take in their sophomore year), which is normed on a representative sample of all students in the country, show no decline since 1963.

I expect that most parents who have sent children through public schools recently won't find these facts surprising. Despite all the laments about low standards, many kids get exposed to far more sophisticated material than was our generation. My two children compiled acceptable but not notable records in high school. Yet one breezed through Ibsen as a junior and the other launched himself on a trajectory in math that reached calculus in his senior year—achievements that I, despite my superior grade record, did not reach until my middle years in college.

Some critics, while acknowledging that average SAT scores are misleading, point instead to a decline in the percentage of students scoring at the highest levels of the SAT. While only 1 percent of males and 1 percent of females score between 700 and a perfect 800 on the SAT-verbal (2 percent of the 1941 group would have scored such), fully 7 percent of males and 2 percent of females score above 700 on the SAT-math. The decline in high scores of the SAT-V probably does reflect a drop in uhhhh, like, you know, verbal skills. But, given the huge increase in SAT-takers, a drop in the percentage of high-scorers still means a big increase in their absolute number.

School Expenditures

A likely retort at this point is that, whatever the record, we ought to be getting better performance because education spending has soared. But again, the data show a different reality. According to U.S. Department of Education figures, we spend only 3.6 percent of our GNP [gross national product] on education, down from 4.2 percent in 1970. A new study by the American Federation of Teachers shows that, using accepted international adjustments for relative purchasing power, the

United States spends less of its resources on education than 11 out of 15 economically advanced nations—although we enroll the greatest number of students.

And, again, the averages don't tell the whole story. To get a true figure for costs of education, we need to separate the costs of *regular* education from the costs of *special* education, keeping in mind that 12 percent of all students are enrolled in federally supported special education programs.

California: A Success Story

One of the best arguments for optimism about American schools is how much some school districts have already achieved. One of the best examples is the state of California. Between 1983 and 1989, twelfth-grade test scores there improved one and a quarter grade equivalents in math and three-fifths grade in reading. Eighth-graders improved one-half grade in all subjects—reading, writing, math, science, and history—in just three years, from 1986 to 1989. Looking at it another way, in 1986 the average Japanese eighth-grader was two years ahead of his American counterpart; California cut the gap by twenty-five percent in just three years.

The state's SAT scores gained almost as dramatically. The proportion of California students scoring over 450 on the verbal portion of the test grew by 19 percent between 1983 and 1989; the fraction scoring over 500 on the math test grew by 28 percent. Average scores went up in every major ethnic group. This occurred though 12 percent more graduates took the test—a less elite group, from whom lower scores might have been expected; though the school system had to cope with an average of 140,000 more students each year; though the number of students living in poverty doubled in the 1980s; though the number of students who did not speak English as a primary language and who are still struggling to cope with it doubled to one in six. And while all this was happening, the dropout rate fell by 18 percent.

Marvin J. Cetron and Margaret Gayle, *Educational Renaissance*, 1991.

Estimates of the costs of special education vary depending on accounting methods from a low of $9,600 per pupil per year to a high, and probably more accurate, $17,600. Using this latter figure and constant 1988 dollars, the costs of regular education have risen scarcely at all since 1970.

International Comparisons

Finally, you might argue, if we're doing so well how come our kids keep getting outgunned on tests by all those Europeans and Asians? But the international comparisons conducted to date have been largely meaningless. The kids aren't the same. Even

30

the language of the test is often spoken only by the better educated segments of some countries.

Only Belgium has a school year as short as ours. Japanese kids are in school 243 days a year. They go to school after school, go to school on Saturdays and have mothers at home to push them. And they fall apart once they get to college. Whether or not American schoolers should attend school 243 days is a legitimate subject for debate, but let's not compare them to students with a calendar that long when American students are in school only about 170 days a year.

The worst fault of the international assessments, however, is that while the great bulk of American students stay in school for 12 years, many are gone by age 13 in many other countries. The Second International Assessment of Educational Progress, IAEP-2, for example, will compare American 13-year-olds to those in Brazil and Mozambique, among other countries. Only 35 percent of the 13-year-olds in Brazil are still in school; in war-torn Mozambique, the number is 5 percent. China hopes to have universal education at the sixth grade by the end of the century.

World Leader

IAEP-2 will be considered important in some quarters because Bush and the state governors have established as a national goal making the United States No. 1 in math and science by the end of the century. But if we consider non-test indicators, we already *are* No. 1. Into the more than 40,000 scientific professional journals, researchers pump articles at the rate of one every 30 seconds, seven days week, 365 days a year. Americans account for 30 percent to 40 percent of all the articles in these journals. No one else even comes close: Great Britain, Japan and the Soviet Union tie for second with 8 percent. These figures have been stable since at least 1973. If our schools provided only sow's ear science education, our universities could not turn it into such a scientific silk purse.

There are plenty of problems in education, plenty of places where the system could be improved, must be improved. No one should take anything I have written as reason for slowing the pace of many reforms in progress around the nation (though there *are* other reasons for wishing some of them would go away). But it seems to me that we cannot solve the problems that do exist if we're distracted by problems that don't exist. Claiming that the system is failing is not only distracting, but creates the wrong climate for improvement—you don't get people to do better by telling them how lousy they are.

"Evidence is growing that year-round schools help improve achievement."

A Longer School Year Would Improve Public Education

Chester Finn

Students in many industrialized countries rank higher academically than U.S. students. Many people attribute this to the fact that these countries, particularly Japan, have longer school years than the U.S. In the following viewpoint, Chester Finn argues that adding more days to the school calendar will benefit American education. Finn maintains that a longer school year will boost student achievement and enhance the quality of the teaching profession. Finn, the director of educational excellence for Vanderbilt University's Washington, D.C. office, is a former U.S. assistant secretary of education.

As you read, consider the following questions:

1. According to Finn, why do people oppose the concept of a year-round school?
2. How would a longer school year offer more employment choices to teachers and students, in the author's opinion?
3. How can school facilities be used more efficiently in a year-round program, according to Finn?

Chester Finn, "Part-Time Schools Aren't Good Enough," *Conservative Digest*, March 1988. Reprinted with the author's permission.

How many parents do you know who need their children around home during the summer to help harvest the crops? Not very many, presumably. Yet we still base our 180-day school year on an obsolete lifestyle adopted in the 19th Century to accommodate parents who needed their youngsters in the fields during the summer months.

It's time to rethink this outmoded calendar and consider keeping the schoolhouse doors open year-round. [Former] President Ronald Reagan and other public figures have advanced this idea of extending the school year, and it is a good one.

This doesn't mean keeping children in school 365 days a year. But it could mean sending them to school 230 or 240 days with breaks of a few weeks every two months or so. Or it could mean setting up a four-quarter school year; requiring all youngsters to attend three quarters; and, *allowing* them to attend the fourth quarter as an elective.

Or it could mean keeping the school building in use all year and letting students and parents choose how they wish to arrange their own 180-day academic year. Many year-round school plans exist, and one may fit a certain community better than another.

Benefits of Extended Term

What's standing in the way of year-round schools? Public opinion, mainly, plus inertia, custom, and fear of the unknown. Schools are one of the most change-resistant institutions in America. We are reluctant to alter routines and lifestyles, even when an alteration might be beneficial. But, before dismissing the notion of extending the school year, consider how such a change could help meet four major challenges facing us today.

• *Education Equity*: All students—rich and poor, slow learners and gifted—deserve full opportunity to meet the higher standards being set in our schools. But that means giving some youngsters more time and extra help to succeed. Year-round schools can do this, and can thus be a powerful benefit for disadvantaged and minority children. Immigrant youngsters struggling with English might use the additional days to improve their language skills. A longer school year would give students with learning difficulties more time to master subjects.

Average students would benefit too. They could use the extra time to pursue such subjects as driver's education, typing, art, or work-experience programs. Gifted students might use the additional time to accelerate their academic subjects, maybe even to graduate from high school a year or two earlier. This would give them extra time to pursue a special interest or to earn money for college.

• *Educational Alternatives*: Many parents want to have more choice over the forms of education available to their children. Think of the combinations of choices that could be available, but aren't today, if the traditional 36-week school year were changed to a more flexible 48-week year.

• *Teacher Professionalism*: Many teachers take non-teaching jobs during school vacations to supplement their salaries. Consequently, teaching is not their sole occupation, a fact that has detracted from efforts to make teaching a true profession. Year-round school could do much to enhance the professional image of teaching.

Teachers who work all year could have more choices. Some years, they would teach all four quarters. But in other years they might use the extra time to take paid sabbaticals or study leaves, develop curricula, or supervise novice instructors. In other words, they could have time during the year, like other professionals, to fine-tune the full range of their skills. Not all teachers want a 12-month work schedule, of course. Those who prefer the shorter year could retain it, even switching seasons for their vacation periods if they wished.

Fiscal Benefits

And there is yet another benefit for teachers: higher salaries. If teachers were paid for a 48-week year at the same rates they are paid today for 36 weeks, their salaries would rise to an average of nearly $35,600 compared with today's average of $26,700.

• *Improved Productivity*: In this time of fiscal belt-tightening it is especially important that we get our money's worth from American schools; lots of people don't think we are. We have been spending an average of $4,300 per student, but it isn't buying enough learning. Although some of what I have suggested will add to education costs, some will yield savings. For example, three teachers who work four quarters get paid as much as four teachers who work three quarters. But you only need three health-insurance policies, three pension plans, and classrooms and support for three teachers.

A child who enrolls for a fourth quarter will add to school costs. But this may be offset by the fact that the school is saving money by operating year-round for those on staggered three-quarter years. And, if funds are tight, the optional fourth quarter need not necessarily be free. I don't think it's unreasonable to suggest that parents pay for this quarter, especially if it is used for acceleration and enrichment, or for helping parents with a child-care problem.

Care and Quality

Besides improving equity, family choice, teacher professionalism, and educational productivity, year-round schools offer other benefits.

34

For one thing, they have the potential of solving the nagging social problem of what to do about children who are home alone during the summer months. Many working parents wince when school doors close in June for three months. Affluent parents may pay for camps, day-care programs, babysitters, or summer schools. But the less affluent don't have so many options. Some will leave their children at home unattended, or "hanging out" in the nearest park, video arcade, or street corner. Year-round school would be a boon to these parents—and their children.

American children need to spend more time learning. The year-round schools would afford them this opportunity. Evidence is growing that year-round schools help improve achievement, especially among low-income and socially disadvantaged students. In 1983, Houston tried a year-round program that resulted in such significant academic improvement among participating students that 25 schools converted to the plan by 1985. (Due to budget constraints, unfortunately, that number was reduced to four in the 1986-1987 school year.)

Extend Time in School

If politicians truly wish to give American students an education equal to the best in the world, they will find the money to extend the school day and year. Our guess—and at this point it can be no more than that—is that by the turn of the century the American school day will have stretched to seven hours, the year to 210 days.

Marvin Cetron and Margaret Gayle, *Educational Renaissance*, 1991.

All the schools in Oxnard, California, have adopted 12-month calendars during the past decade, and student academic test scores there have risen at nearly twice the rate—in several cases, almost triple the rate—of student scores in the rest of the state.

Academic Improvement

The National Council on Year-Round Education surveyed 174 year-round schools in 1982. They found that academic achievement improved in one-third of those schools.

We also know that some students, especially disadvantaged ones, suffer a "summer learning loss." Attending school year-round would likely help these youngsters retain more. They wouldn't be prone to forget as much during shorter breaks as they do during today's three-month summer break.

An Education Department study of Japanese schooling, *Japanese Education Today*, illustrates some of the benefits to youngsters of a longer school year. Japanese schools operate on a 240-day calendar. On a cumulative basis, Japanese students spend 180 more days in school than American students—the equivalent of one added school year—by the time they graduate from high school. And, when you compare test scores, you see that Japanese students learn more.

The 18,000-member American Association of School Administrators, calling the present school calendar an "agrarian model," urged public educators to add four weeks to the school year so that children would be in class 200 days instead of 180. That might be a good start.

School Crowding

Opening our schools year-round can also ease overcrowding. The National Governors Association, in its superb report, *Time For Results*, has concluded there is no reason to leave school buildings sitting idle for half the year while many students are undereducated and classrooms overcrowded. This is especially true in school districts with burgeoning enrollments. A school that is open all year can serve 33 percent more students than one that operates only from September to June. Doesn't it make more sense to use existing facilities to handle enrollment overflows than to spend millions of dollars building new schools? What's more, school buildings that are in use are less apt to be vandalized.

The San Diego School Board, facing a rapidly growing student population and a lack of money for new buildings, voted to implement year-round calendars on a mandatory basis. Under their plan, there will be four sets of students and teachers, with one set always on a three-week vacation. A *Los Angeles Times* editorial supported the plan, explaining that operating year-round schools is the route to go "as long as the student population continues to grow faster than schools can be built."

In 1987, the Los Angeles Board passed and then rescinded a plan to put all its public schools on a year-round schedule. The Chicago and Milwaukee School Boards are also considering extending their school years. At the present time, according to the National Council on Year-Round Education, some 424 schools nationwide operate on extended schedules. Los Angeles and Santa Ana, California; Provo, Utah; and, Las Vegas, Nevada, have all put some of their schools on a year-round schedule.

Solving Problems

There are, of course, some perceived disadvantages to year-round schools, but I view them more as adjustments that need to be made.

The primary impediment is that a number of elements of our society are now organized around the assumption that children

36

will be available during the summer. Much of the tourism and vacation industry, for example, earns its income during the three months children are not in school. Youth camps usually operate during the summer. Baseball teams count on youngsters to help fill the stands. Local recreation, community, and library programs are affected by summer vacation.

Yet many of these interests may actually be better served over the long run by spreading their programs and activities more evenly throughout the year, rather than cramming them all into the summer. Many camps could operate from spring through fall and end up serving more children than they do now. Families with a yen for warm weather could enjoy southern resorts throughout the year rather than fight the beach crowds during the summer. Those who enjoy skiing and other cold-weather activities could take to the northern slopes any time during the winter, instead of having to do all their skiing during Christmas vacation when the kids are out of school.

Specialized Knowledge

Extending the school year makes both educational and economic sense. . . .

The traditional school calendar was not designed to be an educational calendar. It has no particular instructional benefit. It was designed solely to support the 19th century agricultural economy. Change is long overdue.

By altering the traditional calendar and extending the number of instructional days, we help students realize that learning, like the work of adults, is continuous.

Charles Ballinger, *USA Today*, January 12, 1990.

Teenagers wanting to earn money will have more opportunities to work during their school breaks, on the year-round schedule, because they won't all be competing for the same jobs that are available during the summer. . . .

Year-round schools are not a panacea. They cannot substitute for high standards, strong principals, good teachers, parent involvement, and excellent textbooks. But they do offer genuine hope for boosting student achievement, providing better care for the children of working parents, and enhancing the teaching profession. In my view, the time has come again to try year-round schooling.

"Teachers intent on covering ground won't be any better at their craft with 220 days than at 180."

A Longer School Year Would Not Improve Public Education

Colman McCarthy and *The Charlotte Observer*

In Part I of the following viewpoint, Colman McCarthy maintains that increasing the number of school days will not help students learn more because the ineffectiveness of teachers, not the number of school days, is the real cause of America's educational crisis. McCarthy argues that schools need inspired teachers who can motivate students, not a longer school year. In Part II, a *Charlotte Observer* editorial argues that a longer school year would not solve the most serious problems in education nor produce more effective students. Furthermore, the authors maintain that extending the school year would be expensive. This money could be better spent on improving the quality of education. McCarthy is a syndicated columnist and staff writer for the *Washington Post*, a daily newspaper. The *Charlotte Observer* is a daily newspaper in North Carolina.

As you read, consider the following questions:

1. Why is the quality of education more important than a longer school year, according to McCarthy?
2. Why will a longer school year be of no benefit to high school dropouts or students who receive an inadequate education, according to the *Charlotte Observer*?

I

In eight years of teaching high school students in both private and public schools, I've learned that on the subject of education their ideas are often sounder and their opinions sharper than what's coming from the on-high experts and theorists. Two of them, in particular.

Thomas A. Shannon, director of the National School Boards Association, is pushing for a 12-month academic year. No summer idleness, either for students or school buildings. In Massachusetts, Michael Barrett, a state senator, has introduced a bill to extend the school year from 180 to 220 days.

Both of these time-savers are fretting that compared with other countries the United States is encouraging laziness and ignorance by its short school year. Students in Japan, West Germany, South Korea, Israel and Luxembourg all have a minimum of 210 calendar days of class. No slackers there.

Longer Year Theory

Barrett, as if scratching his fingernails on the blackboard to make us dolts understand, writes in the *Atlantic:*

"First, compared with their peers in Asian and European countries, American students stand out for how little they work. Second, compared with Asians and Europeans, American students stand out for how poorly they do." Barrett believes a school year of 220 days is an essential reform—"a superstructure under which other changes can be made."

The unsuper arguments from Shannon and Barrett have been regularly thrown into the education hopper since the late 1940s—and just as regularly rejected. The longer-is-better theorists—Barrett spent a day teaching seventh-graders, so his experiential knowledge is vast—are like teachers who begin each class, "Let's get started, we have a lot of ground to cover." This is the track coach method, substituting pages in a book for yardage.

Teachers intent on covering ground won't be any better at their craft with 220 days than at 180. An inspired teacher can change a student's life—rouse the imagination, stir once-hidden powers of the intellect—in a day, week or month. Extra teaching talent, not extra time, is needed.

Keep Students Enthusiastic

This theme ran through the papers I asked my students at Bethesda-Chevy Chase High School to write. A young man offered this:

"The problem does not lie in the number of days students attend class but in keeping students enthusiastic about learning. . . . Instead of being followers of Japan, South Korea and Taiwan, why doesn't America use its innovative spirit and reconstruct its educational program, not by adding days but by adding stimulation to the classroom."

On the issue that the young waste their time in June, July and August, a senior woman wrote: "Nothing is like experiencing life firsthand by spending a few months in nature, in another country, living with another culture or working at an office or in Congress. I learned more about myself this summer when I traveled with the circus than in four years of high school."

A third student asked: "If people are so concerned about education, why don't they increase the amount of money available for teacher salaries? It is hard to attract good educators to teach when they earn little money."

More Funding

Students are right to resist the call for a longer academic year. They know it means more time in custody, not just in class. The issue is more money, not more schooling. With 70 percent of federal research-and-development funds going into military programs and less than 2 percent to education, the message is obvious: Soldiers are more valued than students, weapons over wisdom.

Making Matters Worse

When I was at the National Institute of Education, one of the education centers we funded conducted a study which concluded that more efficient use of existing school time would be more helpful than longer school years or days.

Many fine teachers are already leaving the profession because of burnout, and more months in the classroom would exacerbate the problem. For students, there would be no summer school available, which many need in order not to fail, and there would be little time for summer employment. Moreover, an increase to an 11-month school year would mean a budget increase of about 16% for teachers' salaries, to install air conditioning, etc., and that would mean a tax increase.

Dennis L. Cuddy, *USA Today*, January 12, 1990.

Despite the generosity of a few corporations, private money to schools is niggardly. Robert Reich reports in the Winter 1991 issue of *The American Prospect* that corporate largess is seldom showered upon public primary or secondary schools: "Of the $2.6 billion contributed to education in 1989, only $156 million went to support the public schools (about 6 percent); the rest went to colleges and universities (especially the nation's most prestigious, which the firms' CEOs were likely to have attended), and to private preparatory schools (ditto)." Public schools received only 1.8 percent of all corporate donations.

Calls for a longer school year are like parents lengthening the time for the family's dinner. If there's little or nothing to eat, why bother? Schools are famished for money. I've never had a student who didn't know that.

II

Michael Barrett [in the *Atlantic*] says that when compared to their peers in Asia and Europe, American students stand out for how little they work and how poorly they do. "The United States faces a time-in-learning deficit every bit as serious as the trade deficit and the balance-of-payments problem," he argues. His conclusion: "Equalizing the time we commit to learning is the way we will begin to come back."

The idea of a longer school year has plenty of supporters. . . . But if the concern is for increased learning—not just increased schooling—a longer year is not the place to start.

The crisis in education is not first a crisis of time. A too-short year is not what drives 25 percent or more of pupils out of school before graduation, or causes many others to get a diploma, but not an education adequate for life, work or higher study. Shorter summers might help some of these students forget less. But a longer school year will not make education more interesting or more effective for them. If one aspirin will not cure a broken leg, will two?

What a longer year will do is cost money: $250 million eventually for a 20-day increase. . . . Cost alone would not deter us were money available and other needs not more urgent. But right now, North Carolina ought to give higher priority to preserving its commitments to school reform and teacher pay, to expanding critical programs for at-risk preschoolers and to underwriting some qualitative changes that would help students more. Don't invest the scarce new money in more aspirin.

It is not just the number of days in class that distinguishes our schools from their foreign competitors. Several recent national studies, for example, talked about higher expectations for all students, better preparation for the world beyond the school, more effective instruction for students who will not go on to college. The status quo is not adequate, but lengthening the school year would do little to correct the most serious flaws. And by consuming dollars and energy, it could in fact preempt more urgent reforms.

Before the reform is done, we suspect, the regular year will be somewhat longer and additional weeks of the summer will be devoted to learning in settings other than the traditional classroom—increasing learning without depriving students and teachers of needed respite. The real issue is timing. This . . . is not the time to put a longer school year first.

41

"Standardized tests undermine school improvement instead of advancing its cause."

Eliminating Standardized Tests Would Improve Schools

D. Monty Neill and Noe J. Medina

Many people, including D. Monty Neill and Noe J. Medina, criticize standardized tests as unfair toward minority students and students from low-income families. In the following viewpoint, Neill and Medina argue that standardized test questions reflect the language and culture of middle- to upper-class whites. Therefore, the authors contend, such tests are unfair to students who speak nonstandard English dialects and students for whom English is a second language. Neill is managing director of the National Center for Fair and Open Testing (FairTest) in Cambridge, Massachusetts. Medina is the director of Education Policy Research, an education improvement consulting firm in Boston.

As you read, consider the following questions:

1. How do standardized tests inaccurately measure students' abilities and skills, according to Neill and Medina?
2. In the authors' opinion, how do standardized tests hinder students' intellectual and social skills?
3. According to Neill and Medina, how can important curricula be ignored by schools that emphasize standardized testing?

Adapted from "Standardized Testing: Harmful to Educational Health," by D. Monty Neill and Noe J. Medina, *Phi Delta Kappan*, May 1989. Reprinted with permission.

In the last two decades, standardized multiple-choice tests have come to dominate the educational landscape in the U.S. From preschool to college, they have become the major criteria for a wide range of school decisions. Test scores limit the programs that students can enter and dictate where students are placed. Test scores are used to assess the quality of teachers, administrators, schools, and entire school systems. Meanwhile, the content and format of standardized tests determine the shape of the curriculum and the style of teaching.

A study by the National Center for Fair and Open Testing (FairTest) estimated that U.S. public schools administered 105 million standardized tests to 39.8 million students during the 1986-87 school year. That's an average of more than $2^1/_2$ standardized tests per student per year. At that rate, by the time a student graduates, he or she has been forced to take 30 standardized tests. . . .

Undermining Education

The FairTest survey revealed that the number of states that mandate testing has increased greatly in recent years. The survey also showed that standardized testing is most prevalent in the southern states and in large urban school systems—locales that tend to serve higher-than-average proportions of minority students and students from low-income families.

Those who favor standardized testing applaud these trends in the public schools. They see tests as "objective" methods of enforcing "accountability"—and thus of improving student achievement, staff competence, and educational quality. Indeed, standardized tests are an essential element of the "school reform movement."

In reality, however, these "objective" instruments often produce results that are inaccurate, inconsistent, and biased against minorities, females, and students from low-income families. By narrowing the curriculum, frustrating teachers, and driving students out of school, these standardized tests undermine school improvement instead of advancing its cause. Instead of promoting accountability, tests shift control and authority into the hands of an unregulated testing industry. Therefore, using standardized test scores as the primary criteria for making important educational decisions will lead to *less* public understanding of the schools and a *weaker* educational system.

The powerful negative effects of standardized multiple-choice tests lead us to emphasize the need to develop high-quality alternative assessment devices that yield educationally useful and accurate results, while strengthening the curriculum and making meaningful accountability possible.

Standardized tests are consistently sold as scientifically developed instruments that objectively, simply, and reliably measure students' achievement, abilities, or skills. In reality, however, the basic psychological assumptions undergirding the construction and use of standardized tests are open to question and often are clearly erroneous. In addition, the studies that are conducted to determine the reliability and validity of standardized tests are often inadequate. Many tests are administered in environments that erase their claims to being "standardized" or that discriminate against minority test-takers and those from low-income families. These flaws undermine the test makers' claims of objectivity and often produce test results that are inaccurate, unreliable, and ultimately invalid. As a result, standardized tests generally fail to provide effective and useful measures of test-takers' achievement, abilities, or skills. . . .

Jimmy Margulies. Reprinted with permission.

Claims that standardized tests exhibit a high level of reliability are usually taken to mean that test results for a given individual will be similar in successive administrations. But in fact, *reliability* is a technical term that encompasses several different concepts.

The type of reliability that is generally measured and reported for standardized tests is internal or inter-form reliability. Consistency over time, which many observers would consider of greater importance, is rarely measured and reported by test publishers. A study of consistency over time generally produces lower reliability coefficients and is more expensive to conduct.

The level of a test's reliability (regardless of the type of reliability measured) is reported as a "reliability coefficient" that ranges from 0 to 1. For most standardized tests, the reported coefficients are very high—often exceeding .8 or .9.

Yet, for an I.Q. test with a reliability coefficient of .89 and a standard deviation of 15, a student has a reasonable likelihood of having a "true score" that is up to 13 points higher or lower than his or her test score. Thus a school system could, for example, bar a student who scores 117 from entering a program for the gifted and talented that requires participants to have I.Q.s of 130—even though that student's "true score" could well be 130. . . .

Test Bias

Test makers claim that the lower test scores of racial and ethnic minorities and of students from low-income families simply reflect the biases and inequities that exist in American schools and American society. Biases and inequities certainly exist—but standardized tests do not merely reflect their impact; they compound them.

Researchers have identified several characteristics of standardized tests that could negatively bias the scores of minority students and of students from low-income families. These tests tend to reflect the language, culture, or learning style of middle- to upper-class whites. Thus scores on these tests are as much measures of race or ethnicity and income as they are measures of achievement, ability, or skill.

To communicate their levels of ability, achievement, or skill, test-takers must understand the language of the test. Obviously, tests written in English cannot effectively assess the performance of those students for whom English is a second and only partially mastered language.

Researchers have also discovered that the elaborated, stylized English commonly used in standardized tests prevents such tests from accurately measuring the achievement, ability, or skills of students who speak nonstandard (e.g., African-American, Hispanic, southern, Appalachian, working-class) dialects.

A related type of bias stems from stylistic or interpretive language differences that are related to culture, income, or gender. For example, African-American students often associate the word *environment* with such terms as *home* or *people*, while white students tend to associate that word with *air*, *clean*, or *earth.* Neither usage is wrong. Yet only one of these two usages—generally the one reflecting the white perspective—will be acceptable on a standardized test.

Similarly, researchers have discovered that individuals exhibit "different ways of knowing and problem solving" that reflect differing styles, not differing abilities. These differing styles are often related to race or ethnicity, income level, and gender. Yet standardized tests (and "standardized" instruction) assume that all individuals perceive information and solve problems in the same way. Again, assumptions about the universal applicability of a style that is exhibited primarily by middle- and upper-class white males limits the reliability of test results. . . .

Impact on Students

Historically, standardized tests were one of several educational tools used to assess student achievement and to diagnose academic strengths and weaknesses. In recent years, however, standardized tests have become not only the primary criteria used by many schools for making decisions that affect students, but also major forces in shaping instruction and assessing the quality of teaching and of the schools.

The use of standardized test scores as the primary criteria for making decisions of any kind is reckless, given the erroneous assumptions that undergird standardized tests, the limited range of skills and knowledge that they measure, their limited reliability, their lack of validity, and the impact that race, ethnicity, family income, and gender exert on test results. Yet just such reckless decisions seriously damage student achievement, the curriculum, and education reform in many schools and school districts.

By controlling or compelling student placement in various educational programs, standardized tests perpetuate and even exacerbate existing inequities in educational services, particularly for minority students and those from low-income families. One clear example is tracking, which has been shown to harm the students placed in lower tracks without necessarily helping those placed in higher tracks to perform better than they would have performed in heterogenous groupings. This is largely due to the fact that students whose test scores are low are presumed to be unable to master complex material and are thus subjected to a dumbed-down curriculum.

The use of scores on standardized tests to determine placement in special education and remedial education programs also causes large numbers of racial and ethnic minorities to be placed in those programs. In 1984, for example, 40% of African-American 5-year-olds in South Carolina failed the standardized tests used in that state to determine eligibility for kindergarten.

Before their formal schooling had even begun, these youngsters were placed in remedial classes because of their scores on unreliable exams. . . .

Children go to school not just to learn basic academic skills, but also to develop the personal, intellectual, and social skills that will enable them to become happy, productive members of a democratic society. Unfortunately, the current emphasis on standardized tests threatens to undermine these broad goals by forcing schools and teachers to focus on narrow, quantifiable skills at the expense of less easily quantifiable and more complex academic and nonacademic abilities.

This outcome is particularly noticeable in the very early grades. As the National Association for the Education of Young Children (NAEYC) noted:

> Many of the important skills that children need to acquire in early childhood—self-esteem, social competence, desire to learn, self-discipline—are not easily measured by standardized tests. As a result, social, emotional, moral, and physical development and learning are virtually ignored or given minor importance in schools with mandated testing programs.

Many schools have embarked on a single-minded quest for higher test scores, even though this strategy severely constricts their curricula. For example, Deborah Meier, the principal of Central Park East public school in Manhattan, testified at a 1981 National Institute of Education hearing on minimum competency testing that students in New York City read "dozens of short paragraphs about which they then answer questions"—an approach that duplicates the form of the tests that the students will take in the spring. Meanwhile, Gerald Bracey, former director of research, evaluation, and testing for the Virginia Department of Education, observed that some teachers did not teach their students how to add and subtract fractions, because Virginia's minimum competency test included questions on the multiplication and division—but not on the addition and subtraction—of fractions.

Impact on Curricula

Sometimes, as Arthur Wise has noted, the curriculum is narrowed simply because "testing takes time, and preparing students for testing takes even more time. And all this time is time taken away from real teaching."

Unfortunately, a closer link between standardized tests and school curricula has become a conscious goal for some school systems. School systems in at least 13 states and the District of Columbia are seeking to "align" their curricula so that students do *not* spend hours studying materials on which they will never be tested—regardless of the value of those materials or the benefits that students might derive from studying them. In other

47

words, aligning curricula with tests subordinates the process of curriculum development to external testing priorities, and, for all intents and purposes, the test becomes the curriculum. The educational price that is paid for allowing tests to dictate the curriculum can be high. Julia Palmer, executive director of the American Reading Council, noted that the major barrier to teaching reading in a commonsense and pleasurable way is the nationally normed, standardized second-grade reading test. Palmer went on to explain that the test questions force teachers and students in the early grades to focus on "reading readiness" exercises and workbooks instead of on reading. As a result, many students become disenchanted with reading.

Mathematics instruction has also been harmed by the emphasis on testing. Constance Kamii notes that standardized tests cannot distinguish between students who understand underlying math concepts and students who are only able to perform procedures by rote (and who therefore cannot apply these procedures to new situations). Thus teaching to the test precludes teaching in a fashion that enables children to grasp the deeper logic. The National Council of Teachers of Mathematics has concluded that, unless assessment is changed, the teaching of mathematics cannot improve.

Just as curricula have been narrowed, so too have textbooks. Diane Ravitch argues that "textbooks full of good literature began to disappear from American classrooms in the 1920s, when standardized tests were introduced. Appreciation of good literature gave way to emphasis on the 'mechanics' of reading." Similarly, a report by the Council for Basic Education (CBE) concluded that the emphases on standardized tests and on aligning curricula to match the tests were two major causes of the decline in the quality of textbooks.

Loss of Real Learning

The narrowing of the curriculum is a virtually unavoidable by-product of placing our emphasis on multiple-choice instruments with limited construct validity. Not only do reading tests not test reading and math tests not test math, but the format militates against their ever being able to measure the essential constructs. As teaching becomes "coaching for the test" in too many schools, real learning and real thinking are crowded out. Among the instructional casualties are the higher-order thinking skills.

Standardized tests (including those that have been mandated by states as part of their school reform laws) focus on basic skills, not on critical thinking, reasoning, or problem solving. They emphasize the quick recognition of isolated facts, not the integration of information and the generation of ideas. As Linda Darling-Hammond concluded, "It's testing for the TV generation—superficial and passive. We don't ask if students can synthesize information, solve problems, or think independently. We measure what they can recognize.". . .

The effects of testing on the curriculum and on student placements lead to educational disaster for many young people. In an all-too-typical scenario, a child who does not test well (often due to cultural background, not academic capability) is tracked—sometimes prior to first grade—into a program for "slow learners" that rests on the assumption that participants cannot or will not learn. The tracking creates a self-fulfilling prophecy, as the child's "achievement" test scores come to correlate with his or her "ability" test scores. . . .

Imperfect Measure

[Standardized tests] can tell us little about a child's ability to learn, to analyze, or to reason—and nothing of the child's judgment, originality, imagination, or creativity. Basing all expectations of a child's abilities on so imperfect a measure would be most inappropriate.

Pat Henry, *NETWORK for Public Schools*, September 1990.

Reflecting its concern about the misuse of standardized tests, FairTest has developed an agenda for testing reform. Making tests fair, accurate, open, and educationally relevant would require major changes in the instruments themselves and sharp controls on their use. However, reducing the most egregious offenses of standardized testing will not be sufficient.

The primary educational needs of the U.S. simply cannot be met by reliance on standardized testing. Albert Shanker argues that education has "never worked well for more than about 20% of our children." To serve the rest, as education must do, will require fundamental changes in curriculum, pedagogy, and management.

At best, standardized testing is hopelessly inadequate for promoting necessary school reform. At worst, such testing will preclude reform. In either case, the continued domination of testing will mean that millions of students—primarily those most in need of improved education—will be dumped into dead-end tracks and pushed out of school. To prevent damage to young people and to allow the implementation of needed school reforms to proceed, testing must become an *occasional adjunct*, used for obtaining certain basic but limited information about education—and for nothing else.

"We should not . . . deprive ourselves and our students of one of the few sources of objective data for evaluating our own performance."

Standardized Tests Should Not Be Eliminated from Schools

Gregory J. Cizek and Ramsay Selden

Most American students have taken standardized tests, which are used to compare the proficiency of different groups of students. In Part I of the following viewpoint, Gregory J. Cizek argues that standardized tests accurately measure students' knowledge and that test scores help identify the best students. In Part II, Ramsay Selden maintains that standardized tests provide information about the academic performance of school systems and thereby help identify schools that need improvement. Cizek is a program associate of the American College Testing Program (ACT), an Iowa City-based organization that produces the ACT college entrance examination. Selden is the director of the State Education Assessment Center of the Council of Chief State School Officers in Washington, D.C.

As you read, consider the following questions:

1. Why is the argument that standardized testing lowers student achievement illogical, in Cizek's opinion?
2. According to Cizek, how do standardized test scores show the quality of classroom instruction?
3. Why is it important for states to know the academic performance of their schools, according to Selden?

Gregory J. Cizek, "Reasoning About Testing." Reprinted with permission from *Education Week*, vol. 9, no. 28, April 4, 1990. Ramsay Selden, "Standardized Testing: Helpful . . . or Harmful?" *PTA Today*, March 1989. Reprinted with permission.

I

Criticism of testing has lately been widespread and multi-faceted. Recently, we have learned of a movement to abolish assessment in early grades and of a coalition formed to combat standardized testing. We have also been offered arguments for reconsidering standards and assessments altogether.

There may be solid grounds for such reappraisal. But the rationale advanced in recent discussions is ill-conceived and poorly defended—the product of sloppy logic. The American public has actually yet to be presented by anyone with a substantial, well-conceived argument for abandoning testing.

Sloppy reasoning has at least three characteristics: It employs grandiose but vacuous rhetoric, makes careless inferences regarding cause and effect, and mistakes faith for fact. While the mere presence of this unholy trinity in this debate is worrisome, more troubling is the possibility that it could actually influence a reform movement.

Emotional Appeal

The abolitionists' use of rhetoric is most noticeable in attempts to capture the moral high ground through emotional appeal. On first glance, what right-thinking person would not want "schools with high standards," an "attitude of excellence," "genuine accountability," more "quality than quantity," "authentic evaluation," or "empowerment for teachers"?

But what does all this jargon really mean? Are any of these phrases meant for any purpose except to make us *feel* bad about evaluation and to make us *feel* good about poorly defined alternatives? I don't think so. In fact, all of the moaning and gloom-saying about current practice suggests a new moniker around which the abolitionists can rally: "genuwhine assessment."

In fairness to the movement, we must ask if the whining is justified. Unfortunately, the argumentation offered in support of this position is mired in careless inferences about cause and effect.

Generally, abolitionists rightly note that testing is not the cause of higher achievement. No one seriously contends that it is. But neither is it logical to argue that testing causes lower achievement. Assessment is simply an attempt to gauge the current state of affairs. The too-frequently invoked medical analogy remains useful in this context, especially given a widespread perception that the education system is ailing: We take the patient's temperature more frequently when there appears to be reason to believe that something is wrong. Such monitoring, we think, will provide a hint about why the patient is sick and tell us whether appropriate therapy is leading to better health.

The cause-and-effect mistake runs even deeper. Researcher Grant Wiggins, for example, has commented that "in the last 20 years, the most massive investment in testing ever undertaken has coincided with a palpable decrease in the quality of education." Sure. And also in the last 20 years, average cholesterol levels have risen, Communist governments have begun to fall, and Nelson Mandela has been freed. Ah, the power of testing!

Teachers Favor Standardized Testing

Studies prove that teachers are *for* standardized testing: As a report from the University of Pittsburgh concluded, "Feeling strongly that they know their own students, teachers think of the tests as yet one more piece of evidence, one further measure of how a child is doing in school. The tests are particularly helpful, the study noted, in assisting teachers in identifying those students who do better on the tests than the teacher had predicted based on his or her observations and experiences with the child."

Sally D. Reed, *A Parent's Survival Guide to the Public Schools*, 1991.

The most plausible cause-and-effect inference regarding testing and educational quality has been overlooked by abolitionists: that the patient's temperature is being taken more frequently because other data suggest that there is a problem. To hypothesize that testing could undermine reform efforts is to wholly misunderstand the problem.

Interestingly, the same abolitionists who claim that a love of testing is the root of all educational evils propose as an alternative merely to substitute different kinds of testing. The newest is "performance assessment," which, we are told, is more "authentic" or "genuine." Or maybe it's "higher order," or "holistic." In any event, opponents of standardized assessment are urging testing companies and the public to read the handwriting on the wall and support the use of something else, something "more real." Indeed. If anything, the public has already read the handwriting on the wall and is reacting negatively because it contains misspellings and poor grammar.

Faith for Fact

Which brings us to the third characteristic of sloppy reasoning: mistaking faith for fact. If this sort of thinking isn't acceptable in teaching about matters as significant as the origin of the world, it shouldn't be permitted in areas of arguably lesser importance, either.

The abolitionists would ask us to be educationally healed by faith in their dogma. While promoting higher standards for education, they suggest that "students with high standards are diligent, thoughtful, engaged, persistent, and thorough—no matter what they learn." Such emotive language might compel the reader to accept blindly the underlying assumption that it doesn't matter what students learn. Are we to accept this premise on faith? Is it sound?

A. Graham Down, executive director of the Council for Basic Education, asserts that alternatives are needed because the traditional tests measure only "knowledge." Now, I suppose I could be accused of being old fashioned, but somehow I'm fixated on the notion that knowledge is still fundamental to learning.

Serious Charges

What about allegations that testing has been particularly harmful for children in the early grades and that, in the words of one abolitionist, "in some schools they spend more time in testing than they do in actual classrooms"? These are serious charges—if true. Such claims must be supported if we are to believe them; we can't simply take them on faith.

Perhaps all of these lapses in reasoning can be explained by the spread of what might be called "evalophobia." In proposing that testing be banned, abolitionists are also implicitly suggesting that we renounce any means of exploring the link between quality of instruction and quality of performance. Of course, standardized tests don't measure *everything* that is valuable or interesting about student achievement. But they do measure some of what is valuable and interesting in an extremely efficient and accurate way.

Reasonable inferences from high scores on a standardized test include the following: High-scoring students seem to be grasping what is taught; they are performing better on the tested material than some other students; and the instruction has been appropriate. Reliance on the proposed "genuine," "empowering" assessments would render such conclusions as the first two tenuous and the third impossible. In fact, much rhetoric surrounding alternative assessment leaves individual students entirely culpable for their educational shortcomings. We should not, for fear of the information provided by testing, deprive ourselves and our students of one of the few sources of objective data for evaluating our own performance.

Keep Stardardized Tests

We should all recognize that we have not achieved technical perfection in assessment; we must also admit that existing instruments address only a portion of what is useful for both our students and ourselves. But we should not jettison the tests we have because they don't do everything we wish they could. At minimum, tests do provide important information about *some* aspects of learning, as everyone should acknowledge. And we should develop new devices to assess other facets of students' intellectual growth.

II

Standardized testing means administering the same test in the same way to two or more pupils. It is a very broad class of uniform testing activities.

Standardized testing is the kind of testing we must use to look at education beyond the context of an individual student. We need such testing whenever we want to get a sense of how two or more entities in the educational process are doing relative to one another. The entities can be children, schools or states. This is for fairness: if we wish to examine *relative* performance, we must use standard procedures that give each child or school or other entity an equal chance to do well.

Is it important to compare? Some believe it is not appropriate to evaluate the performance of children or another entity on a relative scale. They say the child, school or school system should be evaluated and encouraged in terms of his or her (or its) own unique characteristics. Others disagree. They feel that it *is* desirable to review performances in relation to one another for a variety of purposes, such as to know which are doing well or not so well and to select one.

Value of Testing

The vast majority of teachers and parents find some merit in measuring the relative performance of students. Students are given grades by teachers, and millions of parents encourage their children to participate in testing for college admission and to determine their relative achievement.

Most members of the public as well as the policymakers who represent them feel it is valuable to monitor and evaluate the academic performance of their schools and school districts as well as their states and the nation. This enables them to tell, for example, if their school systems are doing better or worse over time and if they are doing better or worse than schools, districts, states or nations whose performance they feel should be similar. If we are willing to decide on goals or values, we can even use test results to tell how our school systems are doing in relation to them.

Let's look at the arguments against standardized testing. First, some critics assert that the failure of some standardized tests to tap important and complex educational skills or the cultural bias of some tests are reasons not to test at all. That premise is based on a view that these shortcomings in tests are rampant and unremediable. But if that perception is wrong it would leave us unnecessarily without any objective information upon which to judge the relative strength of our school systems. Tests are generally developed or chosen to measure as well as possible the skills that are deemed important for the school system. Many states have conscientiously increased the sophistication of the skills their testing programs measure to reflect deeper goals. Also, the creativity of methods used to test in areas such as writing, reading comprehension and science has been improved dramatically in recent years, permitting more effective testing in these areas.

Standardized Tests Assess Effectiveness

Along with other evaluations and measures, tests can be used for assessing the effectiveness of teaching and learning. Results of tests can be used to compare schools, school districts, colleges, states, and even countries in assessing how effective they are in educating students. In making such comparisons, it is clear that tests can be used to hold individuals accountable for leadership, teaching, or learning—or the lack of leadership, teaching, or learning.

Kenneth H. Ashworth, *The College Board Review*, Winter 1989-90.

Good test designers customarily review their programs for cultural bias and stereotyping, and items are regularly eliminated if they reflect large group differences in background characteristics that affect performance on them. Now, group differences have been reduced largely to differences in knowledge or experience that are important educationally and that are difficult to "unconfound" from instruction.

As consumers of education, and as those responsible for the quality of their children's schooling, parents should have and use test results, as long as they are sound. Testing must be done as well as we know how, and we must avoid the shortcomings of poor or expedient testing. There is undoubtedly room to improve, but fair and valid testing is not beyond us. Current tests are not so bad that they should be thrown out while we wait for ideal ones to be developed. We need test data now to know whether our schools are on course.

Test Content

Another criticism expressed by opponents of standardized testing is that the content of tests drives instruction inappropriately. This was of special concern when the Council of Chief State School Officers began to push toward comparative achievement testing among states. The question was whether comparing states would result in an overbearing influence on curriculum from the national level. Or, would state comparisons result in watering down the tests to what could be tested easily? For state comparisons, states agreed on a comprehensive, forward-looking framework for mathematics—the first subject to be tested comparatively—in the National Assessment of Educational Progress (NAEP) for 1990. This framework represents a broad consensus of teachers, policymakers and school administrators who determined what *should* be tested in mathematics, not a least-common denominator. It does not appear to exclude major areas of the subject that some states might wish to emphasize. It allows for great flexibility in what is emphasized and how and when it is taught.

A final argument is that attention to test scores will ignore differences in the conditions under which schools operate and that it will detract from constructive support and improvement of the schools. The chief state school officers have insisted adamantly that states should not be compared simply with other states, but with other states with similar circumstances and needs. They have also called for reporting of achievement indicators in relation to indicators of school processes and inputs, so people can begin to see where to place their efforts to make things better.

States Must Know

In many ways states have become the level of government with the most responsibility for education. They are raising and spending the money, setting many of the standards and spearheading many of the efforts to reform. For states *not* to know how well they are doing in education relative to other states would be like a business not knowing its relative profit margin.

The results of standardized achievement testing should not be the be-all and end-all of educational accountability. But knowing how we are doing—from the individual student to the nation as a whole—in terms of a comparative reference point is appropriate. The relative results of achievement testing programs must be collected through the best-constructed tests we can assemble. There are shortcomings with many of our testing programs, but this does not eliminate the necessity of having them. And, fortunately, the technology for producing them and improving them is already within our grasp.

Distinguishing Between Fact and Opinion

This activity is designed to help develop the basic reading and thinking skill of distinguishing between fact and opinion. Consider the following statement: "Minnesota has the highest high school graduation rate in the U.S." This statement is a fact that could be verified in an almanac. But the statement, "Minnesota produces the most high school graduates because it has the best teachers" is clearly an opinion. It cannot be proven that Minnesota has the best teachers.

When investigating controversial issues it is important that one be able to distinguish between statements of fact and statements of opinion. It is also important to recognize that not all statements of fact are true. They may appear to be true, but some are based on inaccurate or false information. For this activity, however, we are concerned with understanding the difference between those statements that appear to be factual and those that appear to be based primarily on opinion.

Most of the following statements are taken from the viewpoints in this chapter. Consider each statement carefully. *Mark O for any statement you believe is an opinion or interpretation of facts. Mark F for any statement you believe is a fact. Mark I for any statement you believe is impossible to judge.*

If you are doing this activity as a member of a class or group, compare your answers with those of other class or group members. Be able to defend your answers. You may discover that others come to different conclusions than you do. Listening to the reasons others present for their answers may give you valuable insights into distinguishing between fact and opinion.

> O = *opinion*
> F = *fact*
> I = *impossible to judge*

57

1. High school completion rates are at an all-time high.

2. There is no evidence that our education system has ever worked any better than it works today.

3. Year-round school would eliminate summer jobs for many high-school students.

4. A longer school year would give students with learning difficulties more time to master subjects.

5. Year-round schools can be a powerful benefit for disadvantaged and minority children.

6. A National Institute of Education study concluded that a more efficient use of existing school time would be more helpful than longer school years or days.

7. Teachers won't be any better at their craft with 220 days than with 180.

8. California SAT scores increased for every major ethnic group between 1983 and 1989.

9. Home schooling is an educational program that is minimal at best.

10. Studies prove that teachers are *for* standardized testing.

11. Much of the information our children are taught in the public schools is frivolous and unpatriotic.

12. Standardized tests are largely multiple-choice tests that do not adequately measure academic proficiency.

13. Experts estimate that as many as one million American families are teaching their children at home.

14. Home schooling takes away from a child's social skills and isolates children racially and ethnically.

15. Schools don't really teach anything except how to obey orders.

16. The American family is no longer a factor in the education of its own children.

17. Several studies have found that time pressure accounts in part for minorities' low standardized test scores.

Periodical Bibliography

The following articles have been selected to supplement the diverse views presented in this chapter.

Kenneth H. Ashworth	"Standardized Testing: A Defense," *The Education Digest*, November 1990.
Michael J. Barrett	"The Case for More School Days," *The Atlantic*, November 1990.
Jim Bencivenga	"Year-Round Schooling Catches On," *The Christian Science Monitor*, September 9, 1991.
Chester E. Finn	"Real Education Reform for the 1990s," *The Heritage Lectures*, No. 256. Available from The Heritage Foundation, 214 Massachusetts Ave. NE, Washington, DC 20002-4999.
Fortune	Special issue on school improvement, Spring 1990.
David Guterson	"When Schools Fail Children," *Harper's Magazine*, November 1990.
Ronald Henkoff	"For States: Reform Turns Radical," *Fortune*, October 21, 1991.
Tom Morganthau	"A Consumer's Guide to Testing," *Newsweek*, Special issue, Fall/Winter 1990.
Daniel Patrick Moynihan	"Social Science and Learning: Educational Reform Today," *Current*, June 1991.
New Perspectives Quarterly	Special issue on education, Fall 1990.
Newsweek	Special issue on education, Fall /Winter 1990.
Hugh B. Price	"The Bottom Line for School Reform," *Phi Delta Kappan*, November 1990.
Mary Anne Raywid	"The Evolving Effort to Improve Schools: Pseudo-Reform, Incremental Reform, and Restructuring," *Phi Delta Kappan*, October 1990.
Albert Shanker	"Give Students a Reason to Work Hard," *The Wall Street Journal*, July 15, 1991.
Thomas Sowell	"Excuses, Excuses," *Forbes*, October 14, 1991.

How Can the Teaching Profession Be Improved?

EDUCATION
in America

Chapter Preface

As concern about the growing failure of America's schools increases, so does criticism of teachers and the teaching profession. Many critics contend that progress and reform in education require improving the quality of teachers.

Some critics argue that teachers are to blame for poor student performance. They believe that teachers are by and large less capable, with less practical experience, than other professionals.

In response to these criticisms, some states have implemented alternative certification programs. Such programs offer teacher training to enthusiastic people experienced in other professions and allow them the chance to teach. Supporters believe that alternative certification entices more intelligent and more talented people into teaching.

Other critics assert that the blame for student failure lies with the system, not teachers. They argue that teachers are underpaid, overworked, and unappreciated. For example, according to education researchers Marvin Cetron and Margaret Gayle, in 1987 the average starting salary for teachers was $17,500 compared to $21,200 for an accountant, $26,170 for new computer specialists, and $28,500 for engineers. Many experts contend that this disparity in pay deters the best and brightest people from becoming teachers.

Teachers greatly influence how and what children learn. Experts disagree, however, on what problems the teaching profession faces and what solutions would best serve the needs of teachers and children. The authors in the following chapter debate these issues.

"A national certification system that reliably identifies teachers who meet high and rigorous standards can galvanize the entire [educational] system. "

National Teacher Certification Would Improve Teaching

National Board for Professional Teaching Standards

The effectiveness of teachers is often considered the most critical component of education. One way of improving this effectiveness is for teachers to share their knowledge and expertise with one another. In the following viewpoint, the National Board for Professional Teaching Standards (NBPTS) argues that establishing high standards and certifying teachers on a national level improves teacher effectiveness. The NBPTS maintains that national certification will formally recognize the most accomplished teachers and encourage them to impart teaching ideas and skills to fellow professionals. The NBPTS is an organization of teachers and government education officials based in Detroit, Michigan.

As you read, consider the following questions:

1. Which attributes does the NBPTS consider evidence of effective teaching?
2. In the author's opinion, why is it important for teachers to have some control over school resources?

Excerpted, with permission, from "The Challenge to American Education," in *Toward High and Rigorous Standards for the Teaching Profession*, Third Edition, by the National Board for Professional Teaching Standards, © 1991. Greenhaven editors have added subheadings, inserted quotations, and have retitled the material.

The debate about the current level of school performance often misses an important point: However fine or flawed the schools may be, the simple fact is that better results in education are needed. This is not an issue just for inner-city schools, but for all schools.

Better results are necessary because in a world made smaller by science and technology, an educated citizenry is essential to the sound functioning of a democracy and to economic growth. In this knowledge-driven world, a prerequisite for a prosperous and secure national future is a work force that commands more than basic skills. Adults must be able to communicate complex ideas in a compelling manner, take advantage of the latest advances in science and technology, solve problems neither they nor their teachers have ever seen before, and add real value to the goods and services they produce. However positive citizens' attitudes may be toward work, however responsible and reliable they may be, however sterling their work habits, they are essentially unemployable if they are not well-educated. They must be able to think for a living.

The bottom line is that the nation must dedicate itself to producing a kind and quality of education it has never before sought. In the midst of operating a system of "mass" education, it must create schools that treat each child as an individual, that embrace student learning as the highest value, and that foster distinguished teaching by drawing fully on the accumulated wisdom of the faculty. In years past this vision would have been dismissed as romantic; today it is not only desirable, it is a necessity.

No Simple Task

America must have schools in which teachers focus their energies on making the most of the resources at their disposal. When staffed with accomplished teachers, schools should be permitted to operate unencumbered by external prescriptions that overlook the knowledge and expertise that teachers possess about the practices which best serve their students. In such settings innovative materials and methods are used creatively, new breakthroughs in technology are embraced, student initiative and inventiveness are both stimulated and applauded, and expectations are high for all students. Although such schools exist today, they are the exception, not the norm.

Creating such schools is no simple task. Fine-tuning the present system will not suffice. Overnight decrees from on high and exhortations to try harder will, by themselves, prove insufficient. Instead, systemic reform is required, for tinkering will not do. What is required, in fact, is no less than a revolution in teaching and learning.

An essential foundation for this revolution is to make teaching a profession dedicated to student learning and to upholding high standards for professional service and conduct. For too many of our nation's teachers, teaching is still organized essentially as assembly line work. Most teachers who display professional skill do so in spite of, not because of, the way schooling is organized in America.

Catalyst for Change

The National Board cannot single-handedly transform the schools. But the National Board can be a catalyst for lasting change. It can redefine teaching as a career by stimulating new incentive structures, staffing patterns and organizational arrangements. It can bolster reform in teacher education by casting the knowledge base in a richer light. Most importantly, as these related changes both increase the flow of first-rate people into the field and stem the tide of those departing, and as teachers' roles and responsibilities are more sensibly structured, National Board Certification can become a pathway to improved student learning. The National Board must act in concert with other initiatives to make this promise a reality.

Specialized Knowledge

The teachers we seek to recognize as National Board-certified have a rich understanding of the subject(s) they teach. They appreciate how knowledge in their subject is established, organized, linked to other disciplines and applied to real-world settings.

Accomplished teachers command specialized knowledge of how to convey and reveal subject matter to students. They are aware of the preconceptions and background knowledge that students typically bring to each subject, and strategies and instructional materials that work best.

James A. Kelly, speech delivered to the Australian Scholarship Trust, October 25, 1990.

Teaching is at the heart of education, and the single most important action the nation can take to improve schools is to strengthen teaching. A national certification system that reliably identifies teachers who meet high and rigorous standards can galvanize the entire system. Understanding how this might occur begins with understanding the shortcomings of the current system.

Unlike physicians, architects or accountants, teachers have not codified the knowledge, skills and dispositions that account for accomplished practice. Consequently, there are widespread misconceptions about what constitutes good teaching. Some hold that it requires no more than knowing one's subject. Others think that caring about children is all that is essential. Still others believe that just knowing "how to teach" (as if such knowledge can be divorced from the two prior considerations) is sufficient. Actually, all of these attributes are necessary, but even taken together they are not sufficient. Accurately evaluating student needs and progress, translating complex material into language students understand, exercising sound and principled professional judgment in the face of uncertainty, and acting effectively on such judgments are also necessary conditions for teachers to excel.

Cavalier Attitude

Unfortunately, lack of attention to the act of teaching at the college and university level reinforces a cavalier attitude toward teaching in general. Too many Americans—school board members, administrators and many teachers included—believe that any modestly educated person with some instinct for nurturing has the requisite qualifications to teach. The National Board intends to change this view by presenting a compelling case for, and a more accurate description of, accomplished teaching.

Many schools are now organized as if all teachers were peas in a pod, indistinguishable one from another. This strains the imagination. In a profession of 2.5 million people, variations in knowledge and effectiveness are to be expected. Unlike other professions, the schools have, for the most part, been unable to accommodate their practices to account for the diversity that exists within the teaching work force. In no other profession are neophytes thrust into full service without a period of transition; in no other profession are demonstrated competence and success unrecognized and unrewarded; and in no other profession are human resources deployed inflexibly without reference to the needs of the client. Treating teachers as if they were all the same is inefficient and dispiriting. The National Board's ability to identify accomplished professionals in a fair and trustworthy manner can free the schools from a large part of this structural straitjacket.

Countless numbers of accomplished teachers regularly exercise sound professional judgment and practice in a principled and effective manner. But it is rare that such teachers are recognized for their accomplishments or asked to share their expertise with others. An occasional plaque or modest check is no substitute for formal recognition of demonstrated competence that relies on a rigorous process such as the advanced professional certification system the National Board is designing.

The absence of a credible and accepted method to recognize outstanding teaching sends a message that good teaching is not valued, and that the profession does not take itself or its responsibilities seriously. Moreover, because the incentive structure in schools fails to promote the spread of the knowledge and expertise of the most accomplished teachers among fellow faculty members, schools fail to capitalize on these precious resources.

Excellent Teachers

We expect that National Board Certification will lead to better teaching and better learning in both the short run and the long run. This new system of voluntary certification of excellent teachers is being designed by teachers themselves. It is being developed *by* teachers, *with* teachers, *for* teachers—and not *to* teachers.

We're doing it for teachers, yes—but the most important reason we're doing it is for our kids and for the future of our country, so that the quality of education in our wonderful country is worthy of the challenges we face in the 21st century.

James A. Kelly, speech delivered to the Australian Scholarship Trust, October 25, 1990.

This state of affairs has come about not by accident but by design. Schools and the teachers and administrators within them function in the manner that they do as the result of deliberate policy decisions. Many of these decisions have been grounded in the reality that neither labor nor management has trusted the other to make fair distinctions among teachers. Until now, most attempts to recognize accomplished teachers have not only been characterized by limited teacher involvement in their origination, but also have not been based on high standards of professional practice; as a result teachers are understandably skeptical about such programs.

A system of National Board Certification that commands the respect of the profession and the public would make a critical difference in how communities view their teachers. Superintendents would encourage their teachers to acquire National Board Certification and would want to hire Board-certified teachers. No longer would the overriding objective be to fill each vacancy with the lowest-cost teacher; instead, districts that cared about the quality of education being provided to their students would have a strong incentive to see that a solid percentage of their teaching force was National Board-certified.

Perhaps, most importantly, new assignment procedures could be devised to capitalize on the wisdom and ability of the most accomplished teachers. Such behavior is second nature in professional-practice firms in architecture, accounting and law, where the most distinguished professionals accept the most demanding cases. Unfortunately, in many schools, the least experienced teachers are regularly assigned to the most disadvantaged students. Such a practice serves neither teachers nor students. In schools redesigned for improved performance, National Board-certified teachers would not only enjoy greater status, they would likely command higher salaries.

Stimulating Environment

As National Board Certification signals that the teaching force is populated by many practitioners entitled to full professional standing, state and local authorities should find it easier to back away from instructional edicts that limit flexibility and stifle creativity at the school site. Providing more discretion so that those closest to the point of service delivery may use their distinctive knowledge of the client's needs should produce better results for students and yield a more stimulating and professionally rewarding work environment for teachers. . . .

By creating a new and more attractive career path for all teachers, National Board Certification should improve the schools' ability to retain able professionals, make the profession more appealing to bright and enterprising college students who enjoy many other promising options, and attract older Americans seeking new and rewarding careers. Such changes also hold promise for a reversal in the long-term trend of declining minority interest in teaching.

As the labor market has expanded for minority college graduates, many of these able, young people have been attracted to other careers which offer more promising avenues for advancement, greater prestige, and more attractive work environments. The result is that the schools no longer have a captive pool of talented minorities from which to draw. The pool itself has also been constricted by low college completion rates for minority youth. Broad-scale reforms at all levels of American education are required to stem the loss of minority students all along the education pipeline. But even as progress is made on this front, being able to offer a more rewarding career, with decent pay and the prospect of professional standing, respect and responsibility is necessary if sufficient numbers of minorities are to find their way back to the teaching force. . . .

When viewed narrowly, professional certification is a means to enhance the status and pay of teachers. These are worthy objectives in their own right. But when the connections between professional certification and the organization of instruction are examined, the potential to improve student learning can be seen quite directly. Through the potential to transform schooling, to leverage current investment in teaching and to build a system where increasing public investment makes more sense, the full value of National Board Certification is revealed.

"The [national teacher] certification remedy sounds like an effort to cure chills and fevers by devising more accurate thermometers."

National Teacher Certification Would Not Improve Teaching

William Raspberry

Many people oppose national teacher certification because one private group, the National Board for Professional Teaching Standards, would have too much control over how teachers are certified. In the following viewpoint, William Raspberry agrees with this concern and argues that national certification would not enhance teaching skills. National certification is unnecessary to recognize and utilize outstanding teachers, he contends. Raspberry maintains that school principals adequately determine who are the best teachers. Raspberry is a columnist for the *Washington Post* daily newspaper.

As you read, consider the following questions:

1. What major problems prevail in the teaching profession, according to Raspberry?
2. Why does the author doubt that outstanding teachers would be willing to train less effective teachers?
3. According to Raspberry, why will a national teacher certification plan fail to draw more college students and minorities to teaching?

William Raspberry, "Weak Medicine for Teachers," *The Washington Post*, July 19, 1989, © 1989, Washington Post Writers Group. Reprinted with permission.

What's wrong with teaching?

The pay is too low; too few of the brightest college students are attracted to the field; too many of those who are lack the ability to inspire their students; there are too few rewards for excellent teachers; the proportion of minority teachers is shrinking as the proportion of minority students is increasing.

What should we do about it?

The National Board for Professional Teaching Standards has come up with an answer that may not merit the enthusiasm it is likely to provoke. The 64-member board, created by the Carnegie Forum on Education and the Economy in the wake of its 1986 report on public schools, is calling for national certification for outstanding teachers as a way of "ensuring educational excellence in elementary and secondary education."

The certification, which would be an addition to the minimum standards for state licensure, would focus on classroom results—not such ticket-punching procedures as taking the right courses.

And what would it do?

Pie in the Sky

The optimistic—the temptation is to say "pie in the sky"—expectation of the NBPTS is that it would "increase the supply of high-quality entrants into the profession, with special emphasis on minorities," help to provide a better atmosphere for learning and create a "new image for teachers in this country."

It might also increase pay for the best teachers, but that would be up to local school officials. "We're not employers," said James A. Kelly, president and chief executive of the board.

What the NBPTS has in mind is to define the "knowledge, skill and dispositions" required for success in as many as 29 teaching specialties—early childhood education, elementary school science, high school math and so on and to award national certification to those who meet the yet-to-be-devised standards.

The board, whose members include corporate executives, elected officials, teachers' union officials and—the majority—teachers, envisions all sorts of wonderful things flowing from certification.

"In view of their achievement," says Kelly, "board certified teachers might be asked to assume the sort of increased responsibility that adds stimulation to the professional life of a teacher." Or as board member Susan Adler Kaplan, a Providence, R.I., English teacher says, a board-certified teacher "may become a mentor, may provide leadership for her colleagues by demonstrating new teaching methods, evaluating the latest instructional materials or organizing instruction. . . . In

69

short, she will have varied opportunities as a teacher."

But what has board certification got to do with it? Principals know already who their best teachers are, and if they want to use them to strengthen the weaker teachers, what's stopping them?

Another Bureaucracy

There are several very serious drawbacks [to national teacher certification]. First, no certification scheme, especially not a national one, can possibly provide much valid information on the quality of an individual's teaching; assessments will inevitably rely too heavily on standard formal measures and too little on school-level discretionary judgment. Second, voluntary national credentialing would doubtless become cloaked in public authority anyway, as states, districts, and collective bargaining agreements make board certification a requirement for increased pay and educational responsibilities. It would be voluntary only in the sense that it would not constitute a legal barrier to entry. It would, on the other hand, become a legal barrier to career advancement. Third, credentialing by a national board would, in the end, create yet another bureaucracy that teachers and schools would have to contend with in doing their jobs. Making it private or voluntary or teacher controlled does not change its essentially bureaucratic approach to the problem of teacher quality and professionalism. And fourth, this board would be strongly influenced and perhaps dominated by the National Education Association and the American Federation of Teachers, adding to their already stifling hold on educational personnel.

John E. Chubb and Terry M. Moe, *Politics, Markets, and America's Schools,* 1990.

Moreover, why would outstanding teachers want the additional burden of training their colleagues unless it entailed additional compensation? And additional compensation raises the specter of "merit pay," which teachers and their unions have rejected for decades.

Poor Remedy

The results envisioned by the NBPTS make a lot of sense: teachers, led by their most effective peers, organizing instruction, choosing textbooks, setting curricula and in general exercising unaccustomed autonomy.

But it's hard to see how board certification would necessarily produce those results—or how it would inspire bright college students to switch their majors to education or increase the number of minorities entering the field.

Certification by a national board certainly seems preferable to the minimum competency tests most of the states now use. But would it really enhance the skills of teachers?

The problems cited by the NBPTS are the critical problems. But the certification remedy sounds like an effort to cure chills and fevers by devising more accurate thermometers and propounding new standards for bodily temperatures.

"Through evaluation and rewards for our best teachers, we can secure a better education for all our children."

Merit Pay Programs Would Improve Teacher Performance

Lamar Alexander

Some states have instituted merit pay programs to improve education. These programs are designed to reward outstanding teachers by providing salary increases, bonuses, and promotions. In the following viewpoint, Lamar Alexander argues that merit pay programs increase the quality of teaching and education. Alexander maintains that in Tennessee, many of the best teachers remain in the profession because of the financial incentives of the state's merit pay program. As a result, Alexander contends, students' basic skills and achievement test scores have risen. Alexander, now the U.S. Secretary of Education, served as governor of Tennessee from 1979 to 1987.

As you read, consider the following questions:

1. According to Alexander, why have some school districts adopted merit pay programs?
2. How do merit pay programs benefit both teachers and students, according to the author?
3. How can outstanding teachers be objectively evaluated and selected for merit pay, in Alexander's opinion?

Lamar Alexander, "Let's Pay Our Best Teachers More." Reprinted with permission from the April 1988 *Reader's Digest*. Copyright © 1988 by The Reader's Digest Association, Inc.

Bob Bingham, a 33-year-old history teacher in Kingsport, Tenn., was a star of his middle-school faculty, valued by his principal and loved by his students. Yet he had to earn extra money by coaching and, in the summers, by working long hours managing a swimming pool for barely more than the minimum wage. In 1983 he sadly pondered quitting teaching to earn enough to support his growing family.

Today, thanks to an incentive program Tennessee launched in 1984, both Bob Bingham and the state's students are better off. Tennessee has formally recognized Bingham as a Master Teacher, which brings him extra pay for outstanding classroom performance. That rating also enables him to earn thousands more by working beyond the usual ten-month contract, in his case directing a summer school.

When Tennessee began the program, the academic quality of education majors was rock-bottom, and scores on certification tests were embarrassingly low. Moreover, too many of our best teachers were leaving for other jobs—not surprising since our veteran teachers ranked near the bottom of all states in salaries. In addition, a third of our eighth-graders did not possess eighth-grade skills.

Today these trends have been reversed. The number of teachers leaving the profession in Tennessee has dropped. Teacher certification and student achievement scores are both climbing.

In 1983 when I proposed an incentive-pay, "master-teacher" program, not one state paid its teachers a penny more for teaching well. . . .

Better Schools

In 1978, as I walked 1000 miles across Tennessee campaigning for governor, I found a jobs crisis throughout the state. At the ALCOA plant where my father worked to support our family after he left teaching, layoffs were rife because it was cheaper to smelt aluminum in Brazil.

Employment is increasingly dependent on computers. Yet I found precious few places where children were learning to use them.

As governor, I jumped head-on into attracting new industry. But the 30,000 jobs we recruited each year did not replace the estimated 200,000 that had disappeared. M.I.T. economist David Birch told me, "You'll have to grow your own jobs, in good schools that teach people better skills for coping with change."

My own eyes told me he was right. I saw Japanese executives in Chattanooga, Nashville, Knoxville and Memphis start Saturday schools because they wanted their children to learn more math than our schools offered. My speeches began to sound like a broken record: "Better schools mean better jobs.

Schools are the way we as a nation can learn to deal with the enormous changes we face—and do so on America's own terms."

Radical Reforms

After my re-election as governor, I drew on a bipartisan legislative study and submitted a radical package of educational reforms in 1983. Its heart was the new incentive-pay and career-ladder plan to reward and promote the best teachers. The state would evaluate those of our 43,000 eligible teachers who wanted to get on the ladder, granting outstanding performers raises and promotions to master-teacher status, where they could earn $36,000 yearly (more than double the existing $17,800 average for 20-year veterans). The package also called for basic-skills pupil testing and computer training before high school, separate classes for disruptive students, and a 20-percent salary raise for every teacher. To pay the bill, I proposed the largest tax increase in the state's history, to pump one billion dollars more into the schools over three years.

An Innovative Solution

Merit pay simply states that teachers who do the best job should get paid more. Why? Because it encourages more teachers to teach better. In that way, excellence is subsidized and incompetence is punished.

Sally D. Reed, *A Parent's Survival Guide to the Public Schools*, 1991.

Recognizing and rewarding outstanding teachers sounds like a simple idea that would appeal to all, especially teachers. Yet doing so required a year-long battle with the teachers' union—the Tennessee Education Association (TEA), an affiliate of the National Education Association (NEA). NEA executive director Terry Herndon journeyed from Washington to pronounce my master-teacher concept "nonsense" and to pledge NEA's full backing with staff and money to beat it. Their lobbying pressure was so strong that the senate education committee shelved the proposal. The committee chairman, the TEA-backed Democratic candidate in the 1982 gubernatorial primary election, cast the deciding vote.

I decided to challenge the NEA-TEA directly. When the legislature passed an across-the-board teacher pay raise, I vetoed it. "No reforms, no money," I had vowed. "I'll be here four more years and I'll veto any tax hike and teacher raise that does not reward good teaching. Tennesseans will gladly pay more for better schools, but they won't pay more for more of the same."

Indeed, a statewide poll revealed that only 13 percent of Tennesseans would support an across-the-board pay hike, but 69 percent of those with opinions endorsed my tax-and-reform package. And by almost the same margin, they rejected the TEA contention that there is no way to evaluate teachers fairly, and that differential pay would wreck teacher morale.

In January 1984 I called a special session of the legislature. It was a knockdown, drag-out battle. This time the Democratic senate education chairman cast the deciding vote for the bill and became one of its staunchest supporters. Public pressure was so great that the legislature enacted the program and allocated the taxes to pay for it. This included instituting competency testing for students and evaluating teachers, rewarding the best with as much as $7000 in extra pay. House speaker Ned McWherter, a Democrat who later succeeded me as governor, helped pass the performance-pay and career-ladder provisions and declared they are "here to stay."

Quest for Master Teachers

To select Tennessee's master teachers, we asked 106 teachers, who were consensus picks as master teachers themselves, to act as evaluators for candidate selections. After training in the best evaluation techniques we could devise, they went, in three-member teams, to visit the classrooms of the first 3400 applicants for the new career ladder's top rungs. The teams drew on seven sources of information: three classroom observation visits; the candidate's lesson plans; an interview with the candidate; questionnaires given to the principal, students, and peers; and a professional skills test.

Though the state board of education had long had a paper requirement that local boards have evaluation procedures, many ignored it. Our evaluators found principals who could not answer questions about their own teachers. They found teachers who had taught for decades without ever having an administrator offer suggestions for improvement. One fine teacher dissolved into tears, then told an astonished evaluator, "You are the first adult to set foot in my classroom in 16 years, and I just don't know how to handle it."

Altogether, more than 1000 teachers and administrators, about 40 percent of those who applied, made the upper levels on the first try. . . .

Says University of Tennessee Prof. Russell French, who was an adviser on the evaluations: "With four years' experience, we can now demonstrate we have an evaluation process that works well and differentiates clearly and objectively between the many good teachers and the truly outstanding few. It is a powerful new tool for improving education in the United States."

To get their state teaching licenses, students across the country have long been required to stuff their college years with intellectually sterile "education" courses. This prospect has turned many of our best students away from teaching. Tennessee's career-ladder program smashed this teacher-certification bottleneck dramatically.

Ohman. Reprinted by permission: Tribune Media Services.

Once we established a corps of master teachers, Dean Robert L. Saunders at Memphis State University's College of Education used them to launch a one-year postgraduate education program that replaced its undergraduate education major. With a summer of preparation, any arts and sciences graduate who wants to teach can become an apprentice teacher in Memphis-area schools. He or she works directly with a master teacher through the day and returns to the college classroom two evenings a week. At the end of a successful school year, the apprentice gets a teaching certificate.

With a capacity for 50 candidates the first summer, Memphis State had an avalanche of 300 applicants. Its revolutionary program and a comparable one at the University of Tennessee at Knoxville have been so successful that a year after they began, the respected Carnegie Foundation for the Advancement of Teaching recommended a similar program for all teacher certification.

Have better teachers made a difference in student performance? Without a doubt. Student scores in both basic skills and achievement tests have soared. Over three years, eighth-graders increased their number of reading goals mastered by 15 percent and in math by 4 percent. Third-graders consistently scored high in basic skills, and middle-graders gained dramatically.

I wish you could come with me back in the hills to Clay County. Incomes there are half the national average, and nearly 40 percent of the adults over 25 are illiterate. But 9 of the 86 teachers made master-teacher rank, so Superintendent Mayfield Brown can now put his lagging first- to third-graders into summer school with his best teachers. Result: Clay County students who once ranked last among 14 neighboring counties in proficiency tests now score third-highest. Says Brown: "There's no excuse for not educating every child. We've been losing children in the first three grades and never getting them back. Our goal is to have every youngster leaving third grade read at that level or better."

The quality of our teachers and schools will decide America's future in the 1990s. Tennessee has proved that a master-teacher program can work, and our experience in revolutionizing our schools offers lessons for all. Through evaluation and rewards for our best teachers, we can secure a better education for all our children.

"Merit pay, far from improving teacher performance, actually causes far more problems than it solves."

Merit Pay Programs Do Not Improve Teacher Performance

Keith Geiger

Many teachers and teacher associations criticize merit pay programs as unfair systems of teacher assessment. In the following viewpoint, Keith Geiger argues that merit pay programs provide salary bonuses to a fraction of teachers and ignore the financial needs of the rest of the profession. Geiger also maintains that schools do not objectively and equitably identify teachers who deserve merit pay. Consequently, the author contends, merit pay programs cause conflict among teachers. Geiger is the president of the National Education Association (NEA), the nation's largest labor union of teachers, professors, and education administrators.

As you read, consider the following questions:

1. Why do teachers leave the teaching profession, according to Geiger?
2. Why does the author believe it is difficult to identify teachers worthy of merit pay?
3. How can school principals contribute to an inadequate assessment of teacher performance, according to Geiger?

Keith Geiger, "Debate: Do You Believe Merit Pay Would Improve the Performance of Teachers? No," *New York School Boards*, April 1991. Reprinted with the permission of the New York State School Boards Association, © 1991. All rights reserved. No further reprinting without written permission of the publisher.

Merit pay, a system for "rewarding the best teachers with higher salaries": it's an idea that sounds very appealing on its face. Who could argue with such an apparently sensible notion?

No one, it seems—except people in the school districts that have actually tried to implement merit pay! Fairfax County, Virginia, near Washington, D.C.—with nearly 9,000 teachers in 190 schools—is the largest district ever to experiment with a merit pay plan. What happened in Fairfax County illustrates why merit pay, far from improving teacher performance, actually causes far more problems than it solves.

One problem merit pay purports to solve is the exodus of skilled teachers from the classrooms. By paying the best teachers more, the argument goes, we'll induce them not to quit for higher-salaried jobs in private industry.

Our society has never done a good job of providing teachers with adequate compensation for the important work they do. Nationally, today's public school teachers earn an average annual salary of just over $31,331.

While that might sound like a decent salary at first hearing, it's not much when you consider that the average classroom teacher has 15 years of teaching experience and a graduate degree. And in a majority of the states the average teacher salary falls far below this national average. Highly qualified, skilled, and experienced teachers in some states earn as little as $21,300 a year.

Most Teachers Unrewarded

Merit pay completely ignores this grim fiscal reality. In place of appropriate compensation to benefit all teachers, merit pay substitutes a system that rewards a few and ignores the rest.

For the sake of argument let's assume that school systems are able to determine with certainty and objectivity who their "best teachers" are in any given year—a highly dubious proposition. But let's say they can. Even so, competing for merit pay could work as an incentive to keep skilled teachers in the schools only if this occasional, far-from-certain reward is added to salaries that are in the same ballpark as experienced teachers could command in a comparable occupation.

(Meanwhile, polls of teachers who've left the profession consistently show that "poor salaries" aren't the only, or even the main, reason. School districts truly interested in retaining talented teachers need to look beyond pay to school working conditions and a host of other factors that make teachers feel unappreciated and second-class.)

But back to merit pay. While NEA has traditionally opposed the concept, based on 70 years' worth of failed attempts, in the mid-1980s we authorized our local affiliates to give it a new try if they were so inclined. Our Fairfax Education Association (FEA) told its school board, "If you want us to consider merit pay, first we need a healthy round of salary increases to get all teacher paychecks up to a decent level."

In August 1986 the school board agreed to across-the-board raises of over 30 percent for all county teachers over the next three years. The first installment was paid in the fall of 1987, and the final phase was completed with the beginning of the 1989-90 school year. In return, our local Association agreed to work with the school system in developing a more rigorous teacher evaluation system. This system was to enhance the administration's ability to identify both those teachers who did not "measure up" and those who were deserving of merit pay.

Merit Pay Myth

While President Bush admits that "dollar bills don't educate students," his plan for educational reform holds on to the myth that extra money, in the form of merit pay, buys better teaching. . . .

With no objective way to measure excellence, singling out "superior" teachers for extra pay is the surest way to divide all teachers and destroy their morale.

Yaacov Luria, *The Christian Science Monitor*, July 12, 1991.

FEA leaders, looking back, say that one of the main lures was the promise of meaningful teacher evaluations, with or without merit pay. Regular, thorough, thoughtful evaluations are something good teachers welcome—but rarely get.

So the Fairfax plan moved forward, with high hopes on both sides and with the local media reporting every development. But a host of problems soon became apparent. Because the district began stringent teacher evaluation without making any meaningful effort to assure that principals were up to the task, teachers found themselves being judged by principals who were unprepared. Principals who had been recruited with a "program manager" role in mind suddenly found themselves being expected to function as "instructional leaders." They were in no way prepared to fill this new role, and many of them failed miserably.

It may be easy to identify a teacher who isn't doing his or her job effectively. But if you're a principal with several good teachers and you've been told the budget doesn't permit all of them to earn a meritorious rating, how do you decide who'll get it? There's the rub.

The Fairfax County plan set up a review board with a teacher majority to rule on disputed cases of eligibility for merit pay.

But the superintendent could overturn the board's ruling—and did, in almost a third of those cases where the review board upheld a teacher's appeal and said he or she deserved merit pay. (The superintendent never overturned the review board when it supported a principal's decision to deny a meritorious rating.)

FEA surveyed its members and found the competition for merit pay was lowering staff morale, sabotaging collaboration, and encouraging dissension. Teachers reported the advent of jealousies, cronyism, and a "lifeboat" mentality among faculties that had formerly worked well together. Teaching—and ultimately learning—were being undermined.

By February 1989, with the merit pay plan only two-and-a-half years old, the school board had to come to grips with the need to fund the first installment on the merit pay part of the program. Responding to political pressure to find ways to reduce the cost of the plan, the board reneged on its promise to teachers and cut the 10 percent salary increase to a 9 percent one-time merit bonus. Not only did the cut reduce the agreed-to reward, but—even worse—the shift to a bonus, as distinct from salary, eliminated the merit money from any calculation of teachers' retirement benefits.

The board's move to balance its budget on the backs of teachers was the last straw. On top of all the other problems that had surfaced, the board's vote forced the FEA to withdraw its support for the merit pay plan in March 1989. The Association recognized that the plan was broken, and no one knew how to fix it. Today, Fairfax County's merit pay plan is being allowed to die a slow death.

Merit Pay Fails

The simple truth, as revealed in Fairfax and the other districts that have tried merit pay, is that it's a nice-sounding idea that just doesn't work in reality.

School systems almost always find they have more teachers who qualify for merit pay than their budgets can afford to reward. And too often the decisions about who is meritorious are arbitrary by nature or capricious by design. Not only do the rules of the game tend to be inconsistent, but the true goals and standards of merit pay systems often remain undefined.

Clearly, merit pay is not the answer to the problems ailing our schools. Research tells us effective teaching and learning result when teachers work together as teams, when they are encouraged to build strong collegial relationships, and when they have a voice in school decision-making processes. At least as we've seen it implemented to date, merit pay provides none of these positive ingredients that go into improving teacher performance.

"It is essential that teachers be expert in the art of teaching . . . and in the subject area(s) they will be expected to teach."

Extended Teacher Education Produces More Effective Teachers

Robert G. Carroll

University teacher education programs require prospective elementary and high-school teachers to complete the minimum of a bachelor's degree in order to become certified. However, many educators and education researchers contend that this minimum requirement is insufficient to prepare future teachers. In the following viewpoint, Robert G. Carroll argues that extended teacher education programs, such as PROTEACH at the University of Florida, provide the highest quality of instruction necessary to produce the best teachers. Carroll maintains that PROTEACH imparts higher teaching expertise at a time when teachers must become much more knowledgeable. Carroll, a former assistant professor of education at the University of Florida at Gainesville, teaches reading at Fort Clark Middle School in Gainesville.

As you read, consider the following questions:

1. How are the demands placed on teachers greater now than ever before, in Carroll's opinion?
2. According to Carroll, how does the public measure the quality of education?

Excerpted from *Building Bridges for Educational Reform* by Robert G. Carroll, published by Iowa State University Press, 1989. Copyright © 1989 Iowa State University Press, Ames, Iowa 50010. All rights reserved. Reprinted with permission.

PROTEACH (Professional Teacher Program) is the teacher preparation program of the College of Education at the University of Florida. It was implemented in the fall of 1984 after a six-year period of study, debate, and curriculum development. This viewpoint examines the various factors and philosophical positions that affected the development and implementation of PROTEACH. . . .

The initial recommendation to investigate changing the format of teacher education at the University of Florida came from a faculty committee in 1978. A second faculty committee concurred with that recommendation a year later. This launched the college into an extended period of deliberations over not just what changes should be made but whether any changes should be made at all.

High Praise

The preparation programs that existed in the 1970s and early 1980s at Florida commanded a great deal of loyalty from many faculty members. One program had been unchanged for a number of years and most of the faculty seemed content with it. A second program had undergone a significant curricular change some years before that had received national attention and acclaim. The third, due to the nature of its faculty, was in a constant state of self-examination and change and the faculty were confident they were moving in positive directions. Hence, the suggestion of extensively altering these programs did not meet with universal enthusiasm.

Furthermore, the loyalty to the existing programs appeared to be justified. In 1981 the National Council for the Accreditation of Teacher Education (NCATE) had examined the programs at the University of Florida. In its final report the visiting team wrote that Florida's programs were among the best that had ever been reviewed. A year later a State Department of Education review team also praised Florida's teacher-preparation programs, as did a Board of Regents report in 1984. Furthermore, the college was consistently receiving feedback from public school personnel that its graduates were doing quite well. These accolades supported the faculty in its belief that it had already developed strong programs that would continue to produce excellent teachers.

Yet, at the same time that this praise was being received the college was moving toward the reforms of PROTEACH and most of the faculty shared the belief that some form of change in the basic fabric of teacher education was appropriate. In fact, the strength of the existing programs made the PROTEACH reforms possible. Only strong programs and strong faculty can give birth to creative and innovative change.

The reasons that compelled the faculty to investigate making significant changes fell into two complementary lines of thought. The first related to the context of teaching in the foreseeable future and the second related to the status of the research base on teaching.

Nature of Learning

Extending the education program to a graduate level allows time for a broad, general education to be developed, as well as a pedagogy of action. Deciding to become a teacher should be a gradual, well-thought-out process. Establishing education as a graduate degree allows for much-needed self-exploration, the development of an understanding of the interdisciplinary nature of learning, and the pursuit of personal academic interests, and it provides time to investigate how learning and thinking are connected to teaching.

Catherine Twomey Fosnot, *Enquiring Teachers, Enquiring Learners*, 1989.

The demands placed on teachers today are greater than ever before. We continue to crowd the school curriculum with requirements and courses like consumer education, sex education, environmental education, drug and alcohol awareness, and suicide prevention. Certainly all of these are worthy of our attention. However, they are evidence that the schools are being forced to be all things to all people and every minute spent on these requirements is a minute not spent on mathematics, science, and language arts—the subjects in which most parents and the public at large seem to be interested. Furthermore, it is the latter group of subjects that has the more direct impact on SAT scores, the yardstick the public uses to judge the quality of education.

The Art of Teaching

With increased demands for academic excellence and a crowded "cafeteria style curriculum" (National Commission, 1983) it is essential that teachers be expert in the art of teaching, in the efficient use of time, and in the subject area(s) they will be expected to teach. This calls for better training of beginning teachers and better preparation for them in their teaching field than we have ever given them before.

Fifty years ago the possession of a bachelor's degree placed teachers among the most highly educated members of their communities. Today a much greater proportion of the population has graduated from high school, attended some college, obtained a bachelor's degree, or obtained an advanced degree. Meanwhile, the basic requirements for certifying teachers have not significantly changed. As a result, teachers have only slightly more training than a large portion of the public, and an equal amount or even less training than many others.

This deficiency is critical in an information age. The explosion of knowledge and the emphasis on information usage are having dramatic effects on teachers and their students. This can best be illustrated in the role that computers play in the schools. Fifteen years ago computers were esoteric instruments that were used by only a select few; today the schools are expected to help every child become computer literate and more classrooms are getting their own personal computers every day. In fact, many children are now doing their homework using microcomputers to write, edit, and print the final "hard copy."

The demands on teachers arising from life in American society are not limited to the fields of science, mathematics, and language arts; they extend to every facet of the curriculum. For example, the implications of the impact of minority cultures on mainstream America in the coming years are staggering. Social scientists and the teachers of social studies in the public schools must play a crucial role if we are ever to understand and be enriched by each other.

All of this implies that tomorrow's teachers have to be better than yesterday's. They must be better not because yesterday's were bad, but because tomorrow's will be required to know so much more, to have access to so much more, and to display greater expertise in imparting so much more to their students. Yet we are training teachers in essentially the same way and for the same length of time as we did fifty years ago. Surely this justifies a careful examination of the content and processes of preparing beginning teachers. . . .

The PROTEACH Program

PROTEACH is an extended, integrated, five-year program of general and professional studies leading to initial teacher certification and the master of education degree. It is built on a broad-based general background knowledge component. Students come to the College of Education after completing at least sixty-four semester hours of work. The university has set some parameters for thirty-six of these hours in order to guarantee that they be distributed among English; the physical, biological, and mathematical sciences; the social and behavioral sciences; and the humanities. This component is further delineated by the preprofessional requirements of the individual programs within PROTEACH. They each list specific courses that can be used to fulfill some of the general component and others that expand upon it.

As the background knowledge component provides students

with a broad base of general information, the PROTEACH foundational component provides a strong basis in some critical areas of professional knowledge. The foundational component includes thirteen hours of study in the social and historical foundations of education, child development, learning and cognition, measurement and evaluation, and mainstreaming. All students take a course in instructional computing and students in the elementary and special education programs also share a course in parent education. Taken in its entirety, this component provides all PROTEACH students with a shared background of professional knowledge and skills that is essential to the development of prospective educators.

Elementary Education

The elementary education program comprises five years of preparation including six semesters of professional study leading to the master's degree and initial certification. Students in this program are required to complete a twelve-hour specialization in an academic teaching field outside of the College of Education. A second specialization may also be taken outside of the college or inside of the college in a professional specialization such as early childhood, middle grades, special education, or the teaching of reading. The academic specializations were developed in close cooperation with faculty in other colleges in the university, and they represent specific sequences of study beyond that which may have been taken in the general education component.

Precious Resource

In the twentieth century, professional education in all fields has been extended, partly in response to the rapid growth of knowledge underlying practice. The reform of teacher education, then, requires more of that most precious resource—time.

The Holmes Group, *Work in Progress: The Holmes Group One Year On*, 1989.

Students become members of a clinical seminar immediately upon their entry into the college and begin their fieldwork at that time. Ideally, students remain in the same seminar with the same seminar leader throughout their program. The seminar and its members then become a support system, a laboratory for practicing skills, and a forum for feelings and new ideas.

The elementary program emphasizes a dedication to research and to a holistic evaluation of student progress. Courses in educational diagnosis and evaluation and in the research base for teaching are taken early in the program to provide students with a basis for reading and analyzing the professional literature in subsequent courses. A master's level seminar provides each student with the opportunity to pursue a research interest of his or her own that is related to teaching practice. Evaluation practices include a student portfolio that contains written and videotaped evidence of the student's mastery of the FPMS [Florida Performance Measurement System] competencies, evaluations from university and school-based personnel, and the students' own logs, journals, and personal reactions to their field-work. . . .

Secondary Education

The secondary education program is unique among the other PROTEACH programs in that it does not include a bachelor's degree in education. Instead students are expected to complete their bachelor's degree in a teaching field in the College of Liberal Arts and Sciences. They are also required to complete the foundational component described above prior to their entry into the College of Education for a year of professional studies. During that graduate year students take an additional nine hours in their teaching field, a requirement that grows out of a commitment to in-depth training in the subject area and one that exceeds the minimum requirement set by the graduate school at the university.

The graduate year in secondary education is spent primarily in professional preparation for teaching. It features a unique spiraling curriculum and flexible grouping patterns. For example, broad generic teaching competencies such as those in the FPMS are introduced in large interdisciplinary classes. The subject-specific applications of those competencies are then elaborated upon in subject area methods classes. Next, students are sent into the field in teams of two persons from the same subject area to look for specific instances of those competencies learned in their methods classes. Finally, students practice the competencies in microteaching labs with five to eight students from various subject areas. The curriculum and grouping patterns provide a progression from theory to practice and a support system for students as they work towards mastery of each skill.

The foregoing discussion of PROTEACH is only a cursory one. . . . Each program has an element that is skill oriented and that requires the mastery of specific competencies. Each program also has some form of support system built into it to provide for some of the affective needs of its students. The individual course work also reflects both schools of thought in that much attention is given to both the cognitive and affective learning and growth of students. Furthermore, the heavy emphasis on sufficient academic training and on the graduate research function of the college can be seen in the academic specializations, the expansion into the graduate level, and the abandonment of undergraduate degrees in secondary education. Clearly, PROTEACH reflects compromise among the positions, and the overwhelming vote of the faculty to adopt the program indicates a high degree of consensus as well.

It may be self-evident to say that the work of curriculum development does not end with the implementation of new courses. On the contrary, implementation should mark the beginning of a new stage of development and refinement. However, in many cases the real challenge of implementation is to continue the development process once faculty burnout sets in following the strenuous efforts of the design process.

PROTEACH may be subject to such burnout on a greater scale than some other reform efforts because of its overall six-year duration, the intensity of the year-long literature reviews and syntheses, the extended debates, and the concentrated efforts that led to the final design of the program. Whether PROTEACH is typical or atypical in that regard, it is clear that some work remains to be completed. In the opinion of the author critical challenges remain to be met.

Challenges Ahead

PROTEACH offers few concrete assurances that its courses are not offering old wine in new bottles. Certainly, the faculty has done extensive work in reshaping its programs, creating new courses, and identifying the critical knowledge and skills its students must possess. Yet there is no systematic collection of evidence to either support or refute the claim that all of that work has resulted in significant changes in course content and in the methods used to train prospective teachers. Therefore, the first challenge for the college is to monitor the implementation of each new course to insure that its content reflects the research base that has received such strong verbal commitments.

The monitoring of course content is actually a portion of the second challenge. The college must pursue a vigorous agenda of both formative and summative program evaluation. It cannot be presumed that because so much work went into the new program it must necessarily produce better teachers. Only the systematic collection and careful analysis of objective data can answer the hard questions that must be asked in the years ahead. The college has an obligation to the profession and to its students, who are making a substantial commitment of their own to PROTEACH, to assess and to report its successes and failures.

"There is no evidence that extended preparation programs make beginning teachers more effective."

Extended Teacher Education Does Not Produce More Effective Teachers

Willis D. Hawley

In the following viewpoint, Willis D. Hawley argues that postgraduate teacher education programs do not produce better teachers than traditional undergraduate teaching programs because additional courses will not add to the knowledge of teaching. Hawley believes that learning the fundamental principles of teaching is more important than the number of teacher education courses taken. Hawley, the director of the Center for Education Policy at Vanderbilt University in Nashville, Tennessee, is the author of several books, including *Good Schools*.

As you read, consider the following questions:

1. Why do teachers not have higher status, according to Hawley?
2. In the author's opinion, why do extended programs offer less demanding coursework than undergraduate teaching programs?
3. According to Hawley, how can the knowledge of teaching gained in college be lost by teachers on the job?

Adapted from "Should We Extend Teacher Preparation?" by Willis D. Hawley, *Society*, May/June 1989. Copyright © 1989 Transaction Publishing. Reprinted with permission.

As the attacks on teacher education have increased, one reform strategy seems to have gained the most adherents: the proposal to require teacher candidates to have at least five years of
preservice education rather than the four now typically needed
for certification. The five-year teacher preparation movement,
which encompasses many programmatic variations, has powerful proponents. Among them are a special task force of the
American Association of Colleges of Teacher Education
(AACTE), the majority of the members of the National Commission on Excellence in Teacher Education, and the Carnegie Forum on Education and the Economy. The Holmes Group, which
includes the deans of schools of education at most of the nation's research universities, publicly calls for would-be teachers
to complete five years of college and an internship before teaching full-time. Many leading schools of education (such as those
at the University of Chicago and Stanford University, and
Teachers College, Columbia University) now offer teacher training opportunities only at the postbaccalaureate level.

Remarkably, this movement to increase the years of preservice
education for prospective teachers has been proceeding apace
without serious opposition, despite the probability that it could
decrease both the number and the quality of teacher candidates
at a time when we expect a severe teacher shortage. Moreover,
there is no evidence that extended preparation programs make
beginning teachers more effective. . . .

No Evidence of Improvement

We should expect advocates of extended programs to make a
persuasive case that the change they propose will significantly
improve the quality of teaching. No evidence to this effect has
yet been offered. The proponents of extended programs assert
that teachers so prepared will be more knowledgeable and skill-
ful. This argument appears to rest on one or more of the following assumptions about extended programs: (1) there will be
gains in the attractiveness of the profession; (2) students will
learn more in extended programs about teaching and how to
teach; (3) teachers trained in extended programs will be better
prepared in their teaching fields; (4) taking more liberal arts
courses will make students more effective teachers; (5) what
students learn in college about teaching will be reflected in their
classroom performance on the job. Let us briefly examine each
of these assumptions.

Assumption 1 is that there will be gains in the attractiveness
of the profession. Advocates of extended programs have argued
that requiring teachers to have an additional year of schooling
before they are allowed to teach will actually increase the quality of those entering the profession because extended programs

will improve the status of the profession, which in turn will lead to an increase in teachers' salaries. Improved status and higher salaries will attract able students.

Generally speaking, earnings and educational attainment are not closely related once college graduation is assured, especially for women. One can only speculate about the public's willingness to pay teachers more competitive salaries because they have higher degrees. The current market differential for a master's degree is only about $1,600. Teacher salaries declined in the 1970s while increasing proportions of teachers earned master's degrees. (Indeed, teachers are twice as likely as other college graduates to have a master's degree.) Moreover, public funds necessary to implement extended programs would diminish the resources available for teacher salary increases.

No Higher Status

The salary and status arguments are interrelated. Does the requirement of more education for entry lead to higher status for a given profession? Advanced education is correlated with occupational prestige, but many jobs require no more than a college degree for entry and have higher status than does the job of school teaching, including engineering, journalism, and many jobs in business. Education is only one component of occupational prestige, and its contribution seems related, at least in part, to assumptions about the degree to which higher education separates the intellectually able from the less able and transmits knowledge and skills beyond the reach of most people. One reason teachers do not have higher status is that there are so many of them. About 10 percent of all college graduates are needed each year to staff the schools.

The tenuous link between postbaccalaureate education and social status for teachers is nicely illustrated by looking at cultures different from our own. Japan, for example, probably accords its teachers higher status than does any other industrialized country. Yet fewer than 4 percent of Japanese teachers have a master's degree and almost all started to teach upon graduation from college or junior college. The relatively low status of teachers in the United States tells us more about the value we place on good teaching and public servants in general than it does about the relationship between social status and the years of college completed after one receives a bachelor's degree.

The California Program

One way to test the argument that extended programs will lead to higher salaries and higher status is to look at what has happened in California, the one state that has required completion of a fifth year of college before would-be teachers can be fully certified. First, teachers' salaries in California have been similar to those in many nonsouthern states for several years. In 1985-86 beginning teachers' salaries in California took a nonincremental jump to go above the national average. To attribute this salary increase to a requirement that was established more than two decades ago would be wrong. It is much more reasonable to assume that the recent increase in teachers' salaries in California (not so remarkable when the cost of living is taken into account) is the result of concern over the quality and quantity of those who have chosen to teach in that state, given its fifth-year requirements. Many cities in California cannot fill open teacher positions; teaching candidates have ranked very near the bottom of thirty occupations with respect to measures of verbal and quantitative abilities; and close to one-third of the teachers statewide have been hired with temporary credentials because not enough students seek full certification before entry. In short, the lesson to be drawn from California's long experience with extended programs is that they do not increase the status or attractiveness of the teaching profession.

MacNelly. Reprinted by permission: Tribune Media Services.

Assumption 2 is that students will learn more in extended programs about teaching and how to teach. A major argument for fifth-year programs is that teachers so educated will know more about teaching. There are two ways in which this might happen. First, teacher candidates might take more professional coursework. Second, teacher applicants in extended programs will take more sophisticated and more demanding courses.

One-year postbaccalaureate certification programs generally

limit students to fewer education courses than they might take in an undergraduate program. Students might be required to take undergraduate electives in preparation for the fifth year, but such requirements would further complicate entry to the profession because they would further extend the time required to prepare to teach for those who decide to teach after graduation from college or late in their college career.

If teachers' initial training in extended programs would result in a master's degree, the total amount of formal professional education the typical career teacher receives probably will be less than it is now. For example, the typical high school teacher certified upon graduation from college will have taken about sixty semester hours of professional coursework by the time he or she receives the master's degree. The person who receives the master's degree upon completion of a one-year postbaccalaureate training program will take half this much coursework. This argument will not be persuasive to those who discount the value of professional education courses, but such persons are presumably not among the advocates of five-year programs.

Intellectually Demanding?

It might be argued that the "graduate" courses embodied in extended programs will be more intellectually demanding and thus students will learn more about how to teach. Graduate courses required of master's degree candidates in education are not known to be more demanding than undergraduate education courses. Why should they be? They will be taught by the same faculty members. So far as we know, twenty-two-year-olds are not better learners than twenty-one-year-olds. On the other hand, persons pursuing a master's degree or a fifth year of study are likely to be more productive learners if they actually have taught in classrooms because they can then use their experience to frame questions and to organize information. Good teaching involves an enormously complex and demanding set of intellectual tasks. Learning how to perform those tasks is likely to be easier if teachers have a clearer idea about what the process of teaching actually involves.

It seems difficult to argue, either on the basis of existing evidence or on logical grounds, that extended teacher education programs, in themselves, will improve what teachers know about teaching. It may be that extended programs requiring undergraduate education courses could provide teachers with more pedagogical knowledge than four-year programs that insist on a strong liberal arts curriculum and intensive study of the subjects or subject the student will teach. Whether this will make such teachers more effective is a different issue.

Assumption 3 is that teachers trained in extended programs

will be better prepared in their teaching fields. Extended programs requiring undergraduate education courses will not open up much room in the curriculum for subject-matter courses. To the extent that they do, or that postbaccalaureate-only programs do free up time for subject-matter courses, this will permit persons training to be elementary school teachers to take more math, science, English, or social studies courses. But extended programs should have little impact on the number of courses in their subject field that secondary teachers take. In most education schools, secondary teacher candidates already complete a disciplinary major or its equivalent.

Ineffective Response

The idea that five years of preservice education will enhance the quality of teaching is another manifestation of the propensity of social reformers to respond to weaknesses in political institutions by creating new structures rather than reforming the ones found to be inadequate. It is the American way of change but it usually is ineffective because it does not address fundamental problems.

Willis D. Hawley, *Society*, May/June 1989.

The content of the courses they take is more important than the numbers, but this point is not relevant to the debate over the length of preservice teacher education. Moreover, there is reason to believe that the amount of coursework in the subject being taught does not contribute to effective teaching. This last point seems counterintuitive, but it may suggest that once one has ten or so courses in one's field, it is not the number of courses, but whether or not one understands fundamental principles and the structure of the discipline or body of knowledge involved. It seems doubtful that most undergraduate course sequences in any particular field produce these understandings among the students who take them. At most colleges and universities, especially those that educate the greatest number of teachers, undergraduate education seems to be something of a random walk during which course selection is often based on convenience and the desire for free time. As a recent report of the Association of American Colleges concludes, the typical curriculum "offers too much knowledge with too little attention to how knowledge has been created and what methods and styles of inquiry have led to its creation."

Assumption 4 is that taking more liberal arts courses will make students more effective teachers. Some advocates of extended programs, in particular those who argue that teacher preparation programs should begin after undergraduate education has been completed, believe that this reform will make teachers better educated and thus more effective.

Let us assume that undergraduate teacher candidates will take, in addition to the education-related courses they must pass to be certified (some of these are liberal arts courses, in most states), an academic major and satisfy general education or distribution (liberal arts) requirements. Thus most students seeking certification in secondary education will take about three-fourths of their courses outside of education departments and colleges. If no increases in the number of education courses accompanied the implementation of extended programs, requiring five years of college for teacher preparation would mean that students would be freed to take eight to ten electives in lieu of education courses. There is absolutely no evidence that such a change would make students better teachers. The extent to which taking more liberal arts courses would improve teaching would seem to depend importantly on the difference between the intellectual content of the electives and the education courses a student would take. No doubt there are education courses that are undemanding and devoid of the concerns for theory and method of inquiry that characterize the best liberal arts courses, but many students seem to choose their electives on the basis of how undemanding they are. If it is true that many liberal arts courses are more rigorous than many education courses, this speaks to the need to change the content of education courses.

Teachers' Knowledge Undone

Assumption 5 is that what students learn in college about teaching will be reflected in their classroom performance on the job. The movement toward extended teacher education programs, at least among teacher educators, is motivated in large measure by the rapid growth in knowledge about effective instructional practices and teaching behaviors. The argument is that there is now more to know about how to teach effectively than ever before and that teachers should know this information and be able to use it before they enter the classroom. This argument assumes that what teacher candidates learn before they become teachers is often put to good use in the classroom. There is, however, reason to doubt this presumption. Recent research on how teachers learn to teach indicates that much of what teachers learn in the preservice stage of their career is undone or substantially mitigated during the first year or two of teaching and, perhaps, by the "practice teaching" experience. The implication of this reality is that increasing the amount of information and skills teachers learn in college is an inefficient—and perhaps futile—strategy unless ways are devised to enhance the ability of teachers to use what they have learned on the job. Some advocates of extended programs, such as the Holmes Group, have recognized this problem and have advocated the use of intensively supervised paid internships to facilitate induction to the profession. These internships, however, when added to the extended program, will significantly increase the costs of entry for individuals or the public costs of preparing new teachers.

No Improved Performance

In short, the possibility that extended programs will reduce the quality and quantity of teachers is high and the likelihood that they will improve teacher performance is not great. This does not mean that we should not experiment with extended teacher preparation programs but it does mean that such trials should be carefully evaluated. If the risks of extended programs seem high and the benefits uncertain, other strategies for improving teacher education should be explored more aggressively than they have been. Two such alternatives to both the status quo and the extended college-based programs are the reform of undergraduate programs and postbaccalaureate internships. These two strategies would complement each other and, taken together, would almost certainly be more cost-effective than extended programs.

Recognizing Deceptive Arguments

People who feel strongly about an issue use many techniques to persuade others to agree with them. Some of these techniques appeal to the intellect, some to the emotions. Many of them distract the reader or listener from the real issues.

A few common examples of argumentation tactics are listed below. Most of them can be used either to advance an argument in an honest, reasonable way or to deceive or distract from the real issues. It is important for a critical reader to recognize these tactics in order to rationally evaluate an author's ideas.

a. *categorical statement*—stating something in a way that implies there can be no argument.

b. *strawperson*—distorting or exaggerating an opponent's ideas to make one's own seem stronger.

c. *testimonial*—quoting or paraphrasing an authority or celebrity to support one's own viewpoint.

d. *bandwagon*—the idea that "everybody" does this or believes this.

The following activity can help you sharpen your skills in recognizing deceptive reasoning. The statements below are derived from the viewpoints in this chapter. *Beside each one, mark the letter of the type of deceptive appeal being used. More than one type of tactic may be applicable. If you believe the statement is not any of the listed appeals, write N.*

1. The "bigger is better" thinking behind national teacher certification is a ludicrous effort to cure chills and fevers by devising more accurate thermometers.

2. Merit pay plans have never succeeded and will never work.

3. Important organizations such as the National Research Council and the Association of Teacher Educators endorse national teacher certification.

4. Everyone knows that education majors learn more about teaching in five or six years of study rather than in four.

5. Ever since merit pay programs were introduced in Tennessee, student scores have increased.

6. The only way to learn anything about teaching is from classroom experience.

7. Secretary of Education Lamar Alexander, architect of the most successful merit pay program in the U.S., understands that merit pay attracts and rewards the best teachers.

8. Merit pay advocates dangle a "carrot" of a few measly hundred dollars in teachers' faces, expecting them to follow along like they were donkeys.

9. The leading schools of education, such as Stanford University, Columbia University, and the University of Chicago, call for students to complete at least five years of college before teaching full time.

10. National teacher certification would provide not one valid piece of information on the quality of an individual's teaching.

11. Every education student values the importance of learning about teaching.

12. All teachers realize that national teacher certification is another organized effort to centralize education.

13. Teachers are grossly underpaid.

14. The twisted logic of national teacher certification would hoodwink the public into believing that a national board can recognize teaching talent far better than our own schools can.

Periodical Bibliography

The following articles have been selected to supplement the diverse views presented in this chapter.

Aaron Bernstein
: "Letting Teachers Call the Shots," *Business Week*, January 28, 1991.

Susan Chira
: "Efforts to Reshape Teaching Focus on Finding New Talent," *The New York Times*, August 28, 1990.

C. Emily Feistritzer
: "Not Happy Teachers—Better Teachers," *The Wall Street Journal*, October 26, 1990.

Chester E. Finn
: "Accounting for Results," *National Review*, May 27, 1991.

Samuel G. Freedman
: "What Makes a Good Teacher?" *Utne Reader*, September/October 1990.

John I. Goodlad
: "Better Teachers for Our Nation's Schools," *The Education Digest*, February 1991.

Martin Haberman and William H. Richards
: "Why Teachers Quit," *The Education Digest*, April 1991.

Donna M. Kagan
: "Builders of Wooden Boats and the Reform of Teacher Education: A Parable," *Phi Delta Kappan*, May 1991.

David T. Kearns
: "Do Teachers Really Need Licenses?" *The Wall Street Journal*, February 28, 1990.

Connie Leslie
: "The Failure of Teacher Ed," *Newsweek*, October 1, 1990.

Marcus Mabry
: "The New Teacher Corps," *Newsweek*, July 16, 1990.

Amy Saltzman
: "Wooed by the Classroom," *U.S. News & World Report*, February 4, 1991.

Donald J. Stedman
: "Re-Inventing the Schools of Education," *Vital Speeches of the Day*, April 15, 1991.

Richard L. Weaver II
: "The Dynamic Teacher," *Vital Speeches of the Day*, October 15, 1990.

3 CHAPTER

Should Parents Be Allowed to Choose Their Children's Schools?

EDUCATION
in America

Chapter Preface

Perhaps the most debated current educational reform measure is parental school choice. Under school choice programs, geographic restrictions are eliminated and parents are allowed to choose their children's schools. Some choice programs require parents to choose a public school within one district, while other programs include private schools and schools outside of the district. In programs that include private schools, local or state governments pay all or part of a child's private school tuition. Currently only a few cities and states have implemented choice programs, but many others are considering them.

Advocates of choice programs argue that expanding parents' choice of schools will improve public education by introducing competition into the educational system. Because parents could choose the best public or private schools for their children, less effective schools would be forced to improve their quality to compete for students and to remain open. As George Roche, president of Hillsdale College in Michigan, writes, "Where choice experiments have been tried it has been an outstanding success. . . . Test scores have skyrocketed."

Opponents argue that school choice would harm public schools because parents would choose schools that matched their children's ethnic or social class characteristics. Critics contend such segregation would reverse the progress achieved by years of integration of students of all backgrounds. As former Athens, Ohio, school board member Lois D. Whealey explains, "Plain snobbery and a desire to maintain de facto socioeconomic segregation are often the real underlying reasons for school choice: 'I want my child to be with her own kind,' parents say."

Whether parents should be allowed to choose their children's schools is a controversial issue. The authors in the following chapter debate the pros and cons of school choice.

"Choice is being embraced . . . as a powerful means of transforming the structure and performance of public education. "

Parental School Choice Programs Would Improve Education

John E. Chubb and Terry M. Moe

Critics of public education often complain that schools fail because there is no incentive for them to improve. John E. Chubb and Terry M. Moe, the authors of the following viewpoint, agree with this view. Chubb and Moe propose allowing parents to choose their children's schools, thereby forcing schools to compete for students. If parents could choose, the authors maintain, individual schools would improve the quality of education to attract students. Chubb and Moe are the authors of *Politics, Markets, and America's Schools*, from which this viewpoint is excerpted. Chubb is a senior fellow in the governmental studies program at the Brookings Institution, a think tank in Washington, D.C. Moe is a political science professor at Stanford University in Palo Alto, California.

As you read, consider the following questions:

1. Why must educational reform eliminate states' authority over schools, according to Chubb and Moe?
2. In the authors' opinion, why must private schools be included in school choice programs?

Excerpted from *Politics, Markets, and America's Schools* by John E. Chubb and Terry M. Moe, published by The Brookings Institution, 1990. Copyright © 1990, The Brookings Institution. Reprinted with permission.

The most innovative and promising reforms to have gained momentum during the late eighties fall under the heading of "choice." In the past, educators tended to associate this concept with the privatization of public education, aid to religious schools, and racial segregation, portraying it as a subversive notion that threatened the common school ideal and virtually everything else the public system had traditionally stood for. In recent years, however, choice has come to be viewed very differently, even by many in the educational establishment.

This new movement puts choice to use as part of a larger set of strategies for reform *within* the public sector. It is not about privatizing the public schools, nor is it a surreptitious way of giving aid to religious schools. Choice is being embraced by liberals and conservatives alike as a powerful means of transforming the structure and performance of public education—while keeping the public schools public. In the process, it is being used to combat racial segregation; indeed, it has become the preferred approach to desegregation in districts throughout the country—in Rochester and Buffalo (New York), Cambridge (Massachusetts), and Prince George's County (Maryland), to name a few.

Support for Choice

Support for public sector choice is widespread. Surveys reveal that the vast majority of public school parents want to choose the schools their children attend—and that, when choice plans are implemented and people have a chance to exercise their newfound freedom, popular support for choice grows. Not surprisingly, many public officials are also singing the praises of choice, with support running particularly strong among political executives. Their broad, heterogeneous constituencies, their uniquely central role in policymaking, and the public's inclination to hold them singularly responsible for effective government all make them more willing (than legislators) to take bold, unconventional actions that provoke opposition from the established interests.

At the federal level, Presidents Ronald Reagan and George Bush have been enthusiastic supporters of educational choice, although there is not a great deal the federal government can do on its own. More consequentially, given the primary role of the states in public education, the National Governors' Association has come out strongly for choice in its report on education, *Time for Results*—and reformist governors, Democrats and Republicans alike, have typically been in the forefront in pressing for real change. . . .

Without pretending to have an optimal plan up our sleeves, we would now like to outline a brief proposal for a choice system that we think is equipped to do the job. Offering our own proposal in this way has a certain practical value, for it allows us to illustrate in some detail what a full-blown choice system might look like, as well as to note some of the policy decisions that must be made along the way in building one. But more important, it also allows us to suggest in specific terms what our institutional theory of schools actually entails for educational reform—and to emphasize, once again, how essential it is that reforms be founded on theory. The absence of a clear, well-developed theory—and the triumph, in its stead, of platitudes and surface plausibility—leads inevitably to the grab-bag. And to failure and disappointment.

Educational Excellence

We can encourage educational excellence by encouraging parental choice. The concept of choice draws its fundamental strength from the principle at the very heart of the democratic idea. Every adult American has the right to vote, the right to decide where to work, where to live. It's time parents were free to choose the schools that their children attend. This approach will create the competitive climate that stimulates excellence in our private and parochial schools as well.

George Bush, taken from a White House speech delivered on April 18, 1991.

Our guiding principle in the design of a choice system is this: public authority must be put to use in creating a system that is almost entirely beyond the reach of public authority. Because states have primary responsibility for American public education, we think the best way to achieve significant, enduring reform is for states to take the initiative in withdrawing authority from existing institutions and building a new system in which most authority is vested directly in the schools, parents, and students. This restructuring cannot be construed as an exercise in delegation. As long as authority remains "available" at higher levels within state government, it will eventually be used to control the schools. As far as possible, all higher-level authority must be eliminated.

What we propose, more specifically, is that state leaders create a new system of public education with the following properties.

The Supply of Public Schools

The state will have the responsibility for setting criteria that define what constitutes a "public school" under the new system. These criteria should be quite minimal, roughly corresponding to the criteria many states now employ in accrediting private schools—graduation requirements, health and safety requirements, and teacher certification requirements.

Any group or organization that applies to the state and meets these minimal criteria must then be chartered as a public school and granted the right to accept students and receive public money.

Existing private schools will be among those eligible to participate. Their participation should be encouraged, since they constitute a ready supply of often-effective schools. (Our own preference would be to include religious schools as well, as long as their sectarian functions can be kept clearly separate from their educational functions.) Any private schools that do participate will thereby become public schools, as such schools are defined under the new system.

District governments can continue running their present schools, assuming the latter meet state criteria. They will have authority, however, only over their own schools and not over any of the others that may be chartered by the state.

The Funding of Public Education

The state will set up a Choice Office in each district, which, among other things, will maintain a record of all school-age children and the level of funding—the "scholarship" amounts—associated with each child. Schools will be compensated directly by this office based on the specific children they enroll. Public money will flow from funding sources (federal, state, and district governments) to the Choice Office and then to schools. At no point will it go to parents or students.

As it does now, the state will have the right to specify how much, or by what formula, each district must contribute for each child. Our own preference is for an equalization approach that requires wealthier districts to contribute more per child than poor districts do and that guarantees students in all districts an adequate financial foundation. The state's contribution can then be calibrated to bring total spending per child up to whatever dollar amount seems desirable; under an equalization scheme, this would mean a larger state contribution in poor districts than in wealthy ones.

While it is important to give parents and students as much flexibility as possible, we think it is unwise to allow them to supplement their scholarship amounts with personal funds. Such "add-ons" threaten to produce too many disparities and inequalities within the public system, and many citizens would regard them as unfair and burdensome. . . .

Each student will be free to attend any public school in the state, regardless of district, with the relevant scholarship—consisting of federal, state, and local contributions—flowing to the

school of choice. In practice, of course, most students will probably choose schools in reasonable proximity to their homes. But
districts will have no claim on their own residents.

To the extent that tax revenues allow, every effort will be made
to provide transportation for students that need it. This is important in helping to open up as many alternatives as possible to all
students, especially the poor and those located in rural areas.

Success Story

The earliest evidence of choice working came from New York's
East Harlem school district. In 1974, the school district gave
teachers the ability to plan curriculum and gave parents the right
to choose among diverse programs the teachers had created. The
resulting competition increased education quality. Graduation
rates shot up to more than 90 percent from less than 50 percent;
the district, which ranked last of New York City's 32 districts,
climbed to 16th in basic skills testing; community morale soared
as the choice program brought parents and teachers together to
work on behalf of their children.

Jeanne Allen, *Heritage Foundation Talking Points*, November 21, 1990.

To assist parents and students in choosing among schools, the
state will provide a Parent Information Center within its local
Choice Office. This Center will collect comprehensive information on each school in the district, and its parent liaisons will
meet personally with parents in helping them judge which
schools best meet their children's needs. The emphasis here
will be on personal contact and involvement. Parents will be required to visit the Center at least once, and encouraged to do so
often. Meetings will be arranged at all schools so that parents
can see first-hand what their choices are.

The applications process will be handled in simple fashion by
the Parent Information Center. Once parents and students decide which schools they prefer, they will fill out applications to
each, with parent liaisons available to give advice and assistance
(including filling out the applications themselves, if necessary).
All applications will be submitted to the Center, which in turn
will send them out to the schools.

Controlling Admissions

Schools will make their own admissions decisions, subject
only to nondiscrimination requirements. This is absolutely crucial. Schools must be able to define their own missions and
build their own programs in their own ways, and they cannot
do this if their student population is thrust on them by out-

106

siders. They must be free to admit as many or as few students as they want, based on whatever criteria they think relevant—intelligence, interest, motivation, behavior, special needs—and they must be free to exercise their own, informal judgments about individual applicants.

Schools will set their own "tuitions." They may choose to do this explicitly—say, by publicly announcing the minimum scholarship they are willing to accept. They may also do it implicitly by allowing anyone to apply for admission and simply making selections, knowing in advance what each applicant's scholarship amount is. In either case, schools are free to admit students with different-sized scholarships, and they are free to keep the entire scholarship that accompanies each student they have admitted. This gives all schools incentives to attract students with special needs, since these children will have the largest scholarships. It also gives schools incentives to attract students from districts with high base-level scholarships. But no school need restrict itself to students with special needs, nor to students from a single district. . . .

School Structure

The state must refrain from imposing *any* structures or rules that specify how authority is to be exercised within the school. This is meant to include the district-run schools: the state must not impose any governing apparatus on them either. These schools, however, are subordinate units within district government—they are already embedded in a larger organization—and it is the district authorities, not the schools, that have the legal right to determine how they will be governed.

More generally, the state will do nothing to tell the schools how they must be internally organized to do their work. There will be no requirements for career ladders, advisory committees, textbook selection, in-service training, preparation time, homework, or anything else. The schools will be organized and operated as they see fit. . . .

This proposal calls for fundamental changes in the structure of American public education. Stereotypes aside, however, these changes have nothing to do with "privatizing" the nation's schools. The choice system we have outlined here would be a truly public system—and a democratic one.

We are proposing that the state put its democratic authority to use in creating a new institutional framework. The design and legitimation of this framework would be a democratic act of the most fundamental sort. It would be a social decision, made through the usual processes of democratic governance, by which the people and their representatives specify the structure of a new system of public education.

"What's wrong with this proposal to combine vouchers with radical deregulation? Everything."

Parental School Choice Programs Would Harm Education

Bill Honig

Programs allowing parents to use government funds to choose their children's schools are unnecessary because current educational reforms are working and student performance is improving, Bill Honig argues in the following viewpoint. Honig maintains that choice programs would unfairly allow private schools to selectively exclude public school students who do not meet their academic standards. In addition, the author contends that using government funds for private schools, such as religious schools, will violate constitutional restrictions. Honig is the superintendent of California's public schools.

As you read, consider the following questions:

1. Why does Honig believe it is important for students to learn common democratic values in public schools?
2. According to the author, how will school choice result in more bureaucracy?
3. What school improvement strategies are more effective than choice programs, according to Honig?

Bill Honig, "Why Privatizing Public Education Is a Bad Idea," *The Brookings Review*, Winter 1990/91. Reprinted with permission of The Brookings Institution.

One of the loudest salvos in the ongoing battle over "choice" in public schools came from theoreticians John E. Chubb and Terry M. Moe in the *Brookings Review.* Chubb and Moe propose to transform our public schools from democratically regulated to market-driven institutions. They argue that the past decade has seen the most ambitious period of school reform in the nation's history, but that gains in test scores or graduation rates are nil. Their explanation: government, with its politics and bureaucracy, so hampers schools' ability to focus on academic achievement that improvement efforts are doomed.

Using data from the early eighties, Chubb and Moe contend that freeing schools from democratic control boosts performance a full grade level. Thus, they would give students scholarships for any public, private, or newly formed school; prohibit states or school districts from establishing organizational or effective curricular standards or assessing school performance; and allow schools to restrict student entry. They assert that parent choice alone will assure quality.

Totally Wrong Proposal

What's wrong with this proposal to combine vouchers with radical deregulation? Everything.

In the first place, Chubb and Moe's basic charge that current reform efforts have not succeeded is dead wrong and, consequently, the need for risky and radical change unjustified. While their data say something useful about the dangers of rigid bureaucracy and the overpoliticization of education, their findings cannot be used to judge the reform effort, since the students in their study were tested before reforms began. Evidence gathered more recently points to substantial gains.

For example, in 1983 California began refocusing on academic excellence, reducing bureaucracy, enhancing professional autonomy, and moving away from a rule-based to a performance-driven system. We raised standards; strengthened curriculum and assessment; invested in teacher and principal training; established accountability, including performance targets and incentives for good results and penalties for bad; provided funds for team building at the school; pushed for better textbooks; and forged alliances with parents, higher education, and the business community.

The result of this comprehensive approach has been real progress. In 1989, in reading and math, California high school seniors scored *one year* ahead of seniors in 1983, the exact improvement that Chubb and Moe say their proposal would achieve and just what they argue could not be accomplished within the existing system.

Since 1986, California eighth grade scores have risen 25 percent, the pool of dropouts has decreased 18 percent, and the number of high school graduates meeting the University of California entrance requirements has risen 20 percent. Since 1983, the number of seniors scoring above 450 in the verbal section of the Scholastic Aptitude Test has grown 19 percent, the number scoring above 500 has increased 28 percent, and the rate of seniors passing Advanced Placement tests has jumped 114 percent—to more than 50,000 students a year.

Harvell/*Greenville Piedmont*. Reprinted with permission.

California educators achieved these results even though the number of students in poverty doubled, the number of those who do not speak English doubled to one out of five, and California's student population grew explosively.

National Progress

Impressive gains were also made nationally during the 1980s. The dropout pool shrunk by a third; the number of graduates attending college grew 18 percent; and on the National Assessment of Educational Progress, the number of 17-year-olds able to solve moderately complex problems increased 22 percent in mathematics, and 18 percent in science. Reading and writing scores, however, grew less.

Further evidence of improvement in the performance of college-bound American youngsters is that Advanced Placement courses taken have nearly doubled since 1982. The number of students taking the more demanding curriculum, suggested by *A Nation at Risk*, of four years of English; three years of social studies, science, and math; and two years of foreign languages more than doubled between 1982 and 1987, from 13 percent to 29 percent of high school graduates. In science, the number of graduates taking chemistry grew 45 percent to nearly one of every two students, and the number taking physics expanded 44 percent to one of every five students.

Certainly, these gains are not sufficient to prepare American youngsters for the changing job market, to reach their potential, to participate in our democracy, or to keep up with international competition. We still have a long way to go. But that is not the issue. Educators are being challenged on whether we have a strategy that can produce results. We do, and this nation should be discussing how best to build on this record and accelerate the pace of reform—not how to dismantle public education.

Democracy Jeopardized

It is no exaggeration to say that Chubb and Moe's ideas for change would jeopardize our youngsters and this democracy. Any one of the following objections should be enough to sink their plan.

First, the proposal risks creating elite academies for the few and second-rate schools for the many. It allows schools to exclude students who do not meet their standards—almost guaranteeing exacerbation of existing income and racial stratification. We had such a two-tiered system in the 19th century before mass public education helped make this country prosperous and free. We should not go back 100 years in search of the future.

Second, cult schools will result. Nearly 90 percent of American youngsters attend public schools, which are the major institutions involved in transmitting our democratic values. By prohibiting common standards, Chubb and Moe enshrine the rights of parents over the needs of children and society and encourage tribalism. Is it good public policy to use public funds to support schools that teach astrology or creationism instead of science, inculcate antiminority or antiwhite attitudes, or prevent students from reading *The Diary of Anne Frank* or *The Adventures of Huckleberry Finn*? Absent democratic controls, such schools will multiply.

Third, their plan violates the constitutional prohibition against aiding religious schools.

Fourth, the lack of accountability and the naivete of relying on the market to protect children is alarming. In the 19th century the slogan was "let the buyer beware," and meat packers sold tainted meat to consumers. In the 20th century deregulation produced the savings and loan debacle. Nobody seriously proposes rescinding environmental safeguards—why should our children not be similarly protected? Look at private trade schools. Regulation is weak, and scholarships are available. The results: widespread fraud and misrepresentation. Similar problems occurred when New York decentralized its school system. Corruption and patronage surfaced in its local boards of education. All across the nation there are calls for *more* accountability from our schools, not less.

Fifth, the plan would be tremendously chaotic. Vast numbers of new schools would have to be created for this plan to succeed; yet most new enterprises fail. Many youngsters will suffer during the transition period, and with no accountability we will not even know if the experiment was successful.

Sixth, taxpayers will have to pay more. Chubb and Moe maintain that competition will produce savings, but they offer no proof. A potent counter-example: colleges compete, yet costs are skyrocketing. Furthermore, if this plan is adopted nationwide, a substantial portion of the cost of private school students—about $17 billion a year—currently paid for by their parents will be picked up by taxpayers (unless public school expenditures are reduced 10 percent, which would make the plan doubly disastrous). In addition, the proposal includes expensive transportation components and the creation of a new level of bureaucracy—Choice Offices. These offices will include Parent Information Centers, where liaisons will meet with parents and students to advise them on what schools to choose. But how many employees will be necessary for this process if parents are to receive the information they need in a timely manner?

Better Investments

If this country is willing to spend billions to improve education, there are much better investments with proven returns than Chubb and Moe's fanciful idea. One is providing funds to bring teachers up to speed in math, science, and history. Investing in team-building efforts, technology, improving assessment, Headstart programs, or prenatal care also offers proven returns for the dollar spent.

Chubb and Moe misread the evidence on choice and claim it is the only answer. We *should* give public school parents more choice, either through magnet schools or through open-enrollment plans. Choice builds commitment of parents and students and keeps the system honest. But limits are necessary to prevent skimming of the academic or athletically talented or furthering racial segregation.

"Voucher plan[s] . . . generate competition among public schools. And, let us face it, the public schools are the ones that need it."

Government Should Offer School Vouchers

Sally D. Reed

School choice proposals often include the use of government-provided education vouchers, which parents could redeem for their child's education at the public or private school of their choice. In the following viewpoint, Sally D. Reed argues that vouchers help disadvantaged children who otherwise must rely on poor neighborhood schools. Vouchers offer these children an education at better public or private schools. Reed contends that because disadvantaged children are often minorities, giving them access to schools in better neighborhoods also increases racial integration. Reed is the founder and director of the National Council for Better Education, an Alexandria, Virginia-based organization that supports localized control of public schools.

As you read, consider the following questions:

1. According to Reed, how does parents' use of vouchers create competition among schools?
2. In the author's opinion, how do school vouchers neither aid nor discourage parents who might choose religious schools for their children?
3. Why does the author think that powerful teachers' unions and other education organizations oppose school vouchers?

Excerpted, with permission, from *A Parent's Survival Guide to the Public Schools* by Sally D. Reed, published by the National Council for Better Education, 1991.

In November of 1985 the United States Congress began debate on an issue which could reverse the course of elementary and secondary education in America.

The issue: educational vouchers. The debate: whether or not the elements of choice and competition are to be injected back into the American education process. The success or failure of the November proposal will determine whether, at long last, the ball will really start rolling on education reform.

It was a bit of a gamble on the part of the powers that be. Those who cast their votes in favor of vouchers were making an important assumption about the American parent. They were assuming that, given a choice, American parents would seek the highest quality education available for their children. "Yes" voters also assumed that the American parent has the ability to recognize and reject the gimmicky, the unsubstantial and the mindless—in other words, the kinds of trivia that have been passed off as solid subject matter for the past several decades.

Reagan's Voucher Plan

In 1985, under the Reagan Administration, the Department of Education introduced a voucher initiative called TEACH, the Equity and Choice Act of 1985. It was designed to allow recipients of the standard federal assistance package for the disadvantaged, called Chapter One or the compensatory education program, to use an education voucher to secure alternative educational services at another public school within their own district, at a public school outside their own district, or as partial tuition at a private school of their choice. In other words, the intent of the TEACH bill was to voucherize special education aid for disadvantaged children by allowing their parents to purchase remedial mathematics and reading help (which is what Chapter One funds have traditionally been used for) from either the public or private sector.

Because the federal government was already funding Chapter One, it was able to prescribe the conditions under which such funding would be disseminated. Had federal funds not been involved, the federal government would have been inhibited from initiating any choice proposals. It is somewhat ironic that those who had worked the hardest over the years to ensure the federal government did become involved in education (as the NEA's [National Education Association] lobbying for Jimmy Carter and a DOE [Department of Education]) became the loudest critics of this, and all positive steps aimed at education's improvement.

But with the election of Ronald Reagan in 1980 and again in 1984, the tables were turned. Instead of a mouthpiece for their own left-wing political agenda and a rubber stamp for their outrageous spending initiatives, NEA union leaders got instead a dedicated champion of high standards, Secretary William J. Bennett, who dared to suggest that the goal of education should be excellence, not simply fun, and that parents deserved a say in how their children were educated.

Until 1985, education reformers had all but despaired of ever designing a plan capable of energizing America's ailing education system. All the legal avenues to reform seemed to have been plugged by an overbearing and condescending bureaucracy which told grassroots America, in effect, that they were too stupid to make education decisions for their own children.

Let the System Work

With the voucher initiative, Secretary Bennett and the DOE managed to capitalize upon President Reagan's "let the system work" philosophy and at the same time defuse the liberals' favorite oppositionist maneuver of denouncing any conservative-administration program as an attack on the poor, or, as the NEA called it, "a cruel hoax."

For here was an idea specifically targeted to help disadvantaged families. And, if it worked for the disadvantaged, its success would undoubtedly encourage the states and locals, sooner or later, to come up with the voucher or choice plans of their own—something all parents can use. The 1985 choice plan, which was admittedly only experimental, could serve as a first step toward a full-scale transformation of public school expenditures into educational vouchers. And this was the very reason the NEA was so adamantly against it.

More Academic Success

One reason poor and minority parents are becoming interested in educational choice is dissatisfaction with the education their children receive. Private schools generally have more academic success than public schools. A voucher system makes these schooling options more accessible to families from all income levels and encourages public schools to improve.

James D. Foster, *Christianity Today*, August 19, 1991.

For example, the NEA quickly released a five-page statement in October of 1985 condemning the voucher initiative. Among the many bogus arguments used was that the voucher plan "could undermine public support and funding for public schools, ultimately weakening and destroying them"; that it "could potentially violate the principle of separation of church and state"; that it "could lead to racial, economic and social isolation of children"; and that it shifts attention away "from the nation's most critical issue: the lack of adequate funding for high quality public education."

Apparently, the assumption of the first argument was that, given a choice, all parents would flock away from the public schools as fast as possible and place their children in private and parochial schools. Aside from what such an assumption says about union leaders' view of public education (and what the parents think of it), the TEACH proposal was not intended to cover the entire cost of tuition at a private school, since it applied only to the amount allotted for Chapter One compensatory education funds. Secondly, in many areas of the country, private schools are not available, so, in that case parents would be left with only two options: transferring their children to another public school inside their own district, or transferring their children to a public school outside their district.

Generating Competition

The 1985 voucher plan was intended to generate competition among *public* schools. And, let us face it, the public schools are the ones that need it; private schools already have that benefit. That is why they do so well.

The separation of church and state argument was equally off-base. In the first place, the voucher was designed only to encourage freedom of choice, not to either aid or discourage those who choose religiously oriented schooling for their youngsters. And there is nothing unconstitutional about having a choice—at least not yet. In the second place, the argument of separation of church and state is fallacious, since that term never appears in the Constitution but, rather, comes from a private letter sent by Thomas Jefferson to the Danbury, Connecticut Baptist Association in 1802. Liberals and atheists have taken the term entirely out of context in an effort to remove theism, not sectarianism, from both our nation's schools and public places. The First Amendment was never intended to separate God from country. It was meant to ensure that a state church, such as the Anglican church of England, would not be imposed upon the entire population. But thanks to the excesses of the anti-God forces of this country led by the A.C.L.U., we now indeed have a state religion. It is atheism, or humanism as its advocates call it, and it is imposed upon all the people regardless of their own beliefs.

To suggest that vouchers "could lead to racial isolation of children" was, perhaps, the most intellectually dishonest of all the charges made against the idea. Education vouchers would produce precisely the opposite result because parents would, in fact, no longer have to beat the bushes finding the "right" neighborhood for their children's schooling. Since the disadvantaged can rarely move to the "right" neighborhoods, the 1985 TEACH proposal was especially beneficial to them. No, the real fear for education liberals has nothing to do with "racial isolation" or the plight of the poor; what the liberals are afraid of is that with choice in education they may eventually lose their ability to pit racial, economic, and social groups against each other because they all will begin to mingle more naturally.

The Funding Issue

Finally, there was the charge that the voucher issue shifts attention away from the supposed lack of adequate funding issue. Notice that naysayers like the NEA never remind us about all the wonderful things we have received with "adequate" funding—such as bilingual education, whereby a child goes through twelve years of schooling without ever learning how to speak English; or teen health clinics, whereby Mommy's little girl can have a sample of her urine carted over to a Planned Parenthood clinic for analysis; or MACOS (Man: A Course of Study), a social studies text that specialized in denigrating the United States.

The "give us more money" liberal educationists always claim to be progressive while they are busy denouncing every positive or constructive suggestion to come down the pike. Their solution to education's problems is a tired, broken record that we have all lived with for a number of unimpressive years. Indeed, the NEA has raised "shifting focus away from an issue" to the level of a new art form, so it is with some audacity that union leaders and their cohorts should charge the pro-Choice forces with disguising, or clouding the issue.

Fortunately, both President Bush and former Education Secretary Lauro Cavazos came out in favor of Choice programs. Mr. Cavazos called parental choice the "cornerstone" of the Bush Administration's educational policy and President Bush labeled Choice the "single most promising idea" in education today.

Clout of Vouchers

Promising it is. [As Lee A. Daniels wrote in the *New York Times*,] "Minnesota, Arkansas, Iowa and Nebraska already have in place statewide 'open enrollment' plans giving parents wide discretion in choosing schools. Scores of cities around the country have for years offered magnet and alternative schools that extend options beyond neighborhood schools," and these are the schools that have been the most effective in raising student test scores.

Minnesota is one state that takes particular pride, as well it should, in the Choice programs offered in its public schools. [According to Suzanne Fields in the *Washington Times*,] in Minnesota a child or parent "can choose a school in any district, restricted only by available space and considerations of racial balance. Juniors and seniors in high school can attend classes at colleges, universities or vocational schools. Dollars follow students, forcing schools to be competitive in what is legitimately described as educational 'entrepreneurships' requiring truth in marketing."

Statistics seem to indicate that this is a popular notion with both parents and students. For example, "In 1987 only 137 students used the open-enrollment law in Minnesota. About 440 students used it the following year. This year (1989), 3,500 students applied to schools outside their districts, usually choosing better courses, better teachers and higher standards."

Tool for Integration

There is no reason to expect any significant change in present enrollment patterns under a voucher system. If anything, vouchers can serve as a powerful tool for integration by giving minorities the opportunity to choose schools which they cannot attend now as a result of the public "neighborhood school" system. In addition, most voucher proposals limit or prohibit add-ons whereby families could add to the voucher value in order to afford selective, more expensive schools.

Americans for Educational Choice, *Education Voucher Fact Sheet*, 1988.

[Fields continued,] "It's easy to see where Minnesota, whose graduation rate of 91.4 percent is the highest in the nation, might benefit from school choice. But it works in less prosperous places, too. When choice was introduced in a district in East Harlem, the graduation rate in one high school rose from 7 percent to more than 90 percent."

Even though school Choice programs have exhibited remarkable success in addressing the myriad problems that exist in the current structure of the NEA-guided public schools, President Bush will face stiff opposition to his policy of gradual inclusion of Choice.

The Education Monopoly

The biggest problem President Bush or anyone else will have to face in getting a Choice plan through Congress is that we have let the liberals frame the debate not only on the Choice issue but on the voucher issue as well. Like the NEA, to whom several key members of Congress (including Congressman Augustus Hawkins, Chairman of the powerful House Committee on Education and Labor) erroneously believe they owe their careers, many of the liberal camp do not want Choice in education. A few of these, of course, sincerely believe the average American parent just has not enough sense, or judgment, or expertise, to exercise such a choice. But the greatest, and most vocal, of those who oppose Choice do so because they know that competition in education will signal an end to the education monopoly in this country. And if the monopoly is broken, that means a lot of those people who have a stake in the status quo will lose their power. Remember, former Indiana legislator Joan Gubbins did not call public education the most reform-proof special interest in the country for nothing.

Like the union leaders of the NEA, these people are not interested in improving education, reforming education, or bringing new ideas to it. Like the NEA, they do not care about education. They care about keeping the power structure intact, and the sooner the American people understand this, the better able they will be to significantly change what is wrong with the American educating process.

It is relatively easy, once one knows what to look for, to see through these kinds of questions to the real objections to Choice. In the case of the NEA, one needs to look at its annual legislative agenda. There is found year after year a blanket condemnation of any and all voucher and tuition tax credit concepts—in other words, all "Choice schemes," as they like to put it. Looking further, the reader will find that what the union leaders are objecting to in reality is competition—merit, grading, testing, professional evaluations, and so on.

Free Enterprise

The sad fact is that many in our country find the ideal of competition uncomfortable. That becomes particularly critical in an education environment, where we are supposed to be teaching youngsters how our system, economic and otherwise, works. Competition is one of the bases of our democracy, and the values that go with it—like initiative, perseverance, determination, self-reliance—are what make our free enterprise system work.

So, Congress and the American people need to think long and hard about what a Choice plan, even a limited one like the Bush proposal, will mean to them and to the future of this country. For the outcome of this issue will in many ways be a statement about the course we want to pursue as a nation.

"The voucher plan is based on a consumer economics, marketplace model that is not appropriate to education."

Government Should Not Offer School Vouchers

House of Representatives Subcommittee on Elementary, Secondary, and Vocational Education

Educational voucher programs would allow parents to use government funds to enroll their children in public or private schools of their choice. In the following viewpoint, the House of Representatives Subcommittee on Elementary, Secondary, and Vocational Education argues that government should not issue school vouchers because they would not help poor families. The subcommittee asserts that since vouchers provide merely a portion of the average private school tuition, poor parents would have no actual choice between public and private schools. The subcommittee contends that private schools would selectively admit public school students on the basis of academic performance, thus rejecting disadvantaged students with low academic proficiency. The subcommittee is part of the House Committee on Education and Labor.

As you read, consider the following questions:

1. Why is government better suited to provide education services than the private sector, according to the subcommittee?
2. In the author's opinion, why should parents be wary of transferring their children from public to private schools?
3. According to the author, how would vouchers allow private schools to operate without accountability to government?

Excerpted from *Problems Concerning Education Voucher Proposals and Issues Related to Choice* by the U.S. House of Representatives Subcommittee on Elementary, Secondary, and Vocational Education, government printing office, 1990. Public domain.

Some voucher plans would require local school districts to take Federal (possibly Chapter 1) funds which they now receive to provide special remedial services to low-achieving children in poor areas and instead give those funds in the form of a voucher to the parents of these children, at the parents' request. The voucher would then be used by the parents toward the tuition of a private school or the cost of another public school. For several reasons, this represents a deception for parents and a disaster for public policy.

The voucher plan would harm public education by transferring public money to private schools at a time when federal resources for education are shrinking. This "anti-public education" bias is consistent with Administration efforts to eliminate the Federal role in public education by cutting funds and proposing block grants and phase-outs of education programs.

Even assuming that a voucher bill would double the percentage of the student population attending private schools to 20%, we would still need a strong public educational system for that remaining 80%. Universal public education came about because a haphazard assemblage of private and community schools was unequally able to prepare children for their roles as citizens; a voucher bill ignores this history.

If the Administration were truly committed to quality in education, it would be increasing funding for public schools to improve them, not bribing people to abandon them.

Unproven Assumption

A voucher bill is based on the unfounded assumption that "anything is better" than the current system. Some voucher proposals assume that private schools, without being required to do so, will do a better job serving disadvantaged students than public schools have done with mandates to serve such students.

It also implies that disadvantaged students would receive a better education in the "regular" program of the private school than in a special program in a public school.

The voucher plan is based on a consumer economics, marketplace model that is not appropriate to education. Assuming that fostering competition will, by definition, improve education ignores the reality that some services or institutions are not responsive to marketplace forces, but are better provided on a large scale by government. Imagine issuing vouchers for defense on the assumption that everyone could hire his own militia.

A consumer choice such as purchasing a washing machine does not have the lasting effect on both the consumer and society at large as is the case with education.

The "healthy rivalry" between public and private institutions that the Administration envisions will occur under the voucher bill is really an unfair match in which one competitor—the private school—does not have to play by the same rules as the other. The private schools do not have to enroll all students who desire to be enrolled, and do not have to meet the accountability standards required of public schools.

Parental Involvement Rhetoric

Aiding poor parents is not the Administration's primary goal. A potential Chapter 1 voucher is just a way station en route to the "voucherization" of all education.

Both the previous Administration and the current Administration have espoused the rhetoric of parental involvement even as they have consistently sought to and often succeeded in eliminating requirements for parental involvement in existing Federal programs. If Administration officials were truly concerned about parental involvement, they would strengthen the parent provisions in existing laws and regulations instead of wiping them out.

Abandoning Public Schools

The attraction of voucher payments would lead many parents to their church schools, leaving the public school to the few. For those who look upon the public school as a vital force in readying students to live in a multicultural, diverse society, such easily forseeable developments bode ill.

Robert W. Carr, *The Wall Street Journal*, May 2, 1991.

The parents receiving vouchers would not all be poor. Once funds flow to the poorest schools, children are selected for participation in Chapter 1 based on educational deprivation, not income.

Vouchers ignore other benefits of public education. The goals of exposing students to a common culture, preparing them for citizenship, providing equal opportunity, and offering education in the best interests of the child will not be better served by a voucher system.

For example, if parents under a voucher plan selected schools with pupils whose backgrounds are the same as their children's, the result could be more stratification and less tolerance rather than the greater diversity some Administration officials claim.

No Choice for Poor Parents

The voucher amount does not cover enough of the costs of private education to give the poorest families a meaningful choice. The $563 expended per pupil under Chapter 1 in the school year 1983-84 is only 38% of the average private school tuition of $1,480 in fall of 1983 (the last year for which data is available); according to the Congressional Research Service in the Library of Congress. Where are poor parents, with little to no disposable income, to obtain the other 62%?

There is a tremendous range of expenses; the National Association of Independent Schools reports that in school year 1989-90, the median tuition of its member institutions ranges from $5,100 to $5,900 for grades 3 through 6 and is $7,200 for grades 9 through 12. These schools wold be out of the question for voucher parents.

The voucher amount would vary widely from State to State, and this would unfairly constrain choices. A voucher of $280 in California would hardly make a dent in the tuition of the average private school.

LEAs [local educational agencies] could decide to pay no transportation costs, which would make certain schools even more out of range for poor parents.

The schools that charge tuition closer to the average voucher amount of $600 are largely parochial schools. Many parents may not want to send their children to a parochial school where they will be taught a religion different from their own.

The costs for educating disadvantaged children are often higher than average, so private schools would have to subsidize costs beyond their tuition charges, which they may be unwilling to do.

There is nothing to prevent a religious school receiving a voucher from charging higher tuition to non-church members. This may make sense for the church but is not equitable public policy.

The average per pupil expenditure for public schools was $3,997 in the school year 1986-87. Many public school districts charge tuition to non-resident students, so the voucher would be inadequate to cover this amount.

Choice Constrained

Parental choices will be constrained by a number of other factors. The 69% of the eligible children who are not receiving services under Chapter 1 would have no voucher choice at all, because the funding is inadequate to serve all poor or low-achieving children.

Selective admissions requirements would keep disadvantaged students out of some of the best private schools. Enrolling low-achieving children would be counter-productive for private schools whose drawing cards are selectivity and high-achievement scores.

Private schools are not evenly distributed across geographic regions. Some areas have few private schools, or the ones that exist are too far away to transport children to.

The various plans offer no protection for students who enroll in a private school and are later expelled or dismissed.

Parents' choices will be limited by the types of information they receive about their options. As the Alum Rock, California, experiment on vouchers demonstrated, even in its fourth year, one-quarter of the parents still did not know that the voucher program existed, and many more lacked accurate information about it.

Over half of the poor families in the country are headed by a person without a high school diploma. These educationally disadvantaged parents will need assistance and special information to make informed choices.

Inadequate Communication

Many poor parents may have limited English proficiency. Some school districts have a multiplicity of language groups in their attendance areas, and information would have to be provided in every language if these parents are to be well-informed about their choices.

Some voucher proposals provide only that the LEAs inform parents in writing of voucher options and hold an annual public meeting. The information needed for school selection is too complex and varied to be adequately communicated in this fashion to disadvantaged parents.

Parents may be taken advantage of by profiteers and choose a school with the most aggressive promoter instead of the best program.

Parents often choose schools for reasons other than the instructional program. In the Alum Rock experiment, parents primarily used non-educational criteria to decide on schools. Even with the provision of transportation geographic location was the most important factor. . . .

Unfair Exemption

A voucher bill could unfairly exempt private schools receiving vouchers from the requirements governing public school Chapter 1 programs. The private schools might not be required to provide a Chapter 1 program—or *any* special services—to the voucher students. They could use the funds to redecorate the principal's office if they wanted.

Private schools might not have to evaluate or report disadvantaged students' progress and achievement as public schools do, so it would be impossible to verify if the program is accomplishing its objectives.

Private schools might be relieved of the non-supplanting requirement affecting public schools, so parochial schools could use the voucher funds to supplant funds they now receive from the church.

Private schools might be exempted from maintenance of effort, comparability, and other requirements longstanding in the Chapter 1 law to ensure the supplementary nature and integrity of the Federal programs.

Private schools might not have to comply with certain general provisions tied to the receipt of Federal aid that affect public schools, including certain civil rights laws, the Buckley Amendment affecting privacy of student records, or even the Hatch Amendment affecting student psychological testing.

If handicapped children are eligible for Chapter 1, the private schools receiving vouchers would not have to meet the Federal requirements to provide free and appropriate education to these children, as public schools do.

Voucher bills leave private schools essentially autonomous, with no entity charged with monitoring the quality of their programs. Private schools in some States do not even have to provide a core curriculum or meet State standards regarding teacher certification, building codes, safety, etc. State Courts in Ohio and Kentucky have struck down State requirements regulating private schools in this manner.

Voucher bills offer no protection for parents from "fly by night" schools that spring up to take advantage of Federal dollars.

In some voucher proposals there is no recourse for parents if a school falsely advertises services it does not deliver or if a school receives the money and then closes. Some bills contain no complaint procedures for dissatisfied parents.

Government Regulation

It is inevitable that greater regulation of private schools will follow the subsidy. The public's concern that tax dollars be wisely spent and the parents' concern that their children receive a quality education will surely lead to pressure to increase accountability and regulation of the private schools.

Other countries, such as the Netherlands, that provide substantial public assistance to nonpublic schools enforce a relatively high degree of government regulation of these schools, according to a Congressional Research Service paper on vouchers.

If regulation occurs, the independence and special character that makes private education attractive to some individuals would be lost. As researcher K. Alan Snyder commented in an analysis of a Canadian program of public aid to nonpublic schools, "No longer did the private schools seem special in any way. They became clones of the public schools."

If the LEAs, the States, or the U.S. Department of Education failed to develop regulatory assurances and accountability standards, it is inescapable that the courts would, when disgruntled parents brought suit against schools that misuse or abuse Federal dollars. . . .

Voucher bills would have to prohibit discrimination by private schools on the basis of sex, handicapping condition, or religion. Any provision that stated that the voucher does not constitute Federal aid could be construed as an attempt to exempt private schools from the civil rights requirements that are now tied to receipt of Federal aid by public institutions, including Title IX (prohibiting sex discrimination) and Section 504 (prohibiting handicapped discrimination).

Undermining Democracy

Vouchers would subvert public democracy. By subsidizing church schools, vouchers would threaten the separation of church and state. And more important, by funding private schools at the expense of public schools, they could imperil the only school system that is open to everyone, regardless of background, income, and ability.

John B. Judis, *In These Times*, September 18-24, 1991.

Voucher bills would have to contain adequate protections against racial discrimination. The annual, uncontrollable movement of students among schools could wreak havoc on desegregation plans.

Voucher proponents claim that their proposals would promote voluntary desegregation; just the opposite could occur. The voucher could encourage "white flight." These white parents could use the voucher to send their children to a private school with few minorities, leaving the public schools less desegregated. If minority parents send their children to a private school, it may improve the diversity of that particular private school (which is not affected by court or voluntary desegregation plans) but have a negative impact on the racial balance of the public schools, which may be under obligation to desegregate.

"Because they cannot afford private schooling, many parents are forced to send their children to schools that violate their religious convictions."

Choice Programs Should Include Religious Schools

Myron Lieberman

The success of private schools in providing a higher-quality education is one reason given for including such schools in choice programs. In the following viewpoint, Myron Lieberman agrees and adds that private schools would also protect students' freedom of religion. Lieberman argues that public schools are biased against religious students. By including private schools in choice programs, Lieberman maintains, religious parents could send their children to schools that are compatible with their beliefs. Lieberman, a leading education analyst, is the author of *Privatization and Educational Choice*, from which this viewpoint is excerpted.

As you read, consider the following questions:

1. According to Lieberman, why do some religious parents object to public schools?
2. In the author's opinion, how does school choice reduce conflict over the type of education offered by government?
3. How are parents of children in private schools unfairly taxed by government, according to Lieberman?

In recent years the real or alleged deficiencies of public education have stimulated proposals that would enable parents to choose the school their children will attend. One type of proposal is educational tax credits, more commonly referred to as tuition tax credits. Such proposals call for income tax credits or tax deductions for the expenses of sending children to school. Another type of proposal is for government to provide parents with educational vouchers, redeemable for tuition and perhaps other expenses at a school chosen by the parents. Collectively, tuition tax credits and vouchers are widely known as family choice proposals. Their underlying assumption is that the best way to strengthen parental choice of schools is to strengthen parental ability to pay for education, whether in a public or a private school.

Religious Freedom

Perhaps the most important noneducational argument for vouchers is that they are essential to protect religious freedom. The argument is based on the fact that education is compulsory in every state. Because they cannot afford private schooling, many parents are forced to send their children to schools that violate their religious convictions. A voucher system could avoid this outcome by making it possible for parents to enroll their children in schools of their choice.

The factual premises of the religious rationale are indisputable. Historically, denominational schools have always existed in the United States; typically, they preceded public schools. Prior to 1850 state and local assistance to denominational schools was commonplace. The influx of Catholic immigrants in the latter half of the nineteenth century created a policy dilemma for political leaders, who were overwhelmingly Protestant. State aid to religious schools now required aid to Catholic as well as Protestant schools. Rather than accept this alternative, the dilemma was resolved by compulsory education laws. By simultaneously denying aid to Catholic schools, it was anticipated that most Catholic children would be enrolled in public schools. The latter were not viewed as "nonreligious"; on the contrary, they were permeated with a strong Protestant bias characterized publicly if inaptly as a "nonsectarian" approach to religion.

This bias was most clearly reflected in the Bible-reading statutes. During the nineteenth century Massachusetts was the only state that required Bible reading. In the twentieth century, however, thirty-six states enacted statutes requiring or allowing public school teachers to read passages from the Bible at certain times. These statutes typically prohibited teachers from discussing the passages that were read. For example, Pennsylvania law required that "At least ten verses from the Holy Bible shall be read, without comment, at the opening of each public school on each school day. Any child shall be excused from such Bible reading, or attending such Bible reading upon the written request of his parent or guardian."

In many states Catholic parents objected to Bible reading, and not simply because a Protestant instead of a Catholic edition of the Bible was used. The statutes were consistent with Protestant theology that regards people as capable of interpreting the Bible correctly without intermediaries. They were not consistent with Catholic theology, which holds that the Catholic Church is necessary to reveal and interpret the Word of God.

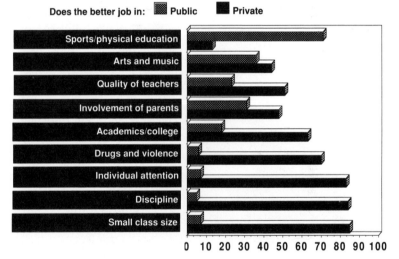

Americans Choose Private Schools

Americans were asked whether private or public schools performed better in several areas. Some said "both" or "neither."

Does the better job in: ▨ Public ■ Private

National Association of Independent Schools survey, January 23-February 11, 1991.

Feeble defenses aside, there was no question about the Protestant bias in the Bible-reading statutes. Nevertheless, out of a total of twenty-five cases on the issue from 1854 to 1924, the protesters, most often Catholic, lost about three out of four cases. This type of bias was reflected in other ways too numerous to be recounted here. What were the aggrieved parents to do? They could—and sometimes did—establish private schools, but such schools had to operate without public financial help. Needless to say, for opponents of Bible reading to appeal for financial help to the very same legislatures that enacted the Bible-reading statutes was not a very promising way out of their predicament.

Response to Religious Restrictions

The Bible-reading statutes were held to be unconstitutional in 1963. Today some of the Protestant denominations that were instrumental in enacting the statutes are expanding their denominational schools as a response to the religious restrictions on public schools. Bible reading is only one of several factors in this situation, but it illustrates two important points. First, whatever public schools do about religious issues, some group is likely to cite the action as a reason to establish private schools. Second, although couched in constitutional terms, the religious rationale is based primarily on the alleged unfairness of compulsory education without financial support for those who object to public education on religious grounds.

Although the religious argument per se has not changed much over the years, several facts pertinent to it have changed. Programs of sex education and restrictions on Bible reading, school prayer, and the teaching of "creation science" have led some Protestant fundamentalists to conclude that public schools are hostile, not merely neutral, to their religious beliefs. This attitude is frequently expressed in charges that public schools are promoting "secular humanism"; the latter is said to be a nontheistic religion that emphasizes human instead of divine sources of moral authority. In addition, many parents who think this way believe that public schools are too permissive in matters of drugs, alcohol, dress, language, and manners. The result is that the number of Protestant fundamentalist schools increased rapidly during the 1970s and 1980s; their rate of increase outstripped every other denominational category. Paradoxically, Christian fundamentalist school officials tend to be more hostile to government regulation than Catholic school leaders, who are more likely to recognize the legitimacy of state regulation of private schools.

Choosing Religious Schools

The upsurge in Christian fundamentalist schools has occurred at a time when Catholic schools faced a number of difficult problems. A sharp decline in the number of Catholics entering religious orders has been a major problem. As the number of nuns and priests available to teach in Catholic schools has declined, the schools have been forced to employ a higher proportion of lay teachers. This has led to greater financial strains on Catholic school budgets and increased interest in government assistance.

For our purposes, the important considerations are these:

First, there has been and still is some religious bias in public schools. I make no effort to quantify the bias but simply accept the fact that from time to time and place to place, public school policies and practices violate good-faith religious convictions.

At the same time, it is equally clear that some critics of public schools will not be satisfied with genuine neutrality, whether it takes the form of objective pedagogical treatment or of avoidance of denominational issues entirely. In other words, I see no immediate end of either justified or unjustified criticism of public schools on religious grounds. Whatever the merits, conflicts over religious objections to public education are likely to continue into the foreseeable future. We can, therefore, expect a religious base of support for family choice no matter what public schools do. . . .

Vouchers Reduce Conflict

In *Capitalism and Freedom*, Milton Friedman argues that education vouchers are desirable as a means of reducing social conflict. As he points out, education, like public policy generally in the United States, is often characterized by intense political, religious, economic, and cultural conflict. Conflict over sex education, prayer in schools, and abortion rights illustrates such conflict.

Real Choice

[Legislators] should insist on choice being extended to private schools. Failure to include private schools may result in denying real choice for those who need it most—low income Americans attending the most dismal public schools. In the inner cities, restricting choice to the public schools effectively would shrink the supply of good schools available to disadvantaged children, and dilute competition. Only by including existing private schools and new providers to open schools will these parents have a real choice.

Jeanne Allen, *The Heritage Foundation Issue Bulletin*, June 28, 1991.

When government provides a service like education, it tends to provide the same service for everyone. Consequently, the only way *A* can get the kind of education *A* wants is to force *B* to have it also; unfortunately, *B* may be strongly opposed and prefer a kind of education to which *A* is strongly opposed. Family choice is therefore viewed as a means of reducing social conflict. If parents could afford the kind of education they want for their children, there would be much less incentive for them to impose their educational views on others. Such imposition is unavoidable when government monopolizes educational services. For this reason, it is better to have their disagreements resolved through the marketplace instead of the political process.

Political Argument for Vouchers

The political rationale is clearly an independent argument for vouchers. One might reject all other arguments but still conclude that vouchers are needed to reduce political conflict over education. Furthermore, the political rationale need not be based solely or even primarily on religious conflict. Its existence might be an important element of the political rationale, but the latter is not necessarily dependent on any particular kind or source of educational conflict. As a matter of fact, many citizens who are indifferent to religious issues have strong convictions about political, economic, or social issues that arise in schools. Parents who have strong convictions about economic issues may not care one way or the other whether public schools have a moment of silent meditation or conduct Christmas pageants with Christian orientation or include "creation science" in the curriculum.

The political argument for vouchers is also based on a concept of equity. All citizens are taxed to support education. Arguably, it is unfair to subject parents to "double taxation" because they choose one type of school over another for reasons of conscience. The alleged inequity gives rise to political conflict as those excluded from the benefits seek redress. Presumably, a voucher system would eliminate this inequity and therefore this source of political conflict.

6 VIEWPOINT

"Choice plans that include nonpublic schools must be seen for what they are . . . scams aimed at wrecking church-state separation. "

Choice Programs Should Not Include Religious Schools

Americans for Religious Liberty (ARL)

Some critics argue that including religious schools as part of government-funded school choice programs raises constitutional issues of separation of church and state. In the following viewpoint, Americans for Religious Liberty argues that such a practice has already been declared unconstitutional by the U.S. Supreme Court. Furthermore, ARL maintains that including private schools in choice programs would drive up education costs. ARL is a Silver Spring, Maryland, organization that supports the separation of church and state.

As you read, consider the following questions:

1. Why does ARL believe it is important for all Americans to be concerned about school choice proposals?
2. In the authors' opinion, how will the inclusion of private schools in choice programs lead to social fragmentation?
3. Why are private school costs per student lower than those of public schools, according to ARL?

Americans for Religious Liberty, "School Choice: Panacea or Scam?" *Voice of Reason*, Winter 1991. Reprinted with permission.

Choice is a good word, an excellent word. It resonates favorably with nearly everyone. We favor choice when it comes to careers, spouses, friends, elections, religion, entertainment, and brands of cars and toothpaste. Most Americans favor choice of options when women face problem pregnancies.

Choice, however, is now being touted as a cure-all for the ills, real and/or imagined, of our public schools. If families could only choose their children's schools, the argument runs, then "bad" schools would dry up and blow away, all children would get better education, and we will march joyfully into Utopia.

The Bush administration, the Catholic bishops, the Brookings Institution (via John Chubb and Terry Moe's 1990 book *Politics, Markets, and America's Schools*), former Delaware governor Pierre duPont, and a host of propagandists and sectarian special interests have hopped on the school choice bandwagon.

Concern over Choice

School choice proposals are of concern to all Americans. We the people, we the taxpayers, will have to pay the bills, and the kind of educational arrangement we pay for will profoundly affect our lives, our children's lives, our economy, and the future of our society and our democratic public education system.

School choice can mean many different things. Confined strictly to public schools, it could be positive and manageable, on the one hand, or, on the other, unmanageable, chaotic, and wildly expensive. Extended to include nonpublic schools, choice plans raise fundamental constitutional issues, would surely create far more serious problems than they are supposed to cure, and would raise school costs to unprecedented levels.

As applied to nonpublic schools, tax supported choice is clearly improper. In the 1970s the U.S. Supreme Court ruled unconstitutional all but the most peripheral and "minor" forms of tax aid. Specifically rejected were such schemes as tuition reimbursements via tax credits or vouchers and providing educational services in sectarian schools. The minor and peripheral forms of parochiaid not ruled unconstitutional by the Court, which cost federal and state taxpayers over $1 billion annually, include transportation service (except for field trips), textbooks and equipment "loans," remedial education offered off the private school campus, and diagnostic exams.

Constitutionality aside, tax aid for nonpublic schools means tax support for the denominational instruction or indoctrination found in virtually all sectarian schools. Of the slightly less than 11% of elementary and secondary students in the U.S. who attend nonpublic schools, well over 90% attend pervasively sectarian schools in which sectarian instruction is almost always mandatory, even for students of other faiths.

Women's rights supporters, incidentally, will note that the overwhelming majority of nonpublic students attend schools operated by denominations which refuse to ordain women and which oppose freedom of conscience for women on reproduction.

The Power to Choose

Promoters of choice plans that go beyond public schools talk about families choosing schools for their children. But they are putting the cart before the horse. Families may *apply* to have their children admitted to a nonpublic school, but it is the nonpublic schools that really do the choosing. They choose which students to admit or retain and which to reject or expel, which teachers to hire and which to reject, and which religion or ideology will permeate the school program. Now many of these schools want to choose tax support for themselves expressly by denying taxpayers the right to choose which religious institutions they, the taxpayers, will support.

Edd Doerr and Albert J. Menendez, *Church Schools and Public Money*, 1991.

Because they are pervasively sectarian and generally mandate participation in sectarian instruction, nonpublic schools tend strongly toward denominational homogeneity. In plain English, Catholic schools rarely appeal to Protestants, Jews, or Muslims; fundamentalist schools rarely attract Catholics, mainstream Protestants, or Jews; Jewish schools seldom attract non-Jews; and Muslim schools almost never attract non-Muslims.

In addition to being religiously rather homogenous, nonpublic schools tend to practice other types of selectivity and discrimination. They enroll fewer children with handicaps than public schools. A large percentage of private secondary schools discriminate by gender in admissions. Most nonpublic secondary schools enroll mainly college-bound students; they usually require entrance exams and their curricula tend to be college-prep and to ignore vocational subjects. Nonpublic schools seldom retain students with discipline problems, so it is common for expellees from nonpublic schools to turn up in public schools, which are generally required to accept them. Many private schools use religious and other criteria not allowed in public schools in hiring staff. Catholic schools generally do not tolerate teachers who are divorced and remarried or who are known to support freedom of conscience on abortion. A fundamentalist school in southern California once fired its principal because he was "thinking about" hiring a Catholic teacher.

Promoters of school choice plans talk about students and their families choosing schools. But they have the cart before the horse. It is the nonpublic schools which do the choosing. They choose which students to admit and which to reject. Including nonpublic schools in choice plans means that the nonpublic schools, or the religious bodies which run them, choose their students, choose what religion or ideology to teach them, and then choose that the taxpayers will pay for them. Since nonpublic schools, unlike public schools, are not subject to democratic control by those who pay for them, the taxpayer is stuck with "taxation without representation" and is deprived of the choice of which religions he or she will support. Many taxpayers would be funding private schools that would exclude them from their faculties.

Including nonpublic schools in choice plans means increasing the costs of taxes to pay for elementary and secondary education by at least 11%. Most nonpublic schools today may be able to operate at a lower per-student cost than public schools, but that is due to the fact that they pay teachers less, seldom serve severely handicapped children (whose education in public schools can often cost as much as six times that of non-handicapped children), and seldom offer expensive vocational courses. If nonpublic schools had to offer the same levels of programs and teacher salaries as public schools, their per-student cost would at least equal public school costs. And since nonpublic schools tend to be much smaller in enrollment than public schools, their lower economies of scale would make their per-student costs even higher.

The Transportation Dilemma

Transportation costs are another complicating factor. About half of all public students are bussed to school, either because the schools are too far away for walking or because students would have to cross dangerous streets and highways. If students were allowed to go to the public school of their choice within their own school district, obviously a much larger percentage of students would have to be bussed, and bussing costs would increase. If students could attend public schools in other districts, as some choice plans would allow, transportation costs would go still higher. If nonpublic schools are included in choice plans, bussing costs would rise astronomically. Pennsylvania already requires that students be bussed to nonpublic schools miles outside their public school districts and even across state lines into Ohio, Delaware, and New Jersey, at enormous cost to hard-pressed public school districts. Howard County, Maryland, busses students to five church schools within the county (which in Maryland is coterminous with the school district); it costs precisely twice as much to bus a student to a church school as to a public school. In northern Ohio, a school district is required to transport two students *by airplane and taxi* from an island in Lake Erie to a church school on the mainland, even though the island has its own public schools; the transportation alone for the students costs more than Ohio spends per year educating a student.

Segregation Academies

While George Bush's plan to allow "choice" may sound reasonable, it would, in reality, have regressive effects on American education.

It could lead to federal funding for religious schools, or to "segregation academies," private schools set up by racists as alternatives to integrated public schools.

Moreover, subjecting the nation's schools to market competition will simply mean that those parents with the resources or ability to send their children to private schools will do so with the federal government's help.

Lance Selfa, *Socialist Worker*, May 1991.

Who will pay for the transportation to "schools of choice"? If the taxpayers pick up the bill, the costs will be astronomical, and this at a time when states and cities from coast to coast are having to slash school budgets, cut programs, increase class size, lay off teachers, and freeze salaries. If the public does not pay the transportation bills for getting students to schools of choice, then only children whose parents can drive them to school will be served.

Social Fragmentation

Choice plans, whether they include nonpublic schools or not, would surely add to school administrative complexity and costs.

With public school budgets either static or shrinking in most of the country's nearly 16,000 school districts, choice plans, with or without the inclusion of nonpublic schools, can only increase costs or force reduction in already underfunded public school programs.

Even in the extremely unlikely event that choice plans did not increase school costs, most choice plans would be objectionable for other reasons. By further dividing children along creedal, ideological, social class, ethnic, academic ability level, and other lines, they would increase social fragmentation. The great virtue of the American comprehensive school is that it tends to bring all sorts of children and teachers together in a democratic and democracy-enhancing enterprise.

Choice in education can be positive when it functions within a democratically controlled public school system. The comprehensive secondary school offers students many choices in the curriculum and also in extra-curricular activities. A single elementary or secondary school could contain two or more separate public schools. In some cases, two or three public schools could offer differing modes of education. The important thing is that no choice system that is publicly supported should be allowed to promote division and divisiveness among students.

What Needs to Be Done

The bottom line is that most of the vocal promoters of educational choice today are less interested in improving public education than in securing tax support for nonpublic, mainly sectarian education. School choice is offered as a cheap, painless panacea for problems both real and imagined. It is being touted as a way to improve education without having to find new sources of revenue.

We know a great deal about what is wrong with American education and what needs to be done about it. For instance, we need to fully fund the proven successful Head Start program for bringing disadvantaged children as close as possible to a level playing field by the time they are ready to start school. We need to fully fund the remedial education programs aimed at keeping as many students as possible up to grade levels. We need to lower class sizes, especially in inner city schools. We need to enrich our school programs in sex and family education, both to better prepare young people for the responsibilities of adulthood and parenthood and to reduce the problem of teens having children. Other educational reforms, such as improving education in reading, writing, science, languages, math, etc., can then follow more easily. Beyond the schools, we must treat the social pathologies associated with poverty, inadequate housing and medical care, drugs, and crime. Our whole society and each of us will benefit from these real reforms.

Doing what needs to be done will obviously cost billions annually. In addition to eliminating government waste, we will surely need to have higher, and hopefully more equitably assessed, taxes. Among the leading 16 industrial nations, the U.S. ranks thirteenth in the level of our effort in supporting elementary and secondary education. The U.S. cannot long remain a world leader at that rate.

Meanwhile, painless panaceas like choice plans that include nonpublic schools must be seen for what they are—devices for distracting our attention from our real problems, scams aimed at wrecking church-state separation, democratic public education, and the fundamental right of citizens not to be forced to support religious institutions.

a critical thinking activity

Evaluating Sources of Information

When historians study and interpret past events, they use two kinds of sources: primary and secondary. Primary sources are eyewitness accounts. For example, a public school principal's description of how school choice has hurt her school is a primary source. A *Time* article that used her description would be a secondary source. Primary and secondary sources may be decades or even hundreds of years old, and often historians find that the sources offer conflicting and contradictory information. To fully evaluate documents and assess their accuracy, historians analyze the credibility of the documents' authors and, in the case of secondary sources, analyze the credibility of the information the authors used.

Historians are not the only people who encounter conflicting information, however. Anyone who reads a daily newspaper, watches television, or just talks to different people will encounter many different views. Writers and speakers use sources of information to support their own statements. Thus, critical thinkers, just like historians, must question the writer's or speaker's sources of information as well as the writer or speaker.

While there are many criteria that can be applied to assess the accuracy of a primary or secondary source, for this activity you will be asked to apply three. For each source listed on the following page, ask yourself the following questions: First, did the person actually see or participate in the event he or she is reporting? This will help you determine the credibility of the information—an eyewitness to an event is an extremely valuable source. Second, does the person have a vested interest in the report? Assessing the person's social status, economic interests, professional affiliations, nationality, and religious or political beliefs will be helpful in considering this question. By evaluating this you will be able to determine how objective the person's report may be. Third, how qualified is the author to make the statements he or she is making? Consider what the person's profession is and how he or she might know about the event. Someone who has spent years being involved with or studying the issue may be able to offer more information than someone who simply is offering an uneducated opinion; for example, a politician or layperson.

Keeping the above criteria in mind, imagine you are writing a paper on school choice. You decide to cite an equal number of primary and secondary sources. Listed below are several sources that may be useful for your research. *Place a P next to those descriptions you believe are primary sources. Place an S next to those descriptions you believe are secondary sources.* Next, based on the above criteria, *rank the primary sources, assigning the number (1) to that which appears the most valuable, (2) to the source likely to be the second-most valuable, and so on, until all the primary sources are ranked. Then rank the secondary sources, again using the above criteria.*

P or S		Rank in Importance
_____	1. A *Wall Street Journal* article outlining several school choice programs in the U.S.	_____
_____	2. A book review of *Politics, Markets, and America's Schools.*	_____
_____	3. An interview with a parent who says a local school choice program helped her children to enroll in a better school.	_____
_____	4. A television reporter's description of a state committee debate on the merits of parental school choice.	_____
_____	5. A researcher's study determining that many families who participate in Minnesota's school choice program choose schools for convenience rather than academics.	_____
_____	6 A *Newsweek* article describing the U.S. Department of Education's support for parental school choice.	_____
_____	7. A journal article written by the executive director of the Council for American Private Education who argues that school choice programs should include private schools.	_____
_____	8. The text of Wisconsin state representative Polly Williams' bill providing educational vouchers to low-income families in Milwaukee.	_____
_____	9. A radio program that discusses California school superintendent Bill Honig's opposition to school vouchers.	_____
_____	10. A speech by George Bush who says that parental school choice will improve public education by making schools compete for students.	_____

Periodical Bibliography

The following articles have been selected to supplement the diverse views presented in this chapter.

Jeanne Allen	"Nine Phoney Assertions About School Choice: Answering the Critics," *The Heritage Foundation Backgrounder*, September 13, 1991. Available from The Heritage Foundation, 214 Massachusetts Ave. NE, Washington, DC 20002-4999.
William Bainbridge and Steven Sundre	"School Choice: The Education Issue of the 1990s," *Children Today,* January/February 1991.
John G. Boswell	"Improving Our Schools: Parental Choice Is Not Enough," *The World & I,* February 1990.
Owen B. Butler	"Some Doubts on School Vouchers," *The New York Times*, July 5, 1991.
Susan Caminiti	"A Bigger Role for Parents," *Fortune*, Spring 1990.
Robert W. Carr	"Markets Can't Fix Schools' Problems," *The Wall Street Journal*, May 2, 1991.
John E. Chubb	"A Blueprint for Public Education," *The Wall Street Journal*, June 6, 1990.
John E. Chubb and Terry M. Moe	"America's Public Schools: The Need for Choice," *Current*, December 1990.
Dennis L. Evans	"The Mythology of the Marketplace in School Choice," *Education Week*, October 17, 1990. Available from 4301 Connecticut Ave. NW, Washington, DC 20008.
James D. Foster and Frank C. Nelsen	"Parental Choice: Will Vouchers Solve the School Crisis?" *Christianity Today*, August 19, 1991.
Tom Gibson	"School Choice: The Answer to Education," *The Saturday Evening Post*, May/June 1991.
Bill Honig	"School Vouchers: Dangerous Claptrap," *The New York Times*, June 29, 1990.
John B. Judis	"Why Bush Voucher Plan Would Be a Poor Choice," *In These Times*, September 18-24, 1991.
Deborah Meier	"Choice Can *Save* Public Education," *The Nation*, March 4, 1991.
Abigail Thernstrom	"Hobson's Choice," *The New Republic*, July 15 & 22, 1991.
Lois D. Whealey	"Choice or Elitism?" *The American School Board Journal*, April 1991. Available from 1680 Duke St., Alexandria, VA 22314.

Should Education for Minority Students Emphasize Ethnicity?

**EDUCATION
in America**

Chapter Preface

America's public schools are becoming increasingly diverse racially and culturally. In some cities, such as Los Angeles, public school students represent more than seventy cultures, from Nepalese to Guatemalan. As new immigrants continue to stream into the U.S., this diversity is likely to increase. Such change has spawned an interest among teachers and administrators to teach more about different cultures, languages, and customs. This movement, called multiculturalism, takes many forms, some of which are highly controversial.

For example, students might study the value of African civilization as opposed to Western civilization, or may focus on the importance of native American culture. Proponents of such courses believe that an understanding of world cultures helps children from all backgrounds dispel damaging ethnic stereotypes and empathize more with one another. This in turn decreases racism and conflict between students of different cultures. In the words of Enid Lee, author of *Letters to Marcia: A Teachers' Guide to Anti-Racist Education*, "Multicultural or anti-racist education equips students, parents, and teachers with the tools needed to combat racism and ethnic discrimination."

Many educators, however, assert that multiculturalism may do more harm than good. These critics charge that highlighting ethnic and cultural differences causes factionalism by encouraging students to group other children according to race or nationality, rather than considering them as individuals. Criticizing such teaching, noted historian Arthur Schlesinger Jr. writes that multiculturalism "exaggerates differences, intensifies resentments and antagonisms, and drives ever deeper the awful wedges between races and nationalities."

Whether emphasizing ethnicity has a positive or negative impact on children's attitudes is a matter of debate. The authors in this chapter give several thought-provoking arguments for both sides.

"Weaving multiple cultural perspectives into the social studies curriculum is important to the education of all students."

Multiculturalism Benefits All Students

New York State Social Studies Review and Development Committee

Proponents of multicultural education argue that studying the world's ethnic populations will benefit students of all races by increasing their awareness of different cultures. In the following viewpoint, the New York State Social Studies Review and Development Committee agrees and proposes emphasizing multicultural education in social studies courses for the state's 2.5 million public school students. The committee maintains that in the U.S., which is becoming more ethnically diverse, multicultural education is necessary to improve communication and understanding among the country's different ethnic groups. The proposal, which affects one of the largest state school systems in the U.S., marks New York as one of the foremost states advocating multicultural education. This viewpoint is an excerpt from the committee's recommendation to the New York State Education Department concerning the state's social studies curriculum.

As you read, consider the following questions:

1. According to the committee, how do social studies develop students' intellects?
2. Why does the committee believe that cultural identity is important?

Adapted from *One Nation, Many Peoples: A Declaration of Cultural Interdependence* by the New York State Social Studies Review and Development Committee, published by the New York State Education Department, June 1991. Public domain.

It is fitting for New York State, host to the Statue of Liberty, to inaugurate a curriculum that reflects the rich cultural diversity of the nation. The beacon of hope welcomes not just the "wretched and poor" individuals of the world, but also the dynamic and rich cultures all people bring with them.

Two centuries after this country's founders issued a Declaration of Independence, focused on the political independence from which societies distant from the United States have continued to draw inspiration, the time has come to *recognize cultural interdependence*. We propose that the principle of respect for diverse cultures is critical to our nation, and we affirm that a right to cultural diversity exists. We believe that the schoolroom is one of the places where this cultural *interdependence* must be reflected. . . .

This Committee affirms that multicultural education should be a source of strength and pride. Multicultural education is often viewed as divisive and even as destructive of the values and beliefs which hold us together as Americans. Certainly, contemporary trends toward separation and dissolution in such disparate countries as the Soviet Union, South Africa, Canada, Yugoslavia, Spain, and the United Kingdom remind us that different ethnic and racial groups have often had extraordinary difficulty remaining together in nation-states. But national unity does not require that we eliminate the very diversity that is the source of our uniqueness and, indeed, of our adaptability and viability among the nations of the world. *If the United States is to continue to prosper in the 21st century, then all of its citizens, whatever their race or ethnicity, must believe that they and their ancestors have shared in the building of the country and have a stake in its success.* Thus, multicultural education, far from being a source of dissolution, is necessary for the cultural health, social stability, and economic future of New York State and the nation.

Aims of Social Studies

The Committee believes that to achieve these ends, the teaching of social studies should emphasize the following:

First, beginning in the earliest grades social studies should be taught from a global perspective. The earth is humankind's common home. Migration is our common history. The earth's peoples, cultures, and material resources are our common wealth. Both humankind's pain and humankind's triumphs must be shared globally. The uniqueness of humankind is our *many ways of being human*, our remarkable range of cultural and physical diversity within a common biological unity.

Second, the social studies will very likely continue to serve nation-building purposes, among others, even as we encourage global perspectives. With efforts to respect and honor the di-

A Spiral Curriculum for Multicultural Education

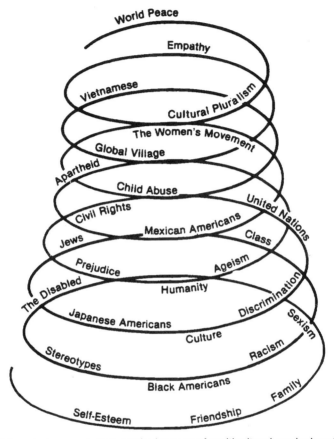

This spiral represents a particular type of multicultural curriculum that begins with self-esteem and includes varied topics of study to promote children's understanding and empathy for others.

From Pamela L. Tiedt and Iris M. Tiedt, *Multicultural Teaching: A Handbook of Activities, Information, and Resources, Third Edition. Copyright © 1990 by Allyn and Bacon. Reprinted with permission.*

verse and pluralistic elements in our nation, special attention will need to be given to those values, characteristics, and traditions which we share in common. Commitment to the presentation of multiple perspectives in the social studies curriculum encourages attention to the traditional and dominant elements in our society, even as we introduce and examine minority elements which have been neglected or those which are emerging as a result of new scholarship and newly recognized voices.

Third, the curriculum must strive to be informed by the most up-to-date scholarship. It must be open to all relevant input, to new knowledge, to fresh perspectives. Human history is to be seen as ongoing, often contradictory, and subject to reasonable differences based on contrasting perceptions and distinct viewpoints.

Inspiring Children

Fourth, students need to see themselves as active makers and changers of culture and society; they must be helped to develop the tools by which to judge, analyze, act, and evaluate.

Fifth, the program should be committed to the honoring and continuing examination of democratic values as an essential basis for social organization and nation-building. The application of democracy to social organization should be viewed as a continuing process which sometimes succeeds and sometimes fails, and thus requires constant effort.

Sixth, one of the central aims of the social studies is the development of the intellect; thus, the social studies should be taught not solely as information, but rather through the critical examination of ideas and events rooted in time and place and responding to social interests. The social studies should be seen not as some dreary schoolroom task of fact mastery to be tested and forgotten, but as one of the best curricular vehicles for telling the story of humanity in a way that motivates and inspires all of our children to continue the process of responsible nation-building in a world context. . . .

A Changing Society

Debate concerning change in New York State's social studies curriculum often implies that the curriculum stands as a fixed and unchanging prescription for the classroom, its stability protecting the inculcation of basic values from shifting political and economic winds. Closer examination, however, reveals that the curriculum has grown and been transformed over time in response to societal change, as a few examples will show.

Unlike literature and languages, the social studies and their parent disciplines of history and geography were not a major part of the mainstream of the school curriculum until the present century. In 1899, a Committee of Seven of the American Historical Association (founded in 1884) made a recommendation which led to the study of European and American history and government in schools, including those of New York State. Other subject-matter organizations, as they were formed, also began to press for inclusion in the school curriculum (the American Political Science Association and the American Sociological Association, for example, founded respectively in 1903 and 1905).

In the second decade of this century, the need to accommodate the surge of immigration led to the view that the schools should help students develop the attitudes and skills necessary for good citizenship. In 1916 a Committee on the Social Studies of the American Historical Association declared this to be the goal of schooling, bringing the term "social studies" into formal use. In 1951, responding to the mood of national insecurity reflected in McCarthyism, New York State dropped the term "social studies" in favor of "citizenship education," and the amount of American history in the secondary curriculum was greatly increased ("social studies" re-emerged in 1960). Between 1965 and the late 1980s, as international communication and commerce increased, the curriculum was enlarged to include more global studies, such as year-long courses in Asian and African Studies (grade 9) and European Studies (grade 10). Since 1987, these in turn have been replaced by a two-year global studies sequence.

Minorities and American History

One cannot understand our complex society without understanding the history and culture of its major ethnic and cultural components. We must, of course, understand our immediate origins in the nation-states of Europe and in their philosophic and political roots. But as Gunnar Myrdal has taught us, we cannot understand American history, nor many of the social and political phenomena of the present, without also understanding the African American experience throughout that history. And the same is true of the Native American experience and the experience of Latino and Asian peoples, as well as all of the varied groups who have helped to shape our institutions and our sensibilities.

Thomas Sobol, letter to the New York Board of Regents, February 2, 1990.

Indeed, the processes of contest, debate, and transformation are integral parts of the rich history of education in the United States. That history has reflected the society of which it is a part, and societal changes over the past 30 years have brought with them rising interest in the study of diverse cultures in the United States and the world. In the universities, scholarly attention has turned to previously neglected groups (those that have historically been minorities in the United States and women) and topics (social history, ethnic and cultural studies). Such scholarship has brought to light much that had been omitted from U.S. and world history, as traditionally studied.

In the 1970s and early 1980s, elementary and secondary schools, like colleges and universities, were faced with the recog-

148

nition that much of the experience, cultural values, and collective pasts of their students was not identified or represented in the curriculum. Corresponding to what James A. Banks has termed the "demographic imperative" of increasing numbers of minority students enrolled in public schools, parents, students and communities served by the schools became more forceful in demanding that their children learn about their own pasts. There was a new recognition that the teaching of social studies as a single officially sanctioned story was inaccurate as to the facts of conflict in American history, and further, that it was limiting for white students and students of color alike.

Assimilation and Culture

Much of the heat of the debate concerning the importance of valuing cultural difference in the schools arises from divergent opinions on whether preparing students to become members of U.S. society necessarily means assimilation. While the goal of assimilation has historically been relatively explicit in American schooling, in recent years many thoughtful writers and educators have argued against assimilation when interpreted as erasure of distinctive cultural identities. *Education must respond to the joint imperatives of educating toward citizenship in a common polity while respecting and taking account of continuing distinctiveness.* Even more, as we have argued, the perspectives of a number of major groups in American society must be recognized and incorporated. Nor is assimilation essential to educate citizens who value this country's ideals and participate in its polity and economy.

Weaving multiple cultural perspectives into the social studies curriculum is important to the education of all students. By including preparation in multicultural education in its standards, the National Council for the Accreditation of Teacher Education (NCATE) correctly recognized in the late 1970s what we appear to need to "discover" again: that multicultural education has powerful pedagogical repercussions critical to both white students and students of color, quite apart from issues of assimilation and loss of identity. NCATE suggested in 1979 that multicultural education provided

> preparation for the social, political, and economic realities individuals experience in diverse and complex human encounters. These realities have both national and international dimensions. This preparation provides a process by which an individual develops competencies for perceiving, believing, evaluating, and behaving in different cultural settings. Thus, multicultural education is viewed as an intervention and an ongoing assessment process to help institutions and individuals become more responsive to the human condition, individual cultural integrity, and cultural pluralism in society.

149

Over the past two decades, elementary, middle, and secondary schools and postsecondary institutions have seen efforts to restructure the curriculum in order to represent more adequately the diverse cultures of the student body and the world in which students must eventually function. Shifts in curriculum design in such states as California, Oregon, Iowa, Ohio and Florida reflect an increasing awareness that children and society are inadequately served when study is limited to the intellectual monuments of Western civilization. Comprehensive study of multiple cultures is increasingly recognized as having critical relevance for students who will face a national economy and political structures that grow more globally interdependent and increasingly diverse.

Curriculum Change

New York State has successfully embarked upon a number of investigations and efforts to revise the curriculum to include the study of multiple perspectives and diverse cultures, both within and outside the U.S. Since 1970 the Board of Regents has issued a series of policy statements seeking to ensure that, in the words of a 1983 report on education for a global perspective, "all students should have a knowledge and understanding of the cultures of this nation and of the world and that more students should possess communication skills necessary to meet their personal, academic and professional objectives" in both their own and other cultures and languages. In keeping with this long-standing policy, and in response to the report, "A Curriculum of Inclusion," by an earlier task force appointed to investigate the extent to which the New York State Social Studies syllabi are responsive to the facts of diversity in this State, the Board of Regents has decided to consider recommendations designed to

> increase students' understanding of American culture and history; the cultures, identities and histories of the diverse groups which comprise American society today; and the cultures, identities and histories of other peoples throughout the world.

"It is surely not the office of the public school to promote ethnic separatism and heighten ethnic tensions."

Multiculturalism Promotes Ethnic Separatism

Arthur Schlesinger Jr.

Arthur Schlesinger Jr., an acclaimed author and Pulitzer Prize-winning historian, is a professor of humanities at the City University of New York. Schlesinger served on the New York State Social Studies Review and Development Committee, whose report appears in the opposing viewpoint, and criticized the committee's proposal. Schlesinger argues that schools should not stress multicultural education because it divides society and accentuates ethnic characteristics. He maintains that the reinforcement of group differences threatens unity among Americans by perpetuating ethnic and racial subcultures. Schlesinger believes that schools should teach children a common American culture.

As you read, consider the following questions:

1. Why does Schlesinger believe it is important for the U.S. to create its own national identity?
2. Why does Schlesinger believe that it is not the role of public education to promote cultural awareness?
3. In the author's opinion, how have Western democratic ideals inspired people globally?

Arthur Schlesinger Jr., "Toward a Divisive Diversity," *The Wall Street Journal*, June 25, 1991. Reprinted with permission.

It is unquestionably necessary to diversify the syllabus in order to meet the needs of a more diversified society. It is unquestionably necessary to provide for global education in an increasingly interdependent world. Our students should by all means be better acquainted with women's history, with the history of ethnic and racial minorities, with Latin American, Asian and African history. Debate, alternative interpretations, "multiple perspectives" are all essential to the educational enterprise. I welcome changes that would adapt the curriculum to these purposes. If that is what the report means by multicultural education, I am all for it.

But I fear that the report implies much more than this. The underlying philosophy of the report, as I read it, is that ethnicity is the defining experience for most Americans, that ethnic ties are permanent and indelible, that the division into ethnic groups establishes the basic structure of American society and that a main objective of public education should be the protection, strengthening, celebration and perpetuation of ethnic origins and identities. Implicit in the report is the classification of all Americans according to ethnic and racial criteria.

These propositions are assumed rather than argued in the report. They constitute an ethnic interpretation of American history that, like the economic interpretation, is valid up to a point but misleading and wrong when presented as the whole picture.

A New Identity

The ethnic interpretation, moreover, reverses the historic theory of America—which has been, not the preservation and sanctification of old cultures and identities, but the creation of a new national culture and a new national identity. As Secretary of State John Quincy Adams told a German contemplating migration to these shores, those who would settle in America must recognize one necessity: "They must cast off the European skin, never to resume it. They must look forward to their posterity rather than backward to their ancestors."

Of course students should learn more about the rich variety of peoples and cultures that have forged this new American identity. They also should understand the curse of racism—the great failure of the American experiment, the glaring contradiction of American ideals and the still crippling disease of American society. But we should also be alert to the danger of a society divided into distinct and immutable ethnic and racial groups, each taught to cherish its own apartness from the rest.

The republic has survived and grown because it has maintained a balance between *pluribus* and *unum*. The report, it seems to me, is saturated with *pluribus* and neglectful of *unum*.

The first paragraph of the preamble notes that "no other coun-

152

try in the world is peopled by a greater variety of races, nationalities, and ethnic groups." It continues: "But although the United States has been a great asylum for diverse peoples, it has not always been a great refuge for diverse cultures." Both points are correct—but the report is oblivious to the historical fact that the second sentence explains the first.

Cultural Assimilation

Why has the U.S. been exempt from the "trends toward separation and dissolution" that, as the report later notes, are having such destructive effects in the Soviet Union, Canada and elsewhere? Obviously the reason the U.S. is still the most successful large multiethnic nation is because, instead of emphasizing and perpetuating ethnic separatism, it has assimilated immigrant cultures into a new American culture.

Most immigrants came to America precisely in order to escape their pasts. They wanted to participate in the making of an American culture and an American national identity. Even black Americans, who came as involuntary immigrants and have suffered—still suffer—awful persecution and discrimination, have made vital contributions to the American culture.

Divisive Words

The war of words on multicultural education concerns me as a historian and a teacher. The divisive "isms" are the problem: tribalism versus Anglo-Saxonism. Conformism versus elitism. Particularism versus multiculturalism.

These words are not teaching tools. They encourage a territoriality, a commodification of curricular content that inhibits the process of education.

Marcia Carlisle, *The Christian Science Monitor*, September 6, 1991.

The preamble rejects "previous ideals of assimilation to an Anglo-American model." Of course America derives its language and its primary political purposes and institutions from Britain. To pretend otherwise is to falsify history. To teach otherwise is to mislead our students. But the British legacy has been modified, enriched and reconstituted by the absorption of non-Anglo cultures and traditions as well as by the distinctive experiences of American life. That is why America is so very different a nation from Britain.

The report does on occasion refer in general terms to the need for *unum* as well as for *pluribus*. The preamble observes, "Special attention will need to be given to those values, characteristics, and traditions which we share in common." I do not, however, find this concern much reflected in the body of the report or in the proposals for syllabus revision. Part II begins by describing "the search for common cultural grounds" as "more important than ever." This comment, if true, should give that search a much higher priority than it receives in the report. Buried toward the end is a comment on the importance of examining with care "what the elements are that hold together a nation or culture in spite of what are often great differences. This surely is one of the central questions to be considered in any course in American history." It surely is, but it receives practically no attention in the proposals for curricular revision.

Stressing Ethnic Differences

A basic question is involved: Should public education seek to make our young boys and girls contributors to a common American culture? Or should it strengthen and perpetuate separate ethnic and racial subcultures? The report places its emphasis on cultivating and reinforcing ethnic differences. Students, the report says, should be "continually" encouraged to ask themselves what their cultural heritage is, why they should be proud of it, "why should I develop an understanding of and respect for my own culture(s), language(s), religion, and national origin(s)." Would it not be more appropriate for students to be "continually" encouraged to understand the American culture in which they are growing up and to prepare for an active role in shaping that culture?

Am I wrong in sensing a certain artificiality and inauthenticity in all this? If the ethnic subcultures had genuine vitality, they would be sufficiently instilled in children by family, church and community. It is surely not the office of the public school to promote ethnic separatism and heighten ethnic tensions. The bonds of national cohesion in the republic are sufficiently fragile already. Public education should aim to strengthen, not weaken, them.

Western Ideals

Our democratic ideals have been imperfectly realized, but the long labor to achieve them and to move the American experiment from exclusion to participation has been a central theme of American history. It should be a central theme of the New York social studies curriculum.

And it is important for students to understand where these democratic ideals come from. They come of course from Europe. Indeed, Europe is the unique source of these ideals— ideals that today empower people in every continent and to which today most of the world aspires. That is why it is so essential (in my view) to acquaint students with the Western history and tradition that created our democratic ideals—and why it is so wrong to tell students of non-European origin that Western ideals are not for them.

I regret the note of Europhobia that sometimes emerges in vulgar attacks on "Eurocentric" curriculums. Certainly Europe, like every other culture, has committed its share of crimes. But, unlike most cultures, it has also generated ideals that have opposed and exposed those crimes.

Self-Defeating Strategy

Though the educational establishment would rather die than admit it, multiculturalism is a desperate—and surely self-defeating—strategy for coping with the educational deficiencies, and associated social pathologies, of young blacks. Did these black students and their problems not exist, we would hear little of multiculturalism. There is no evidence that a substantial number of Hispanic parents would like their children to know more about Simon Bolivar and less about George Washington, or that Oriental parents feel that their children are being educationally deprived because their textbooks teach them more about ancient Greece than about ancient China.

Irving Kristol, *The Wall Street Journal*, July 31, 1991.

The report, however, plays up the crimes and plays down the ideals. Thus, when it talks about the European colonization of Africa and India, it deplores "the eradication of many varieties of traditional culture and knowledge." Like infanticide? slavery? polygamy? subjugation of women? suttee? veil-wearing? footbinding? clitorectomies? Nothing is said about the influence of European ideas of democracy, human rights, self-government, rule of law.

The Schools' Function

I also am doubtful about the note occasionally sounded in the report that "students must be taught social criticism" and "see themselves as active makers and changers of culture and society" and "promote economic fairness and social justice" and "bring about change in their communities, the nation, and the world." I very much hope that, as citizens, students will do all these things, but I do not think it is the function of the schools to teach students to become reformers any more than I ever thought it the function of the schools to teach them the beauty of private enterprise and the sanctity of the status quo. I will be satisfied if we can teach children to read, write and calculate.

"If African American children were taught to be fully aware of the struggles of our African forebears, they would find a renewed sense of purpose. "

Afrocentrism Promotes Black Self-Esteem

Molefi Kete Asante

Afrocentrism is used in schools to teach history and culture from the black point of view. Many black educators and others believe that U.S. schools do not adequately teach black history and that this negatively affects black students' academic performance. In the following viewpoint, Molefi Kete Asante argues that Afrocentrism is necessary for black children to develop self-esteem and a strong sense of identity. Asante maintains that the teaching of black history from white teachers and authors has forced blacks to perceive themselves as inferior to whites. He believes that teaching about blacks' African heritage and cultural contributions will improve black students' progress in school. Asante is chairman of the African-American Studies department at Temple University in Philadelphia, Pennsylvania.

As you read, consider the following questions:

1. How does Afrocentricity differ from Eurocentricity, according to Asante?
2. In the author's opinion, why do children have little understanding of black history?
3. According to Asante, how can Afrocentrism benefit children of all races?

From "The Afrocentric Idea in Education" by Molefi Kete Asante, *The Journal of Negro Education*, Spring 1991. Reprinted with permission.

Many of the principles that govern the development of the Afrocentric idea in education were first established by Carter G. Woodson in *The Mis-education of the Negro* (1933). Indeed, Woodson's classic reveals the fundamental problems pertaining to the education of the African person in America. As Woodson contends, African Americans have been educated away from their own culture and traditions and attached to the fringes of European culture; thus dislocated from themselves, Woodson asserts that African Americans often valorize European culture to the detriment of their own heritage. Although Woodson does not advocate rejection of American citizenship or nationality, he believes that assuming African Americans hold the same position as European Americans vis-à-vis the realities of America would lead to the psychological and cultural death of the African American population. Furthermore, if education is ever to be substantive and meaningful within the context of American society, Woodson argues, it must first address the African's historical experiences, both in Africa and America. . . .

The Afrocentric Approach

Afrocentricity is a frame of reference wherein phenomena are viewed from the perspective of the African person. The Afrocentric approach seeks in every situation the appropriate centrality of the African person. In education this means that teachers provide students the opportunity to study the world and its people, concepts, and history from an African world view. In most classrooms, whatever the subject, Whites are located in the center perspective position. How alien the African American child must feel, how like an outsider! The little African American child who sits in a classroom and is taught to accept as heroes and heroines individuals who defamed African people is being actively de-centered, dislocated, and made into a nonperson, one whose aim in life might be to one day shed that "badge of inferiority": his or her Blackness. In Afrocentric educational settings, however, teachers do not marginalize African American children by causing them to question their own self-worth because their people's story is seldom told. By seeing themselves as the subjects rather than the objects of education— be the discipline biology, medicine, literature, or social studies—African American students come to see themselves not merely as seekers of knowledge but as integral participants in it. Because all content areas are adaptable to an Afrocentric approach, African American students can be made to see themselves as centered in the reality of any discipline.

It must be emphasized that Afrocentricity is *not* a Black version of Eurocentricity. Eurocentricity is based on White supremacist notions whose purposes are to protect White privilege and advantage in education, economics, politics, and so forth. Unlike Eurocentricity, Afrocentricity does not condone ethnocentric valorization at the expense of degrading other groups' perspectives. Moreover, Eurocentricity presents the particular historical reality of Europeans as the sum total of the human experience. It imposes Eurocentric realities as "universal"; i.e., that which is White is presented as applying to the human condition in general, while that which is non-White is viewed as group-specific and therefore not "human." This explains why some scholars and artists of African descent rush to deny their Blackness; they believe that to exist as a Black person is not to exist as a universal human being. They are the individuals Woodson identified as preferring European art, language, and culture over African art, language, and culture; they believe that anything of European origin is inherently better than anything produced by or issuing from their own people. Naturally, the person of African descent should be centered in his or her historical experiences as an African, but Eurocentric curricula produce such aberrations of perspective among persons of color.

True Multiculturalism

Multiculturalism in education is a nonhierarchical approach that respects and celebrates a variety of cultural perspectives on world phenomena. The multicultural approach holds that although European culture is the majority culture in the United States, that is not sufficient reason for it to be imposed on diverse student populations as "universal." Multiculturalists assert that education, to have integrity, must begin with the proposition that all humans have contributed to world development and the flow of knowledge and information, and that most human achievements are the result of mutually interactive, international effort. Without a multicultural education, students remain essentially ignorant of the contributions of a major portion of the world's people. A multicultural education is thus a fundamental necessity for anyone who wishes to achieve competency in almost any subject.

The Afrocentric idea must be the stepping-stone from which the multicultural idea is launched. A truly authentic multicultural education, therefore, must be based upon the Afrocentric initiative. If this step is skipped, multicultural curricula, as they are increasingly being defined by White "resisters," will evolve without any substantive infusion of African American content, and the African American child will continue to be lost in the Eurocentric framework of education. In other words, the African American child will neither be confirmed nor affirmed in his or her own cultural information. For the mutual benefit of all Americans, this tragedy, which leads to the psychological and cultural dislocation of African American children, can and should be avoided. . . .

Why has Afrocentricity created so much of a controversy in educational circles? The idea that an African American child is placed in a stronger position to learn if he or she is centered— that is, if the child sees himself or herself within the content of the curriculum rather than at its margins—is not novel. What is revolutionary is the movement from the idea (conceptual stage) to its implementation in practice, when we begin to teach teachers how to put African American youth at the center of instruction. In effect, students are shown how to see with new eyes and hear with new ears. African American children learn to interpret and center phenomena in the context of African heritage, while White students are taught to see that their own centers are not threatened by the presence or contributions of African Americans and others.

Including African-American Children

Afrocentricity aims to locate African-American children in the center of the information being presented in classrooms across the nation. Most African-American children sit in classrooms, yet are outside the information being discussed. The white child sits in the middle of the information, whether it is literature, history, politics or art. The task of the Afrocentric curriculum is finding patterns in African-American history and culture that help the teacher place the child in the middle of the intellectual experience.

Molefi Kete Asante, *Newsweek*, September 23, 1991.

Institutions such as schools are conditioned by the character of the nation in which they are developed. Just as crime and politics are different in different nations, so, too, is education. In the United States a "Whites-only" orientation has predominated in education. This has had a profound impact on the quality of education for children of all races and ethnic groups. The African American child has suffered disproportionately, but White children are also the victims of monoculturally diseased curricula.

During the past years many White students and parents have approached me after presentations with tears in their eyes or expressing their anger about the absence of information about African Americans in the schools. A comment from a young White man at a major university in the Northeast was especially striking. As he said to me: "My teacher told us that Martin Luther King was a commie and went on with the class." Because this student's teacher made no effort to discuss King's ideas, the student maliciously had been kept ignorant. The vast majority of White Americans are likewise ignorant about the bountiful reservoirs of African and African American history, culture, and contributions. For example, few Americans of any color have heard the names of Cheikh Anta Diop, Anna Julia Cooper, C.L.R. James, or J.A. Rogers. All were historians who contributed greatly to our understanding of the African world. Indeed, very few teachers have ever taken a course in African American Studies; therefore, most are unable to provide systematic information about African Americans.

Afrocentricity and History

Most of America's teaching force are victims of the same system that victimizes today's young. Thus, American children are not taught the names of the African ethnic groups from which the majority of the African American population are derived; few are taught the names of any of the sacred sites in Africa. Few teachers can discuss with their students the significance of the Middle Passage or describe what it meant or means to Africans. Little mention is made in American classrooms of either the brutality of slavery or the ex-slaves' celebration of freedom. American children have little or no understanding of the nature of the capture, transport, and enslavement of Africans. Few have been taught the true horrors of being taken, shipped naked across 25 days of ocean, broken by abuse and indignities of all kinds, and dehumanized into a beast of burden, a thing without a name. If our students only knew the truth, if they were taught the Afrocentric perspective on the Great Enslavement, and if they knew the full story about the events since slavery that have served to constantly dislocate African Americans, their behavior would perhaps be different. Among these events are: the infamous constitutional compromise of 1787, which decreed that African Americans were, by law, the equivalent of but three-fifths of a person; the 1857 Dred Scott decision in which the Supreme Court avowed that African Americans had no rights Whites were obliged to respect; the complete dismissal and nonenforcement of Section 2 of the Fourteenth Amendment to the Constitution (this amendment, passed in 1868, stipulated as one of its provisions a penalty against any state that denied African Americans the right to vote, and called for the reduction of a state's delegates to the House of Representatives in proportion to the number of disenfranchised African American males therein); and the much-mentioned, as-yet-unreceived 40 acres and a mule, reparation for enslavement, promised to each African American family after the Civil War by Union General William T. Sherman and Secretary of War Edwin Stanton. If the curriculum were enhanced to include readings from the slave narratives; the diaries of slave ship captains; the journals of slave owners; the abolitionist newspapers; the writings of the freedmen and freedwomen; the accounts of African American civil rights, civic, and social organizations; and numerous others, African American children would be different, White children would be different—indeed, America would be a different nation today. . . .

Educational Sense

Although we students didn't say it this way, my teachers at Howard [University] were "Afrocentric," and they were passing on that "Afrocentric" legacy to us. And yes, their efforts did build up the self-esteem of the young black men and women in those classrooms. But their efforts enriched the lives of Howard students of other racial and ethnic backgrounds who sat in those classrooms as well.

To regard Afrocentricity simply as a means to help African-American youth feel "good about themselves" is to take the narrow view. The key measure of Afrocentricity's validity is that it makes educational sense.

Franklyn G. Jenifer, *The Washington Post National Weekly Edition*, November 26-December 2, 1990.

No wonder many persons of African descent attempt to shed their race and become "raceless." One's basic identity is one's self-identity, which is ultimately one's cultural identity; without a strong cultural identity, one is lost. Black children do not know their people's story and White children do not know the story, but remembrance is a vital requisite for understanding and humility. This is why the Jews have campaigned (and rightly so) to have the story of the European Holocaust taught in schools and colleges. Teaching about such a monstrous human brutality should forever remind the world of the ways in which humans have often violated each other. Teaching about the African Holocaust is just as important for many of the same reasons. Additionally, it underscores the enormity of the effects of physical, psychological, and economic dislocation on the African population in America and throughout the African diaspora. Without an understanding of the historical experiences of African people, American children cannot make any real headway in addressing the problems of the present.

Certainly, if African American children were taught to be fully aware of the struggles of our African forebears they would find a renewed sense of purpose and vision in their own lives. They would cease acting as if they have no past and no future. For instance, if they were taught about the historical relationship of Africans to the cotton industry—how African American men, women, and children were forced to pick cotton from "can't see in the morning 'til can't see at night," until the blood ran from the tips of their fingers where they were pricked by the hard boll; or if they were made to visualize their ancestors in the burning sun, bent double with constant stooping, and dragging rough, heavy croaker sacks behind them—or picture them bringing those sacks trembling to the scale, fearful of a sure flogging if they did not pick enough, perhaps our African American youth would develop a stronger entrepreneurial spirit. If White children were taught the same information rather than that normally fed them about American slavery, they would probably view our society differently and work to transform it into a better place. . . .

Aim of Afrocentrism

This nation has long been divided with regard to the educational opportunities afforded to children. By virtue of the protection provided by society and reinforced by the Eurocentric curriculum, the White child is already ahead of the African American child by first grade. Our efforts thus must concentrate on giving the African American child greater opportunities for learning at the kindergarten level. However, the kind of assistance the African American child needs is as much cultural as it is academic. If the proper cultural information is provided, the academic performance will surely follow suit.

When it comes to educating African American children, the American educational system does not need a tune-up, it needs an overhaul. Black children have been maligned by this system. Black teachers have been maligned. Black history has been maligned. Africa has been maligned. Nonetheless, two truisms can be stated about education in America. First, some teachers *can and do* effectively teach African American children; secondly, if some teachers can do it, others can, too. We must learn all we can about what makes these teachers' attitudes and approaches successful, and then work diligently to see that their successes are replicated on a broad scale. By raising the same questions that Woodson posed more than 50 years ago, Afrocentric education, along with a significant reorientation of the American educational enterprise, seeks to respond to the African person's psychological and cultural dislocation. By providing philosophical and theoretical guidelines and criteria that are centered in an African perception of reality and by placing the African American child in his or her proper historical context and setting, Afrocentricity may be just the "escape hatch" African Americans so desperately need to facilitate academic success and "steal away" from the cycle of miseducation and dislocation.

"The premise of the Afrocentric curriculum is absurd, and its promise of self-esteem is doomed to fail."

Afrocentrism Does Not Promote Black Self-Esteem

Anne Wortham

Supporters of Afrocentrism in schools argue that it helps increase black students' appreciation of black history and culture and thereby improves self-esteem and proficiency in school. In the following viewpoint, Anne Wortham argues that Afrocentrism cannot bestow self-esteem on black children because self-esteem can only be developed through individual effort. Wortham believes that self-esteem is the product of an individual's self-confidence and sense of personal worth. For black children to gain self-esteem, Wortham contends, they must be taught how to think independently and derive satisfaction from individual achievement, rather than take pride in the accomplishments of the black race. Wortham is an associate professor of sociology at Illinois State University in Normal, Illinois and a continuing visiting scholar at Stanford University's Hoover Institution in Palo Alto, California.

As you read, consider the following questions:

1. Why does Wortham believe that blacks should avoid linking their personal identities to their ancestors?
2. In the author's opinion, how can Afrocentrism harm intergroup relations among Americans?
3. According to Wortham, why should the contributions of important blacks be viewed as individual rather than group efforts?

Adapted from "Restoring Traditional Values in Higher Education: More than Afrocentrism," a speech given by Anne Wortham at The Heritage Foundation in Washington, D.C., February 22, 1991. Reprinted with permission.

Before I examine the content of Afrocentric education, let me take this opportunity to be politically incorrect and say that I am not an African; calling myself African would make no more sense than a white Australian calling himself English because his ancestors were English prisoners deported to the Australian continent. Neither am I part of any "African diaspora." I am a native of this land—an indigenous American and thoroughly Western. This is my home; I desire no other, either symbolically or existentially.

What exactly is Afrocentrism anyway? My comments are drawn basically from Professor Malefi Asante's 1987 book, *The Afrocentric Idea*. He writes that Afrocentricity means "placing African ideals at the center of any analysis that involves African culture and behavior." The Afrocentric idea is "a commitment to a historical project that places the African person back on center" in a cultural analysis; as such it becomes an "escape to sanity." Asante argues that Afrocentrism is not just an artistic or literary movement; neither is it just an individual or collective quest for authenticity through the history of a people. Above all, he says it is "the total use of a method to effect psychological, political, social, cultural and economic change." It involves overthrowing "Eurocentric icons" and exorcising them from the life and thought of African-Americans whose minds have been colonized by Europeans. The Afrocentric idea goes beyond the decolonizing of the mind that began with the black power movement to something else—the quest for an authentic mindset that one can speak of as Afrocentric.

Emphasizing the Contribution of Blacks

According to the Afrocentric perspective of education, the way to improve the educational achievement of black children is to improve their self-image by requiring that teachers include or emphasize the contribution of blacks in art, science, mathematics, language arts, social studies and music. This approach, known as the "Afrocentric curriculum" has gained in popularity and is being variously implemented around the country. In the District of Columbia, where enrollment is 90 percent black, a group of parents and businessmen founded an organization called, ironically, Operation Know Thyself, which lobbies school officials and pushes for the integration of an Afrocentric curriculum in all courses from kindergarten through high school.

The name Operation Know Thyself is paradoxical because the premise underlying the organization's promotion of an Afrocentric curriculum is that self-esteem is dependent on cultural heritage, and that the self is a group phenomenon rather than personal identity expressed in personality and character. The tragic irony in this approach is that the attempt to derive self-esteem from the knowledge of black cultural contributions requires that one's sense of personal identity be tied to the thinking and actions of people with whom one happens to share some racial ancestry and ethnic history; it is a recipe not for increasing self-esteem, but for perpetuating the kind of other-oriented dependency that is one of the primary obstacles to positive self-esteem.

Prescription for Chaos

No self-esteem can be achieved by the distortion of history embodied in the Afro-centric curriculum and the racist view of history upon which it is predicated. It is a dead end, which will leave minority students in poverty, trapped in the inner city, forever blaming others for their condition. Whatever the motives of its advocates may be, it is a prescription for educational chaos and disaster.

Allan C. Brownfeld, *Human Events*, June 1, 1991.

A very controversial Afrocentric approach in education is the teaching program known as African-American Baseline Essays, an outline used by several inner-city public schools around the country. The central claim of the Baseline Essays is that ancient Egypt was a black nation. One of the essays asserts that Europeans "invented the theory of 'white' Egyptians who were merely browned by the sun. According to Baseline: 1) Africa was "the world center of culture and learning in antiquity." Ancient Greece derived significant aspects of its culture largely from blacks. 2) Ramses II and King Tutankhamen were black. Aesop was probably black. Cleopatra was partly black. 3) "Since Africa is widely believed to be the birthplace of the human race, it follows that Africa was the birthplace of mathematics and science."

Tolerance and Racism

According to the New York State Board of Education's 1989 Task Force on Minorities, the value of the Afrocentric approach is not only that it will cause children of minority groups to have "higher self-esteem and self-respect," it will also cause children from European cultures to have "a less arrogant perspective." This idea is an inversion of the argument made during the 1950s by social scientists, who took the position that segregated schools contributed to the low self-esteem of black school children. Together these propositions amount to saying that the self-image of black students is dependent on having white classmates who must disprove their own alleged racism by tolerating the ethnocentrism of blacks. When white students incorporate the notion that their self-esteem is tied to the approval of minorities, they come to think in the following way: "I want to be good (i.e., tolerant). Minorities tell me I am bad (a racist/Eurocentric). A tolerant person does not contradict the assertions of minorities. So the way to be tolerant is to be racist." This is the self-fulfilling prophecy that teachers encourage when they blindly abdicate their responsibility as educators and subject their students to Afrocentrism.

Tolerance and Understanding

Ayn Rand's condemnation of the double standard that permeated victimization politics of the 1970s is equally applicable to the promoters of Afrocentrism during the 1990s. For such people, wrote Rand:

> "Tolerance" and "understanding" are regarded as unilateral virtues. In relation to any given minority, we are told, it is the duty of all others, i.e., of the majority, to tolerate and understand the minority's values and customs—while the minority proclaims that its soul is beyond the outsider's comprehension, that no common ties or bridges exist, that it does not propose to grasp one syllable of the majority's values, customs or culture, and will continue hurling racist epithets (or worse) at the majority's faces. Nobody can pretend any longer that the goal of such policies is the elimination of racism—particularly when one observes that the real victims are the better members of these privileged minorities.

The Afrocentric curriculum requires not only the complicity of whites in the denigration of the cultural origins of their ethnic groups, but also requires the estrangement of both whites and blacks from the distinct culture they have created in the United States. By using the term "African" to refer to members of the American Negro subculture and the term "European" to refer to members of the many Caucasian American subcultures, Afrocentric education completely distorts the reality of intergroup relations in America. Moreover, it deliberately defines American Negroes as outsiders to the Western experience in defiance of the fact that we are bloody well in it up to our necks! As Earl E. Thorpe pointed out three decades ago:

> Since 1865 practically all colored Americans . . . constantly have viewed this country as their home, and have not wished to be expatriated or colonized. Their political and social faith have been the traditional faith of America, and they speedily and unhesitatingly have risen to the colors when the nation was imperilled by war. By and large, they have been basically American since the early days of slavery, and their so-called racial traits are simply American traits, accentuated here and there by historic circumstance. This does not deny the survival of certain

African words, dances, and similar idioms, but these survivals have become a part of the total national culture.

The premise of the Afrocentric curriculum is absurd, and its promise of self-esteem is doomed to fail. There is no doubt that black children have a need for positive self-esteem. They are not unique in this; the need for self-esteem is inherent in man's nature. (For an exposition on why this is so, I refer you to a work by psychologist Nathaniel Branden entitled *The Psychology of Self-Esteem*.) Self-esteem is the reputation a person has with himself. Branden defines authentic self-esteem as the integrated sum of a sense of personal efficacy (self-confidence) and a sense of personal worth (self-respect). He says that it is "the conviction that one is competent to live and worthy of living." There is only one way that man can make himself competent to live, and that is by the proper exercise of his rational faculty. He needs to have confidence in the reliability of his tool of cognition, and he needs to feel that he is right in his characteristic manner of act-ing—that he is good and fit for happiness. "Man makes himself worthy of living by making himself competent to live," says Branden.

Personal Worth

Since, as Branden points out, "There is nothing a man is so likely to regard as irreducibly and unalterably 'himself' as his manner of thinking," one of the primary tasks of education must be teaching children the method of thinking. They must be taught to attain intellectual independence to free themselves from the dependence on the authority of significant others. They need to achieve the personal autonomy that results from independent thinking, independent judgment and self-responsi-bility. Afrocentric education assumes that personal worth is de-rived from group pride, and in so doing, promises what it can-not deliver.

Studies of the effects of minority status on self-esteem indicate that although it may seem logical that experiences of prejudice, discrimination and economic failure would cause a group to have a lower self-esteem than a group that does not, it is not necessarily the case. Indeed to insist that is to generate another stereotype—that of self-hatred.

The assumption of a direct relationship between self-esteem and discrimination assumes that all blacks adjust to their ethnic status in the same way and that there is no variation in the ef-fect that ethnicity has on their self-concept. To date, studies of the relation of ethnic identity and self-concept show that: 1) no assumptions about self-esteem can be based on race; 2) factors such as social class, school performance and reference groups appear to be more important than race in explaining self-image;

and 3) that self-satisfaction, pride and self-respect are not a monopoly of those of dominant groups.

All students should learn about the contributions to history and culture made by people of different backgrounds. But it is a cruel hoax to suggest that there is any significant linkage between race or ethnicity and self-esteem. When I attended school in a segregated school system in the South, I learned about blacks who had contributed to American culture. However, I was not taught that there was anything special about them except that they were very smart, articulate, creative people who were worth knowing about because of their outstanding human qualities and achievements, because of the role they played in the making of America, and the contribution they made to the uplift of the Negro community.

No Cure-All for Self-Esteem

Many parents view the Afrocentric curriculum as a cure-all for the dire ailments of urban school districts. They hope for increased self-esteem and better academic performance under an Afrocentric curriculum. But self-esteem is not something that can be "taught" in the same way as, say, English or math. In addition, even proponents admit that there is only anecdotal evidence to suggest that changing the curriculum will improve the academic performance of minority children.

David Nicholson, *The Washington Post National Weekly Edition*, October 8-14, 1990.

No one told me that by having this knowledge something positive would happen to my view of myself. The reason was that my teachers, who were black, knew that properly educating me meant teaching me how to function as a human being, not as a black person. They did not tell me this in so many words, but what they taught was a clear indication of their intent. In the face of a society that viewed Negroes only in terms of racial stereotypes, my teachers focused not on teaching me counter-stereotypes, as Afrocentrists would, but on the things I needed to know to fulfill my human potential. In other words, I believe they understood that being a victim of racism did not entitle me to exemption from the standards of human achievement, and it would have been unthinkable for them to give me the impression that I could obtain a sense of worth by secondhand means.

What is more important to the self-esteem of a Chinese-American: to know that tea, paper, paper money and printing originated in China or to acquire the skills necessary perhaps to sell tea and calculate his earnings? What is more important to the self-esteem of a Negro American: knowing that Negro spirituals and folk songs gave rise to what is recognized as American popular music, or learning how to defer immediate gratification when and if necessary and to tolerate unavoidable frustration in order to achieve his goals?

There is no necessary conflict between making students aware of the contributions of many peoples to the culture of their society and understanding that their self-concept has nothing to do with the achievements of people who happen to look like them, or talk like them or worship God as they do. Self-esteem is not a transferable commodity, or something conferred upon one by other people's character and actions. It has to be earned by the individual himself; there is no other way. What children need to learn is the distinction between culture and personality, and between biography and history.

Individuals, Not Group Symbols

This is not to deny the importance of teaching children about the history of American Negroes. But Afrocentrism does not simply claim that Negro American history has been distorted or excluded from school curricula; it wants to substitute any objective account of Negro history for its own selective and self-aggrandizing view. Moreover, in teaching students about the lives and achievements of people like Ralph Ellison, Duke Ellington or Bessie Smith the Afrocentric curriculum intends that students view such persons not as individuals but as symbolic ancestors whose works are the cultural property of Negroes and whose lives were but extensions of all Negroes. Indeed, it demands that they be spoken of not even as Americans but as Africans.

Take another case, that of Booker T. Washington, founder of my alma mater, Tuskegee University. All school children need to know about the life and ideas of Washington, who was an inspiring figure in American history. However, since Washington was an ardent proponent of free enterprise and championed the other ideals of Western civilization, the consistent practice of Afrocentrism requires educators to present Washington as an unfortunate black leader who was a captive of Eurocentric consciousness. Surely, such a distortion of Washington's own worldview and his ideas cannot be seriously offered as education. No doubt he would be excluded from some Afrocentric curricula altogether.

"Those of us who advocate bilingual education have a vision of . . . a people proud and skilled in English and equally proud and skilled in dozens of other tongues."

Bilingual Education Helps Minority Children

Rita Esquivel

In bilingual education programs, children are taught in both English and their non-English native languages. In the following viewpoint, Rita Esquivel asserts that bilingual education is necessary because it helps each minority group appreciate its cultural heritage. Esquivel believes that in the United States, with its rich mixture of cultures and languages, affirming cultural diversity can promote understanding. Esquivel is director of the U.S. Office of Bilingual Education and Minority Language Affairs in Washington, D.C.

As you read, consider the following questions:

1. According to Esquivel, how does bilingual education help the cultural transition of minority students?
2. In the author's opinion, how does the comprehension of other languages help minorities to better understand English?
3. Why do some people oppose bilingual education, according to Esquivel?

Rita Esquivel, speech given to the California Association of Bilingual Education, Anaheim, California, January 31, 1991.

The metaphor of tapestry is a rich one. A tapestry is a work of creativity, but it is often put to very practical uses as carpet or curtain or wall covering. The weave of a tapestry is intricate and complex, yet the visual image it presents is often made simple by its unity. A tapestry is woven of thousands of threads, and still it is one single art object. If you look at a tapestry from the underside, you see what looks like a disorderly tangle of stitches and knots and disconnected figures; if you stand in front of it, you perceive the finished surface, whose patterns are clear, whose segments are related to one another in beautiful designs.

What are we suggesting when we speak of bilingual education as a tapestry of languages? The bilingual education population is multiple and extremely diverse; it is becoming more rather than less so. In the projects funded by Title VII [of the Bilingual Education Act] alone there are currently students who speak 152 different languages. Included are traditional Western languages like Spanish, Italian, and Polish; there are American Indian languages like Arapaho, Cherokee, and Zuñi; there are Asian languages—Cantonese and Cambodian. We find Armenian and Haitian Creole. . . . Some two million children in American schools have a home language other than English. In the midst of this wonderful diversity, all these children are being introduced to a common new language, English, which will become their vehicle of communication and mutual understanding not only with those who speak only English but also with those who speak those multiple tongues I referred to earlier.

Enriching Cultures

In this country, English is the medium of political, cultural, and social unity. Those of us who advocate bilingual education have a vision of a people both diverse and one, a people proud and skilled in English and equally proud and skilled in dozens of other tongues. When I say "a people proud and skilled in English and equally proud and skilled in dozens of other tongues," I'm not talking about knowing the English equivalents of Chinese and Italian words or the Chinese and Italian equivalents of English words. I want and hope for more than that. I hope for a deep comprehension of and respect for the values embedded and transmitted through language. I even hope for the mutual interlacing of cultures in such a way that each is enriched by the others. Learning a new language gives one the power to enter literally a new world. . . . Each language we know allows us access to a worldview, to particular ways of thinking, to a range of feeling, to interpretations of reality unique to that language. You have probably had the experience of searching for a foreign word that will communicate the precise meaning of an English word or expression and realizing suddenly that there is no exact equivalent. There is no exact English equivalent, for example, for the Spanish *simpatico* or the Italian *prego*. *Hogar* and home are, technically, synonyms, but they are not really; they carry a somewhat different emotional content which is critical to the meaning. One language makes it possible for a person to see and understand realities that remain veiled—even invisible—in another language. Back in the late sixties the linguist Benjamin Whorf developed the very persuasive theory that the language we are born into determines what realities we will notice and know and effectively bars us from perceiving and knowing others. Whether the theory is valid or not, it is true that language conditions what we experience and how we interpret it.

Ethnic Changes in the Classroom

Projected percentage of enrolled public school students in 1995 who will be nonwhite, or Hispanic, or both:

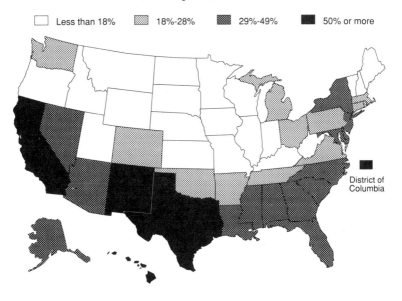

Sources: Western Interstate Commission for Higher Education and the College Board.

Two simple examples come to my mind. A few weeks ago four women of the Office of Bilingual Education were having coffee together. The four were born and grew up in four different Latin American countries; they are fluent in both English and Spanish. One of them mentioned that her sister, who lives in

172

Peru, had told her that the word *privacidad* had surfaced as a newly-coined word in Peruvian newspapers and articles. She remarked to the other staff members that there really is no noun equivalent of privacy in Spanish. That launched a conversation among the four women, who, after searching their respective Spanish vocabularies, agreed that while the language contains the adjective *privado*, there is no direct noun equivalent. The conversation wandered into speculation about privacy and *privacidad*, about the cultural differences communicated by the absence of exact parallels. There is no doubt of the central importance of privacy in American culture, its critical role, for example, in legal arguments about certain social issues. But privacy does not carry the same cultural overtones in Hispanic societies. Another example. My deputy, born and reared in China, mentioned that when her daughters were little, she and her husband made it a habit to teach them Chinese words and phrases. When the girls said something in English, the parents would tell them how to say the same thing in Chinese. One day one of the children tossed off the very ordinary, "I changed my mind." Esther started to repeat the sentence in Chinese and was stumped. The only words she could think of would be appropriate in a solemn, rather weighty situation—for example, if a prime minister changed his or her mind. But the same language would be almost ludicrous if spoken by a child. In Chinese society children don't change their mind. Imagine, on the other hand, an American child who doesn't—or isn't allowed to— change his or her mind! There is a sharp difference in cultural values!

Identity of Bilinguals

What I'm saying is that our students who are learning Spanish and Mandarin Chinese and Armenian are entering another culture just as the students in our bilingual programs who are learning English are entering our common American culture. This is not a matter of substituting hot dogs for Peking duck or abandoning mariachis for Madonna. Rather, taking on a new language means expanding the world within each of the bilingual learners; a new language makes it possible for the learners to come in touch with vast fields of human experience. Taking on a new language means being faced with a set of values— sometimes very different from those we hold and accept as the only valid ones.

What goes on in bilingual education classrooms is not simply the acquisition of English language competence by speakers of Spanish, Japanese, Korean. In those classrooms, students—toddlers as well as teenagers—are forced to come to terms with their heritage. Their language, their customs, their foods and their music, their very identity as this person rooted in Mexico or El Salvador or Taiwan or Cambodia must be renegotiated and integrated with their identity as this person adopting and adopted by a new land. Where cultural values clash—as they frequently do—these students, some of them very young children, are faced with choices that are difficult even for adults. And you who are the teachers and the aides, the principals and the superintendents, the policy makers and the parents, you are guiding a process which is about much more than subjects and predicates. You are guiding a process which is about new identities and the respectful encounter of multiple cultures and values. The work that you do, the way that you do it, the self that you bring to the work has a powerful role in the ongoing creation of the American nation and people. I cannot emphasize too strongly what a critical part bilingual education has to play in this juncture of our history.

Building English Proficiency

Children who learn reading, arithmetic, and other subjects in their native language while they are being taught English will not be as likely to fall behind their anglophone peers, and will have little difficulty transferring their subject-matter knowledge to English as their English proficiency increases. On the other hand, when nonanglophone children or those with very limited English are immersed in English-only classrooms and left to sink or swim, as they were for generations, they will continue to fail at unacceptable rates.

Dennis Baron, *Social Policy*, Spring 1991.

Some in the United States fear the growing linguistic and cultural diversity; they clamor for restrictions and prohibitions of the use of languages other than English; they demand that newcomers learn English before they are allowed into our schools. My office answers many letters from Americans who are troubled by the proliferation of languages and cultures in the United States. They mention the division between English- and French-speaking groups in Canada; they wonder whether the same situation could occur in this country, pitting American against American. They cite the near-impossibility of agreement in the United Nations, where initiatives must somehow incorporate the competing interests of peoples and nations. If we encourage multilingual, multicultural experience, the writers say, are we constructing a society made up of warring interests, incapable of commitment to a shared vision of the common welfare? I don't doubt that some of the opposition to transitional bilingual education and to the use of the home language for instruction is motivated by prejudice. But some reflects honest questioning and legitimate speculation about the relation of unity and pluralism. The theme of the one and the many is, after all, an ongoing human debate; it was a favorite philosophical question among the ancient Greeks: is oneness possible where difference abounds? How much difference can a society absorb and remain united?

Of course, these questions are far bigger than the issue of bilingual education. But bilingual education is an easily identifiable context for debating questions of unity and pluralism. "Doing something about" bilingual education seems manageable. In some ways you in California are right on the cutting edge of the questions, the challenges, and, yes, even the battles provoked by the continuing influx of diverse peoples into the United States. California has the largest body of recent immigrants; California has the largest concentration of students whose language of origin is one other than English. And those languages are multiple. True, there is a preponderance of Hispanics and Asians, but the Santa Monica school where I was the assistant superintendent had children who spoke 28 different languages. It is not an exaggeration to think of California as the new Ellis Island. And there is no doubt that the impact of today's immigration falls heavily on the schools. Bilingual education has become, in a real sense, the field in which language meets language, culture meets culture, values meet values.

Rich in Languages and Cultures

Bilingual education is a tapestry. It is a tapestry of languages. It is equally a tapestry of cultures and values. It brings into one process the multiple treasures of multiple peoples and their long and honorable histories. It introduces the young to the never-completed process of fashioning one people, who at one and the same time take pride in their languages and cultures of origin and honor and delight in the shared language and culture of America.

The world in which we contemporary people have our dwelling is a global expanse. No longer is any aspect of our national life determined solely by us and our interests. No longer is it possible for us—even if we wanted to—to remain insulated from international developments. If we had any doubts before, surely the events in the Middle East have made that crystal clear. Education which makes people bilingual and bicultural—better yet multilingual and multicultural—is no longer a luxury reserved for the socially and economically privileged. It is a matter of survival. The earth's peoples grow daily more interwoven, their lives and fates meshed together for good or ill. Our country will be a purposeful, energetic actor in this movement to the extent that we the people open our minds to the rich human heritage held in the languages and cultures of the entire world. We are very fortunate to have many of them right here in this very nation. This country has a unique potential to become the wealthiest nation in the world—rich in languages, rich in cultures, rich in the new experience which would result from the intermingling and mutual influence of cultures and values. There is no doubt in my mind that bilingual education is one of the keys to such wealth. That is why we must maintain our commitment to excellence and ingenuity in bilingual education. That is why we can believe that our work matters.

"Bilingual education programs . . . have failed to prepare language-minority children for high school graduation."

Bilingual Education Handicaps Minority Children

Rosalie Pedalino Porter

While supporters of bilingual education believe minority children need to be taught in their native languages, opponents such as Rosalie Pedalino Porter argue that the programs inadequately educate minority children. In the following viewpoint, Porter cites as evidence the fact that Hispanics, who comprise the majority of students schooled in bilingual education, have higher drop-out rates than other students. Porter believes bilingual education is harmful and that students need to be immersed in the English language. Porter, the head of bilingual programs for the Newton, Massachusetts, public schools, is the author of *Forked Tongue: The Politics of Bilingual Education.*

As you read, consider the following questions:

1. According to Porter, how can bilingual programs provoke ethnic discord?
2. In the author's opinion, how is bilingual education comparable to segregation?
3. Why does Porter believe that the education of minorities is important to the U.S. economy?

Rosalie Pedalino Porter, "Bilingual Education Trap," *The Washington Post*, April 22, 1990. Reprinted with permission.

In the name of "cultural sensitivity," we are systematically undereducating our language-minority children, severely reducing their opportunities for economic and social advancement.

The politics of ethnicity—in particular, pressure to continue the widely applied experiment called bilingual education, in which children are taught not in English but in their native language—has distorted policy and limited the search for alternatives.

Since bilingual education began, the number of different languages represented in schoolrooms nationwide has grown to 153, and the programs have become the single most controversial area in public education. No wonder: They segregate limited-English children, provide them inferior schooling and often doom them to unskilled jobs as adults.

Increase in Programs

Yet bilingual programs continue to increase, despite striking evidence of their failure:

• In November 1988, Con Edison, the public utility company of New York City, gave an English-language aptitude test to 7,000 applicants for entry-level jobs. Only 4,000 passed—and not one of those was a graduate of the city's bilingual education programs.

Yet a coalition of ethnic activists recently succeeded in convincing the state Board of Regents to pass new regulations that will keep more limited-English children enrolled for more years in native-language classrooms.

• In Los Angeles, which has the largest enrollment of limited-English students in the country (142,000), a survey of teachers in 1988 revealed that they are opposed to bilingual education by a margin of 78 to 22 percent. These results have been ignored and a bilingual master plan imposed on the Los Angeles schools that requires even more teaching in the native language.

• In New Jersey the state Board of Education announced that limited-English students may take the test of basic skills required for high school graduation in any of 12 languages. What the board didn't explain is how a student who has passed math and science tests only in Arabic, for example, can possibly use that knowledge to get a job in our English-speaking society or to qualify for college entrance.

Funding Continues

The U.S. Department of Education—despite its own studies showing bilingual education fails the children it is meant to help—continues to direct the major portion of federal funding for language-minority children into these same bilingual programs.

Millions of children are affected, and their numbers are growing faster than the rest of the school population. Estimates range from 1.5 to 7.5 million—from 5 to 20 percent of total enrollment.

A survey by the Education Department in May 1989 reports that from 1985 to 1988, enrollment of limited-English students in kindergarten through 12th grade increased by 7.1 percent while total school enrollment nationwide declined by 1.3 percent.

Reduced Language Skills

Bilingual education tends to establish a limited English vocabulary and reduced language skills among Hispanics. A student taught in two languages, one intimate, easy and familiar, the other cold, formal and difficult, will naturally tend to use what is most pleasant and easy. As a result, Hispanics without real sensitivity to or capability in the English language will be competing with people who have immensely rich vocabularies in English.

Philip Vargas, *The Washington Post*, April 8, 1991.

Out of a total school population of 39.2 million in kindergarten through 12th grade, the number of limited-English students is reported to be 1,533,520 or 5 percent. But the survey acknowledges that the actual number may be three to six times that many.

Five states reported that as many as 22.5 percent of all their schoolchildren are not able to use the English language well enough to benefit from regular classroom teaching in English.

Origin of Bilingual Education

The Bilingual Education Act of 1968 was designed to remove language barriers to learning. Access to an equal education was the primary goal and early mastery of English was seen as the key to such access.

The act mandated three years of study under a new initiative called bilingual education, which was expected to help students learn English faster, develop self-esteem and master subjects for grade-promotion and high school graduation.

These presumed benefits were entirely hypothetical; there was no evidence that such results would actually occur.

Bilingual advocacy groups soon began to exert pressure at the state level for public schools to provide support for maintaining students' native cultures as well. In some instances, the original program title was changed to "bilingual-bicultural education."

Often schools were urged to hire only teachers of the same ethnic background as the students. Instructors from the Dominican Republic, it was argued, could not "relate" to Puerto Rican students.

179

There were repeated efforts to amend state laws to keep students in bilingual classes beyond the three years originally mandated.

In many cases, political pressure changed what was to have been a temporary, "transitional" program into a permânent vehicle for developing students' native language and culture at the expense of English-language learning and integration into mainstream classrooms.

"The most significant thing about bilingual education is not that it promotes bilingualism," says Stanford University bilingual advocate Kenji Hakuta, "but rather that it gives some measure of official public status to the political struggle of language minorities, primarily Hispanics."

Programs Fail

The two basic premises of bilingual education are that it will make minority children equally literate in two languages while at the same time preserving their cultural identity. Neither in fact is the case.

For two decades, federal- and state-funded bilingual education programs throughout the country have failed to prepare language-minority children for high school graduation, much less for jobs or higher education.

Moreover, they have conspicuously failed to reduce the extraordinarily high drop-out rate for Hispanic students—between 40 and 50 percent nationwide, compared with 25 percent for blacks and 14 percent for non-Hispanic whites, according to the National Association for Bilingual Education.

As a classroom teacher of fifth- and sixth-grade Hispanic students in Springfield, Mass., I found that most of these children had not just arrived from another country but had lived on the U.S. mainland most of their lives.

Yet after five or six years in bilingual classrooms, they were able neither to do math or reading at the proper grade level in Spanish nor to master the English-language skills they needed. My experience was representative of the conditions in other school districts.

A study of the Boston Public Schools' bilingual program completed in 1986, for example, revealed that more than 500 Hispanic students who had been in bilingual classrooms since kindergarten were not able, on entering seventh grade, to take classes in English.

Emphasizing Spanish

When students are taught in Spanish a substantial part of each day, Spanish is the language they will know well, not English. This is not surprising. Educators call it the "time on task" concept—the proven link between the amount of time spent studying anything and the degree of success in learning it.

Two multiyear research projects conducted for the Department of Education in school districts with large Hispanic populations confirm this common-sense principle. In Dade County, Fla., and El Paso, Texas, language-minority students were divided into two groups: One was taught entirely in Spanish; the other received all instruction in an English-language "immersion" program.

Each study showed the same result. Both student groups attained the same levels in math, science and social studies. But the immersion students were far ahead in English speaking, reading and writing skills.

Furthermore, in both cases researchers found no evidence of greater self-esteem on the part of the students taught in their native language.

Across the nation, classroom teachers have learned firsthand how unsuccessful bilingual programs are. But they rarely speak out for fear of being labeled "racist."

Now, however, even supporters of bilingual programs are realizing that linguistically separate education of minority students for most of the school day is difficult to reconcile with our commitment to integrate schools along racial lines.

Ethnic Alienation

Indeed, such programs can provoke ethnic discord. As early as 1977, Alfredo Mathew Jr., a pioneer in bilingual education, warned that "while bilingualism, from a political point of view, is meant to foster the Puerto Rican-Hispanic identity and consequently encourages concentrations of Hispanics to stay together and not be integrated, one also has to be wary that it not become so insular and ingrown that it fosters a type of apartheid that will generate animosities with others, such as blacks, in the competition for scarce resources, and further alienate the Hispanic from the larger society."

Continued exclusive reliance on bilingual programs is also incompatible with another national goal—increased economic competitiveness. In the next 20 years, at least half the new workers entering the labor force will be minorities.

The ability of minority populations to use the language of the majority society is linked directly to their individual opportunity and thus, most basically, to social justice.

Certainly other factors besides language contribute to the failure of language-minority students, including poverty, family instability and overt discrimination.

These students need more supervision and opportunity in their lives and more special help in their schooling if they are to overcome their disadvantages. They need early and intensive help not only in learning the language of the schools and society but in mastering the subject matter of math, science, history and information technology.

Disparate Cultures

Certainly no one argues that these students should be subjected to the old "sink or swim" policies of neglect that earlier ethnic groups experienced.

But neither should we confine them only to traditional bilingual education, given America's astonishing diversity of cultures.

Obstacle to Success

The more time a child spends on a given task, the more likely he or she is to remember the lesson. Hispanic children who spend hours a day listening to Spanish may develop better skills in that language, but they're not likely to learn English as well as students who are given intensive help learning the new language. Because virtually all these students will spend their lives in the U.S., bilingual education may ultimately deprive them of the ability to earn a decent living or move into the social mainstream.

Linda Chavez, *The Wall Street Journal*, May 3, 1990.

To propose that one program can successfully meet the needs of such disparate communities as Cambodians, Navajos, Vietnamese and Russians is either naive or willfully misleading. Spanish speakers alone comprise many distinct communities from more than three dozen countries in Central and South America, the Caribbean and Europe, with members in all economic and social levels. Their goals may be equally diverse.

A national survey of Asian, Cuban, Mexican-American and Puerto Rican parents of limited-English students reveals their very different attitudes. Asians (whose numbers rose 70 percent during the 1980s) are the most likely to cite learning English as one of the three most important objectives of schooling and give a much lower priority to the teaching of the home language in school than the other three groups.

Puerto Ricans and Mexican-Americans are more likely than Asian or Cuban parents to want their children in native-language programs and to expect schools to teach the history and customs of their ancestors. Asian and Cuban parents tend to believe that this is the family's responsibility.

Clearly, we need to give parents and educators a range of alternatives—as well as the right to choose the most effective approaches for their communities and the power to assign public funding to support their choices.

One highly effective alternative has been promoted by Canada and Israel: second-language learning by the technique of "immersing" students in the new language as early as age 5. This method requires trained teachers and a special curriculum.

Comparable "early immersion" programs in the United States are operating successfully in El Paso and Uvalde, Texas; Arlington and Fairfax, Va.; Berkeley and San Diego, Calif.; Elizabeth, N.J.; and Newton, Mass. They use new language teaching techniques that include early immersion in the English language.

The aim of these programs is not primarily the strengthening of the student's native language but is instead pragmatic and double-barreled: Early and intensive English-language instruction together with strong emphasis on computation, analytical mathematics, biological and earth science, history and the study of different cultures.

In addition to our fostering respect for each child's ethnic culture and language, limited-English children must be given the means and the motivation to complete a high school education and to prepare for productive work or for higher education and professions. Such motivation comes only from real achievement.

That means putting aside the segregative and inadequate program of bilingual education and replacing it with a rich, content-filled education in English, the empowering language of our society.

a critical thinking activity

Recognizing Stereotypes

A stereotype is an oversimplified or exaggerated description of people or things. Stereotyping can be favorable. Most stereotyping, however, tends to be highly uncomplimentary, and, at times, degrading.

Stereotyping grows out of our prejudices. When we stereotype someone, we are prejudging him or her. Consider the following example:

Mr. Smith believes that ethnic minorities are too lazy and stupid to learn proper English. Whenever he hears minorities speaking poor English or their native languages he states: "If these people would just knuckle down and study they could learn to speak English just as well as the rest of us. If they're so lazy, why don't they just go back where they came from?" He is unable to understand the difficulty of learning a new language and simply equates poor English with laziness. Why? He has prejudged all minorities and will keep his stereotype consistent with his prejudice.

Part I

The following statements relate to the subject matter in this chapter. Consider each statement carefully. *Mark S for any statement that is an example of stereotyping. Mark N for any statement that is not an example of stereotyping. Mark U if you are undecided about any statement.*

S = *stereotype*
N = *not a stereotype*
U = *undecided*

184

1. Hispanic adults are afraid their children will forget their ethnic heritage.
2. Asians are smarter than whites.
3. Hispanics want to turn this country into Mexico. They want all the benefits of citizenship, but don't think they should have to learn English.
4. Tests scores show that blacks score lower than whites on standardized tests such as the SAT.
5. Blacks speak substandard English because they think everyone should bend over backwards to understand their poor English.
6. Many textbooks analyze subjects such as history from a white European perspective, causing some minority children to perceive themselves as inferior to whites.
7. Black and Hispanic parents do not encourage their children to work hard in school.
8. A larger percentage of Hispanics drop out of school than blacks.
9. American Indian children are among the poorest of all minority students.
10. Whites are genetically more intelligent than members of other ethnic groups.
11. Blacks are unwilling to interact with whites or other minority groups.
12. Whites cheat more on tests than minority students because they know teachers are less likely to suspect them.
13. The contributions of American Indians, blacks, and other minorities are often omitted from school textbooks.
14. Hispanics disagree over whether bilingual education benefits Hispanic children.
15. Minority families tend to have fewer economic advantages than white families.
16. Asian students study harder than Hispanic students. That is why they learn English much quicker than Hispanics.

Part II

Based on the insights you have gained from this activity, discuss these questions in class:

1. Why do people stereotype one another?
2. What are some examples of positive stereotypes?
3. Why are stereotypes harmful?
4. What stereotypes currently affect members of your class?

Periodical Bibliography

The following articles have been selected to supplement the diverse views presented in this chapter.

American Legion	"Barriers of Bilingual Education," October 1991.
Dennis Baron	"English in a Multicultural America," *Social Policy*, Spring 1991. Available from 25 W. 43rd St., Rm. 620, New York, NY 10036.
Richard Bernstein	"A War of Words," *The New York Times Magazine*, October 14, 1990.
Midge Decter	"E Pluribus Nihil: Multiculturalism and Black Children," *Commentary*, September 1991.
Anthony DePalma	"The Culture Question," *The New York Times*, November 4, 1990.
Michel Marriott	"Afrocentrism: Balancing or Skewing History," *The New York Times*, August 11, 1991.
Elizabeth Martinez	"The Politics of 'Cultural Diversity': Old Poison in New Bottles," *Z Magazine*, July/August 1990.
Michael Meyers	"Black Racism at Taxpayer Expense," *The Wall Street Journal*, July 30, 1991.
Newsweek	"African Dreams," Special section on Afrocentrism, September 23, 1991.
Gary Putka	"Curricula of Color," *The Wall Street Journal*, July 1, 1991.
Robert Reinhold	"Class Struggle," *The New York Times Magazine*, September 29, 1991.
Arthur Schlesinger Jr.	"The American Creed: From Dilemma to Decomposition," *New Perspectives Quarterly*, Summer 1991.
Time	"Whose America?" Special section on multi-culturalism, July 8, 1991.

What Role Should Religion Play in Public Education?

EDUCATION
in America

Chapter Preface

Encourage free schools, and resolve that not one dollar of money shall be appropriated to the support of any sectarian school. Resolve that neither the state nor nation, or both combined, shall support institutions of learning other than those sufficient to afford every child growing up in the land of opportunity of a good common school education, unmixed with sectarian, pagan, or atheistical tenets. Leave the matter of religion to the family altar, the church, and the private schools, supported entirely by private contributions. Keep the church and the state forever separated.

Ulysses S. Grant, 1875.

As this quote indicates, arguments over whether religion should be allowed in schools closely parallel arguments that advocate the separation of church and state. Indeed, people that argue for such separation believe, like former president Ulysses S. Grant, that religion should never enter the schools in any form, but should remain a personal family matter. This philosophy has been reinforced several times by the Supreme Court, which has consistently ruled against allowing formal religious teachings and prayer in the schools.

While many Americans argue that religion must be excluded from public schools, others believe that it has a rightful place in the classroom. According to a September 1989 *Parents* magazine poll, 65 percent of respondents said that a daily prayer in public schools would help promote values among children. Many such supporters believe that the presence of religion and prayer in schools would provide students with moral values that would help them avoid problems such as chemical dependency, teenage pregnancy, and juvenile delinquency.

Because a majority of Americans are members of some type of religious faith, the issue of what role religion should play in education is commonly discussed. The authors in the following chapter debate this issue.

"Religion is not being taken nearly as seriously in public education as it should be. "

Public Schools Should Teach Religious Studies

Warren A. Nord

Public school boards sometimes face the decision of whether to include religion as part of the curriculum. In the following viewpoint, Warren A. Nord argues that public schools must teach students about various religions because too little of such teaching is available outside of the school environment. Nord maintains that religious study is important because of its vast influence on world affairs. He believes that religions, like education, are traditions that help people understand the world. Nord is director of the Program in the Humanities and Human Values at the University of North Carolina at Chapel Hill.

As you read, consider the following questions:

1. Why do public schools place a low priority on religious study, according to Nord?
2. According to the author, how is religion important to understanding history and literature?
3. Why does Nord believe it is unfair to exclude religion from public education?

Adapted from "Taking Religion Seriously," by Warren A. Nord, *Social Education*, September 1990. Reprinted by permission of the National Council for the Social Studies.

What students learn about religion in schools is apt to be particularly important because most of them are not likely to learn much about it elsewhere. Newspapers and television tell them little about religion other than that is has something to do with scandals, foreign wars, and terrorism.

Some people argue that home and church are the places where children should learn about religion, but many children do not go to church (or synagogue or mosque) and learn nothing about religion at home. Those who do learn something often do not learn very much, and in any case what they learn will most likely be narrowly limited to the beliefs and rituals of their own particular religion. Home and church provide all too little of what a well educated person should know about religion.

Moreover, the kind of learning fostered in home and church is likely to be quite different from that of public education: home and church (quite properly) "indoctrinate" children by initiating them into their parents' religious tradition, into a particular way of understanding the world. The goal of public education—properly conceived, of course—is quite different: it is to provide students with an understanding of various religious and secular traditions, informing them, but not requiring them to conform to any particular view. Put most simply, the approach of public education is to teach rather than preach.

Include More Religious Study

Unfortunately, too often students can graduate from public schools—in fact they can receive college degrees, M.B.A.'s, J.D.'s, M.D.'s, and Ph.D.'s—without ever having to confront a religious idea. Many educators have come to accept such silence as desirable in a culture where, over the last several decades, the call for religion in school has come to be identified with the Religious Right. Often, religion is thought to be too controversial for politically sensitive public schools. Other educators have concluded that religion is largely irrelevant to education; we live, after all, in a largely secular culture, and it should come as no surprise that our textbooks and curriculum reflect that fact.

In the last few years, however, a series of textbook studies, a few state boards of education, and several national organizations—most prominently the National Council on Religion and Public Education and the Association for Supervision and Curriculum Development—have jointly pressed home the point that religion is not being taken nearly as seriously in public education as it should be. The result has been a growing, now very broad, consensus for incorporating a much greater study of religion into public education. Although there continues to be considerable concern about whether this can be done well in practice, there is widespread—and growing—agreement in principle that religion must be taken much more seriously.

There are only two places in the public school curriculum where there will almost surely be some discussion of religion: in world history courses and in literature courses that are taught historically. Religion has been so central to our historical experience that it cannot easily be avoided.

Our roots are to be found, Matthew Arnold told us, in the Hellenism of Athens and the Hebraicism of Jerusalem. Of course "our" roots are now also to be found in the Meccas and Benares of various non-Western religions as we become an increasingly pluralistic society. What cannot be doubted is that our ways of thinking about nature, morality, art, and society were once (and for many people still are) fundamentally religious, and still today in our highly secular world it is difficult even for the non-religious to extricate themselves entirely from the webs of influence and meaning provided by our religious past.

The Value of Religion

Because religion plays a significant role in history and society, study about religion is essential to understanding both the nation and the world. Omission of facts about religion can give students the false impression that the religious life of humankind is insignificant or unimportant. Failure to understand even the basic symbols, practices, and concepts of the various religions makes much of history, literature, art, and contemporary life unintelligible.

Study about religion is also important if students are to value religious liberty, the first freedom guaranteed in the Bill of Rights.

Association for Supervision and Curriculum, *Religion in the Public School Curriculum*, 1988.

To understand history and (historical) literature one must understand a great deal about religion: on this all agree. Consequently, the relative absence of religion from history textbooks is deeply troubling. World history texts typically give ten times the space to Athens and Rome that they give to Jerusalem, and ancient Egypt and Sumeria are likely to rate more pages than ancient Israel or early Christianity. If the Pilgrims and Puritans are given several pages in an American history text, only a few paragraphs will describe their religious views. All of the textbook studies have commented on the absence of religion from history textbooks. . . .

Any study of government and civics must come to grips with a range of issues having to do with the relationship of law and religion. Perhaps the most extraordinary aspect of our Constitution is that it is a completely secular document; indeed, the United States had the first secular government. (There are, of course, good religious as well as secular reasons why this is so.) But if our formal Constitution is secular, much law has had religious roots and purposes, and it is tremendously important for students to understand the relationship between moral law (or "natural law" or religious law) and civil law. They should understand historical religious arguments for and against democratic government; they need to understand (and appreciate the justifications, religious and secular, for) civil disobedience; they should have to reflect critically on why public education—why *their* education—must be secular; and it is important for them to understand the implications of the conflation of religious and political symbolism in what is often called "civil religion." Moreover, there is much discussion nowadays about whether our society is fragmenting in the legalistic ethos of constant appeals to rights and individualism. To what extent does a democratic society need shared ideals and purposes to give it direction and cohesion—and what role does religion have in providing them?

I trust my point is clear: any study of history . . . and of government must draw on an understanding of religion or the study will remain narrow and superficial. Religion has traditionally informed, and continues to inform and assess, ways in which we think about history, justice, law, and society. (And, of course, religion is equally relevant to the study of psychology, in home economics courses, of nature in science courses, of sexuality in health courses, and so on across the curriculum.)

Religious Liberty

One theme in American history warrants special consideration. Because America is a pluralistic society we disagree about a great deal—religion included (perhaps religion especially). A considerable part of what has bound us together as a nation is an almost universally shared commitment to the Constitution and those democratic virtues that have informed so much of American public life over the last two centuries. A part of this heritage is our commitment to religious liberty—not just religious toleration, but the *right* of people to believe and, within broad limits, act on their religious faith.

There is, no doubt, disagreement over what, precisely, the religion clauses of the First Amendment mean, and I do not want to suggest that nothing important hangs on how we resolve these questions of interpretation. But the general commitment to freedom of conscience, freedom of religious speech and action, is clear and constitutes a powerful ideal. It is tremendously important that students appreciate the significance of religious freedom, for this has not been the usual way of doing things in the world.

There is a rich and exciting story to be told here, with the persecution and religious wars of Europe as a backdrop against which American religious liberty shines so brightly. Yet, as Charles Haynes (1987) has pointed out:

> Most U.S. history texts give regrettably scant and often inaccurate treatment to the development of religious freedom. The reader of these texts might conclude that, after gaining religious freedom, America became free from religion! Absent from the texts are accounts of the contributions of religious groups to the evolution of our nation [and] the struggle of minority faiths for full freedom and acceptance.

Our world continues to be one in which religious violence and wars darken the lives of great numbers of people. Religious liberty is, all things considered, fragile. Zealotry and persecution have the sanction of world history. Perhaps the most important lesson to learn about the American experiment in religious liberty is that religion and politics thrive when religion is not established. Before Thomas Jefferson argued for a "wall of separation" to preserve government from the corruption of religion, Roger Williams argued for a "wall of separation" to protect religion from the corruption of government. We know that the "wall" of separation has many twists, turns, and windows. Few have argued for the separation to be complete. Still, the rough separation provided by the American experience gives evidence for the success of this part of the American experiment.

The location of the religion clauses at the very beginning of the Bill of Rights symbolizes their significance: freedom of conscience, freedom in our ultimate commitments, is at the foundation of our beliefs about what constitutes a just and good society. Students must be taught to appreciate this.

The Purpose of Education

The usual focus of the social studies curriculum on politics, economics, law, and government should not blind us to the larger purposes of education, and the role of social studies in it. Education orients students in the world. Whether intended or not, it serves a moral, indeed a kind of spiritual purpose. It tells students: this is what is important, this is what is normal, this is what is true, this is how people live their lives, this is what is good. It passes judgment—implicitly if not explicitly.

History and literature are the two central subjects of public school education, and it may be worthwhile saying a little about each of them in this regard. History is not simply a chronological sequence of historical events. It is the story of human suffering and human flourishing and what causes each of them. How historians and teachers tell that story is deeply controversial. There are many versions: liberal and conservative, Marxist and Christian, secular and religious.

Moreover, history locates individuals within traditional communities and, as such, provides students with an identity, with certain beliefs and values—as Americans, as human beings, as members of Western Civilization, or as members of particular ethnic groups, for example. Without historical consciousness we are lost in much the way we would be if we suffered from amnesia and could not remember anything for more than an hour. What we make of ourselves and what purposes we have in life, depends on our understanding of who we are, and that is derived in large part from the particular historical communities and traditions which we are taught about and come to identify with.

Literature and Spirituality

Similarly, English is not primarily about achieving literacy (though that is essential for everything that follows); nor is it primarily a matter of coming to understand literature as art—in terms of genre, style, plot, narrative, symbols, etc. The primary reason why literature is so important is that it gets us into the hearts and minds of people different from us: it nurtures empathy, and it broadens our understanding of what is human. It is because great literature grapples with the concerns of human existence in imaginative ways which we can emotionally (as well as intellectually) come to appreciate that it is important enough to require it of students at all grade levels.

How we choose our literature and interpret it, how we tell historical stories, orients us morally and spiritually in the world. This is simply unavoidable. Teachers of history and literature must very self-consciously appreciate the moral and religious significance of what they are doing.

Public education has avoided deeply moral and religious ways of understanding history, human psychology, society, and nature. The alternatives it puts before students are largely desacralized and demoralized. We initiate children into a profoundly secular world governed by economic, political, and technological imperatives, where science and social science provide our only contact with reality. Whether for wanting to avoid controversy, or because of their biases, educators have not laid all of the alternatives before students.

Students must also be introduced to moral and religious ways of experiencing the world. I would not have them taught as truth. Nor would I have it taught as truth that people are essentially utility self-maximizers or that self-actualization is the greatest need of people. Where there is deep cultural conflict I would have students come to understand all of the major alternatives. This is not being done now.

Religions warrant study for their own sake, not just for their influence on wars and social movements; they provide a myriad of ways in which people have made sense of their place in the world. This is what education should be designed to do: help students make sense of the world.

Essential Studies

Where a school does not have a religious studies program, every effort should be made to establish one. Apart from the fact that religious (or religionlike) phenomena are of crucial importance to human beings—we all need a worldview, a way of life, a sense of meaning in life and so forth—religious studies are essential to enable students to understand religious individuals and cultures and deal successfully with conflicts between religious sub-groups and between religious and non-religious people.

Clive Beck, *Better Schools: A Values Perspective*, 1990.

Because truth is so controversial, fairness may be the most fundamental pedagogical virtue. When there is deep cultural or intellectual conflict—as is surely the case regarding the truth of various religious and secular points of view—fairness should be the operative virtue. Contemporary public education provides students with a deep understanding of various secular ways of thinking about the world, but says next to nothing about religion. Much secular thought conflicts with much religious thought. To exclude religious ways of thinking is unfair; it is, more or less, indoctrination by default.

Fairness requires more than mere consideration of a point of view, however. Fairness means letting all of the parties in a conflict *speak for themselves*. It is interesting that in our criminal justice system we give defendants the right to have their day in court, the right to speak for themselves, even when the matter is fairly trivial—as with traffic tickets. Yet at the same time we often do not allow representatives of various religious (and sometimes secular) points of view speak for themselves in the curriculum even when the subject is momentous, but entrust their points of view to third-party textbook authors (and teachers) who often times are not at all sympathetic to the position they may (or may not) feel compelled to describe.

Fairness, then, means letting people tell their own stories. This means much greater use of primary source material in the classroom. And, it means giving advocates of a point of view

195

enough time and space to make sense of their story. It means being open to the emotional "feel" of their story. To understand other people and their religion is not to have memorized a few facts about them; it is to have some imaginative sense of how they see and feel the world.

Living Traditions

There are some on the Religious Right who would have only their brand of Christianity taught in the schools, and there are some in the Secular Left who would have no mention of religion at all—except in safely historical contexts. I have argued for serious, non-indoctrinative study of various religions (along with serious, non-indoctrinative study of secular ways of thinking), not just for their historical significance, but as living traditions that help orient us in a complex and confusing world. This is, after all, the overriding purpose of education: to orient us in the world.

When we think of religion in contemporary Iran and Poland, when we think of the abortion issue, when we think of the role of the church in the struggle for social justice in Latin America, when we think of our own mortality and what gives meaning to life—who can deny Supreme Court Justice Robert Jackson's (1948) assertion of the centrality of religion in "the tragic story of mankind." It is too important to leave out. We must take religion much more seriously.

"The proposal to introduce teaching 'about' religion to the public-school curriculum is the worst of ideas at the worst of times."

Public Schools Should Not Teach Religious Studies

R. Joseph Hoffmann

Religion has no place in public education because teachers are unqualified to teach it, states R. Joseph Hoffmann in the following viewpoint. Unlike other subjects, religion is not easily understood or taught. Furthermore, Hoffmann maintains that public school teachers' approach toward religious studies would be unduly influenced by the religious preferences of school boards and principals. Hoffmann is an author and editor of several books, including *Jesus Outside the Gospels* and *What the Bible Really Says*.

As you read, consider the following questions:

1. How is religion different from other school subjects, such as music or science, according to Hoffmann?
2. In the author's opinion, why are public school teachers unqualified to teach about religion?
3. Why does Hoffmann believe that religion has not improved the human condition?

Adapted from "Religion in the Public Schools?" by R. Joseph Hoffmann, *Free Inquiry*, Winter 1989/90.

The proposal to introduce teaching "about" religion to the public-school curriculum is the worst of ideas at the worst of times. As noted in *Free Inquiry*'s Fall 1988 issue, fourteen educational and religious groups have endorsed a push to teach religion "objectively" in the public schools. A pamphlet released on the program claims that schools can educate without promoting or denigrating any particular religion, and maintains that "failure to understand even the basic symbols, practices, and concepts of various religions makes much of history, literature, art, and contemporary life unintelligible."

There are at least three reasons to ditch the plan, any one of which should be enough to kill it before it involves the educational establishment and that bastion of intellectual mediocrity, the National Educational Association (NEA) in another round of time- and mind-wasting opportunities.

Hazy Subject

First off: Religion is not music, science, or art. Its "subject" matter is hazier than anything currently on the books. All Roman Catholics, Presbyterians, and Jews know (or think they know) what their religion is all about. In practical terms, however, this knowledge means little more than being able to find a parking place on Saturday or Sunday morning and a vacancy in the pew. "Real knowledge" of religious traditions—like the Latin Mass and the refinements of King James's English—has dipped dangerously close to zero among the faithful, and even though the churches chatter endlessly about the beauties of religious tolerance, pluralism, and (that desideratum *non pareil!*) dialogue, the trendy tolerance of the post-Vatican II era really is based on *not* knowing that Catholics, Protestants, Jews, and others believe different things. To put it another way: The catechism of our time, sociologically speaking, is that differences don't matter (in undergraduate language: everybody's entitled to "their" opinion).

It is a tribute to the modern consciousness and to the role of religion in modern life that so little attention is paid to tradition and dogma. In places where tradition matters—where people do know "about" the particularities of religious faith—Catholics and Protestants terrorize innocent citizens with their antics, Jews and Muslims throw rocks and bottles at one another, black Anglicans kill black Presbyterians, Muslim teachers are taunted by Hindu sages. If all of this seems facetious, it is meant rather to be healthily cynical. There is no proof whatever that knowing something about what "other" people believe promotes understanding. And the movement called "ecumenism," or Interfaith Dialogue, is based on a systematic weakening of the doctrinal foundations and practices of all religions—a glossing over of differences, not an examination of why they occur or whence they came. In fact, ecumenism has less to do with the growth of tolerance than with the massive spread of cultural illiteracy.

Propagating Dogma

Religion has always been able to capitalize on illiteracy and has a good deal to gain from the propagation of "soft" dogma: "We Anglicans no longer believe in hell," a foppish vicar announces to the very Romish Father Dudderwell: "And what about you Catholics?" "Oh, we believe in hell all right. It's an article of faith. We just don't believe anybody actually goes there anymore." Contrary to what the churches think has happened in the past generation, the growth of tolerance has had almost nothing to do with dialogue: Tolerance has been promoted through the subtle external influence of secular values (some good, some bad), and the churches have been able to accommodate that influence only by pretending that such values really are the essence of the Judeo-Christian tradition.

First Amendment Restriction

There is and can be no doubt that the First Amendment does not permit the State to require that teaching and learning must be tailored to the principles or prohibitions of any religious sect or dogma.

Abe Fortas, *The Great Quotations on Religious Freedom*, 1991.

Atop the ecumenical mountain—in the developed countries, anyway—sits a guru with bloodshot eyes and the uninspired message, "You are all God's children: Go home and do what you want—just don't hurt anybody." After hearing that, if pilgrims begin to wonder about pilgrimages (and gurus), who can blame them? In any case, public-school students in the United States should feel less good about themselves and even worse about what they don't know and haven't learned. The study of religion, given the state of current priorities, is rather like school prayer—only a distraction.

Teaching Religion

Second: How should religion be taught? I have been involved with the academic study and teaching of religion for years. If there were a good way to teach the subject, I probably would have heard about it. What I see, in the higher reaches of education anyway, is a field beset with uncertainty about what its proper role should be. Retrojecting such study into the lower

199

grades will not solve the problem, and bodes likely to make it worse.

To take the discussion back to our prototype Catholic, Presbyterian, and Jew (we can add a Muslim and a Buddhist): Students come into a classroom knowing their religious affiliation—or lack of it—like they know their grade-point average and gender. Beyond that, they know next to nothing about the tradition they embrace. Those who enroll in religion classes in college usually do so for all the wrong reasons. Religion courses are regarded as "crips," "guts," or payoffs: soft—like the dogma they have learned—and taught by kindly Christian teachers who regard all students worthy of salvation by good grades alone. Students expect to hear nothing new or surprising. They are, on the whole, innocent of the Western intellectual tradition and hence of the religious aspects of that tradition. What religious "knowledge" they have is of the most rudimentary sort: belief in God (sort of); belief in Jesus (usually in some inarticulate, un-Nicene formulation: Jesus is God); belief that the Bible is full of wonderful moral truths—as yet unexplored because, like *Moby Dick*, they haven't actually read it; belief that weird religions like Islam make people do scrungy things like blow up airplanes. And so it goes.

Confusion and Misunderstanding

In too many such classes, professors (especially, perhaps, those who must appease students to get good evaluations and tenure) play to the stands—to the lowest common denominator of adolescent experience ("Well, I was always taught that . . . "). Thus, I have heard from assorted Catholic students, "I was always taught that abortion was okay as long as rape or incest were involved," and from variegated Protestants that there is nothing in the Bible "against" homosexuality. A college classroom—and, by extension, a high school—is no place to sort out the sources of denominational confusion and misunderstanding. A professor in a public university (or a public school) should not have to say to a Good Catholic Kid, "Look, your church's position on abortion is not exactly as you describe it," or to inform students that unwelcome things *are* in the Bible.

The brutal truth is, art historians know their subject matter and how to teach it; English professors know how to dissect a poem; and physicists know how to teach the uncertainty principle. Their respective subject matters remain subject matters, and while ideology may have a part to play in any method used in any field, in no comparable field is the *subject matter* an ideology. Furthermore, doctrine is so disheveled nowadays that no teacher can be expected to keep up with the rapid erosion of the dogmatic foundations of world religions: In short, even if it

200

were desirable that teachers should sort out the essentials of religious faith for their charges, they could scarcely be expected to
do the job properly. . . .

Heightened Confusion

Third: Who would teach religion in the high schools? Even if
none of the foregoing objections had merit, this is an excellent
reason for scrapping the proposal. The confusions of higher education are likely to be trebled when a subject is introduced to
public-school teachers. Remember the "new math" and the
"new English"? Fine for M.I.T. and Stanford, but havoc when
they made their way into the how-to manuals of the educational
schools in Urbana and Tallahassee. Professors at least have the
time to reflect on the methodological cracks involved in teaching about religion. Public-school teachers do not. In general,
they are not the textbook writers, and even more uniformly,
they are not critics of the texts they use. I stare at a shelf full of
introductory college texts in world religions and biblical studies.
The covers are glossy (like high-school textbooks), the pages are
slick. Most are filled with photographs of desert excavations,
mosques, dervishes, and monks, and the various icons and para-
phernalia of the religious "quest" of mankind—to borrow a standard title. Many of these texts are written by colleagues with a
"religious" point of view. Most—even in the field of world religions—are studiously noncritical; the greater share are apolo-
getic: Religion is a good thing. It has a multiplicity of forms. The
religious experience of humanity is a fascinating tapestry of in-
tricately woven patterns. Jesus and Mohammad and the buddha
Gautama were very wise men with great moral lessons to teach.
That's the sort of drivel that fills the space between the pictures. True, there are some excellent introductory texts, but they
are pricelessly rare. And because of their scientific bent or questioning stance (usually straightforwardly historical with many
fewer pictures) they are usually thought unsuitable for introductory classes.

Brainless Approach

I have no doubt what sort of book would make its way into
the public schools. It would have to conform to the religious
predilections of an uninspired school board and a good church-
going principal. It would thus be the scholastic equivalent of
soft dogma, the message of the guru, and the attitude of the
Anglican vicar. Religion would be presented as an assortment
(take your pick) of timeless moral truths acted out in a dizzying
variety of liturgies and contained in books thought by their
devotees to be holy or sacred. It would have lots of pictures
and, as even some of my college texts now do, study-questions
at the end of each chapter that look suspiciously like they were

lifted from Sunday-school workbooks ("Name the mountain where Moses learned of Yahweh's plan for him").

No Business of Government

If the state . . . teaches about the beliefs and practices of religions, it will not only violate the often cited "separation of church and state," but it will also find itself either questioning, undermining or neutralizing students' religious beliefs. That is not the state's business, especially when it has not even taught the three R's well.

Dennis L. Cuddy, *The News and Observer*, January 5, 1989.

Sad to say, this brainless approach to the subject is probably the "best case scenario." The "worst case" is double-edged: On the one hand, teachers imaginative enough to introduce content and criticism will risk their necks and their jobs: "Now, while the Bible thinks of Moses as a historical figure, there is good reason to think that he is really a conglomeration of leaders who presided over the Israelite evacuation of Egypt." Or: "All ancient Near Eastern people regarded mountains as the dwelling place of gods, so it's appropriate that Moses should be depicted as meeting his God on a mountaintop." Let Mr. Jones teach that sort of stuff in his Humanities 101 class at Anytown High and Mr. Jones will soon find himself selling insurance. Furthermore, the unlikely alliance of societies and organizations that support the teaching of religion in the schools have no wish to encourage the likes of a Mr. Jones or to pay his lawyer's fees. What is clearest to me about this proposal is its sappiness: the spongey identification of religion with morality or moral "systems" and the Disneyish small-world-isn't-it notion that by learning about our religious differences we will all get to be good friends and bring peace to the Middle East. I repeat: Religion isn't gender. It isn't skin color. It isn't an intelligence quotient. It is *ideology*—moreover, *inherited* ideology, much of which is based on wrong, discredited, or unproductive world views. Speaking personally, I have not found myself becoming more "tolerant" of Islam lately merely because I have intensified my study of its history. "Travel" said George Bernard Shaw, "greatly narrows the mind." So too with the study of religion.

Inevitable Abuse

As to the other edge of the "worst case," we have Miss Emily Goodpastor of Bibletown, Georgia, who applauds the fact that Baptists have played such a prominent part in getting religion "back into the schools," as she puts it. She has been told (with a wink) by her principal (an elder in her church) and (with a nudge) by the superintendent of schools (a lay preacher) that she must give "equal time" to all religious traditions and show partiality to none. As Miss Goodpastor sees it (and has seen it since the Communists took prayer out of the schools), these paper-principles can be overlooked for the sake of the gospel. This is her chance to talk some sense into those three Roman Catholic students and let the class vote on whether Buddha was as good a teacher as Jesus. (Thus will the six Vietnamese in the tenth-grade class be saved.)

Simply put, there is no way *not* to abuse such teaching, at least given the present look of public-school education in the United States. We have not only the most intellectually impoverished students in the industrialized world, but a teaching profession sadly lacking the wherewithal to enrich them. Whatever the theoretical merits of such a proposal—and they are few—the machinery to implement it has not yet been invented.

I have hardly touched on the potential harm to the constitutional separation of church and state; that harm would certainly come if the "worst case scenario" materialized—as I have no doubt it would. Imagine the spillover: the legal tangles, the outraged parents, the "unlawful dismissal" hearings, the sermons in Miss Goodpastor's church, the tears of the Vietnamese students. Ah! the tolerance that mutual understanding would engender in the best of all possible worlds. But that world is not this, and religion—as a traditional source of division and conflict—has not done very much for its betterment. I say we let God rest on his mountain and not drag him into the classroom.

"Nothing in this Constitution shall prohibit the inclusion of voluntary prayer in any public school program or activity. "

Public Schools Should Allow Formal Prayer

William E. Dannemeyer

One part of the debate about the separation of church and state includes the issue of whether student prayer should be allowed in public schools. William E. Dannemeyer, the author of the following viewpoint, is among many people who argue that formal, voluntary prayer should be allowed in classrooms. Dannemeyer contends that allowing such prayers in public classrooms would instill moral values in children. Part I of the viewpoint is Dannemeyer's question-and-answer description of his Community Life Amendment, which would amend the U.S. Constitution to allow voluntary school prayer. Part II is his proposition that prayers be allowed in schools. Dannemeyer is a Republican U.S. representative from California.

As you read, consider the following questions:

1. How have problems in the home contributed to immorality among youth, according to Dannemeyer?
2. In the author's opinion, how does reinforcing the concept of "a Creator or Higher Authority" benefit children?
3. Why does Dannemeyer believe that a lack of moral values harms children?

Excerpted from Rep. William E. Dannemeyer's remarks to the U.S. House of Representatives as entered into the *Congressional Record*, May 1, 1991. Public domain.

Q. What is the Community Life Amendment?

A. The Community Life Amendment is a joint resolution to amend the U.S. Constitution to allow voluntary prayer in public schools.

Q. Why is this amendment needed?

A. Because a series of Supreme Court decisions, beginning in 1962, have held that formal recognition of a creator is unconstitutional in public schools. These decisions include: Engel (1962—Regent's prayer), Abington (1963—Lord's prayer and Bible reading), Stone (1980—posting the Ten Commandments), and Edwards (1987—teaching the creation of the earth equally with evolution).

Q. What is meant by voluntary prayer?

A. The legislative intent of this bill is to allow in public schools the formal recognition of the Creator of our inalienable rights as stated in the Declaration of Independence. If vocal, prayer must originate from a student, be extemporaneous, and unconstrained in form and content by any governmental or administrative authority. Local communities are left to decide standards dictating a proper time or place in public school settings.

Fundamental Concepts

Q. But aren't kids allowed now to say silent prayers whenever they choose?

A. Yes. What is not allowed is a formal recognition of a creator.

Q. Shouldn't we leave parents and the religious communities of families to teach children these fundamental concepts?

A. Relegating the formal recognition of a creator to its proper place is not enough to effectively influence the active minds of children who spend most of their days away from both home and religion and in an environment that unhesitatingly proclaims that such instruction is antithetical to reasoned thought and intellectual stimulation.

Humanism, by definition, will fail to effectively instruct kids that a creator is the source of their civic and personal liberties. In fact, the moral relativism of humanism will adversely indoctrinate children by teaching them that utility is the only standard whereby actions should be judged. Socialist, Communist, and authoritarian regimes have provided ample evidence of where moral relativism leads a nation.

Q. Would this amendment affect Court rulings on prayers at school graduations or athletic events?

A. Yes. Local communities would be free to allow or disallow such prayers. The format would be the same as in the school room—student initiated and extemporaneous.

Q. How would voluntary prayer in public schools help society?

A. The best answer to this question is to examine the direction of society from the time school prayer was deemed unconstitutional. Mr. David Barton has done his best to study the correlation, if any, between the removal of school prayer and societal decline.

Decline in SAT Scores

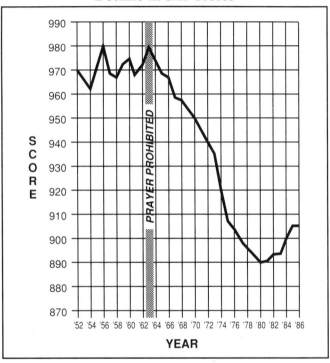

Source: *Congressional Record*, May 1, 1991.

Mr. Barton, in his book *America: To Pray or Not to Pray*, has measured several social indices. For instance, the scholastic aptitude test [SAT] is an academic test measuring the developed verbal and math reasoning skills of students preparing to enter college. These results are used widely to gain admission to colleges and universities. The SAT has been administered to high school seniors since 1926. A scale was established in 1941 to allow comparison of scores from year to year.

Notice the dramatic decline in scores at the time of the initial Court decision prohibiting State-sponsored prayers [see above chart]. A high of 980 in 1963 down to the 1986 level of 905. . . .

Other indices mirror this decline. Tell Mr. Barton that other factors are responsible for these tragedies. Tell him it is due to insufficient social spending or social justice. Tell him it was the adverse effects of the Vietnam war or the advent of television. Just don't tell him 1962 and 1963 were not pivotal years in our social existence.

Mandated Prayers

Q. Don't you really want to push us back to the point of State mandated and written prayers?

A. No. The Community Life Amendment contains the provision that, "Neither the United States nor any State shall prescribe the content of any such prayer." It does not matter what anybody else wants or thinks on the subject—the amendment as passed would prohibit a return to State written and mandated prayers.

A considerable decline in standards and morals can be demonstrated regarding the standing of youth in our society. Any number of social and educational indicators point this out. It does not matter if you examine scholastic aptitude test scores, premarital sexual activity, pregnancies to unwed teenagers, teen suicide rates, sexually transmitted disease prevalence, juvenile crime record, and so forth, the story is the same. American kids are taking it on the chin by and large.

Is there a central cause to these problems? Are these problems mutually exclusive? And why is it that the more prosperous we seem to be as a nation, these problems only get worse?

I hold to the admonition that no success can compensate for failure in the home. The home is where we should begin our search for answers to these problems. Here we will find answers to a large part of our woes. Complementing the social and educational declines of youth are the deteriorating conditions of their parents. Divorce is an epidemic today. Female-headed single parent households, negligent husbands avoiding financial and moral responsibilities, and the resulting economic strain are too much for the remaining familial structure to bear. This stress leads to physical, emotional, and substance abuse. Pretty soon, the term "family" as we know it has ceased.

Moral Value

Unfortunately, there is little that Congress or any other coercive instrument can do to implant the back bone of moral value necessary to prevent dysfunctional families. But moral value is what is needed. Don't get me wrong. Congress tries to help, but the help is sadistic, almost as if tax dollars were going to the Marquis himself to provide therapy to individuals suffering from an inattention disorder. Congressional response to date has only indemnified familial dysfunction.

One area of public policy where Congress has some leverage is education. From 6 to 8 hours per day, 5 days a week, public schoolchildren are open to concentrated influence outside of home and church. I will not spend the time here to catalog the infusion of secular humanism into public education that began, for all intents and purposes, in the 1930's. This influence has been widely broadcast both for good and bad.

Bush Supports School Prayer

I continue to support a belief held by the overwhelming majority of Americans—the right to voluntary school prayer. And so I continue to support a constitutional amendment restoring voluntary prayer. You see we need the faith of our Fathers back in our schools.

George Bush, statement to the National Religious Broadcasters' Convention, January 29, 1990.

But, I do feel compelled at this time to comment on what secular humanism has replaced: Normative moral values based on the Judeo-Christian ethic. Up until 1962, these values were unquestioned as a positive influence in public education. Kids were taught to recognize the moral and historical value of their inalienable rights. The precepts embodied in the Ten Commandments were the mortar that held our laws together, gave them weight, and that fueled individual self-government. The consummate benefit to society, to our moral safety net, was that the concept of a creator or higher authority was reinforced in the minds of public school kids.

Far from being an establishment of religion, formally recognizing a creator as part of the schoolday affirmed no more than the concept that some things in life transcend man. Our Founders called these things "life, liberty, and the pursuit of happiness." Evidently, such verities are no longer important for public school kids to understand.

Should we then wonder why our youth are in such disarray? Should we then wonder why our ability to govern a nation parallels our relative ability to govern ourselves? Would Congress run such massive debts if each Member was instilled with the normative wisdom of the proper role of Government, with frugality, with prudence? Would a citizenry elect unwise rulers if a majority of citizens held these values high in their own lives, if they voluntarily cared for the poor, old, and sick among them? Under these conditions, would we really need an all-encompassing state to use its coercive powers to compel us to do what we ought to be doing voluntarily?

Big Government, high crime, illiterate kids, and dysfunctional families are ultimately a result of moral negligence and a denial of a creator. We have allowed moral values and a creator to be kicked out of public schools, and because most kids attend public school, we are paying a high price.

Inalienable Right

Imagine a public schoolroom where a child is taught that stealing is wrong, not because some adult arbitrarily imposes this opinion, but because the law of the land, given to this student by a creator, says that the child has an inalienable right "to the pursuit of happiness" and therefore frowns disapprovingly on one person taking something that belongs to another person.

Under what circumstances would the child better learn this lesson: (A) where a teacher arbitrarily opines the belief that stealing is bad even though the child has friends who have found great utility in stealing; or (B) where a teacher reinforces home and the religious community of the family to say, regardless of utility, stealing is wrong because the Creator of your rights, rights that could be trampled in a climate of theft, has judged it to be wrong.

Unfortunately, were you to choose (B), schools would not be able to implement programs sufficient to meet this goal. The U.S. Supreme Court has told us so. They have said that to do so is a violation of the first amendment's establishment clause, that to allow class time to be used by students to formally recognize the Creator who gave them their inalienable rights is a contractual breach never intended by the same Founders who insisted that we have such transcendent rights.

I, like many other Americans, believe that the Supreme Court has missed both the juris and the prudence of this issue. To correct this deficiency I am introducing the Community Life Amendment. The amendment says simply:

Nothing in this Constitution shall prohibit the inclusion of voluntary prayer in any public school program or activity. Neither the United States nor any State shall prescribe the content of any such prayer.

The Community Life Amendment reaffirms the inherent constitutional right all Americans have to acknowledge the Creator who gave them their inalienable rights. This constitutional amendment would allow local communities to determine for themselves the matter of voluntary prayer in public school. It says that the Federal Government has no positive role to play in determining these issues.

"A public school may never require religious activities of a devotional or nonacademic nature."

Public Schools Should Not Allow Formal Prayer

Edd Doerr and Albert J. Menendez

Opponents of formal prayer in public schools argue that such a practice would violate the First Amendment by promoting one type of religion over others. Edd Doerr and Albert J. Menendez, the authors of the following viewpoint, agree with this view, contending that it would be impossible to adopt a school prayer policy satisfactory and inoffensive to all students. Doerr and Menendez are the authors of *Religion and Public Education*, from which this viewpoint is excerpted. Doerr is the executive director of Americans for Religious Liberty, an organization in Silver Spring, Maryland that supports the separation of church and state. Menendez is the author of more than twenty books, including *School Prayer and Other Religious Issues in American Public Education* and *Religion at the Polls*.

As you read, consider the following questions:

1. Why has the U.S. Supreme Court ruled against formal school prayer, according to Doerr?
2. How can public school students voluntarily pray during school, in the authors' opinion?
3. Why do Doerr and Menendez find mandated "moments of silence" for prayer in public schools objectionable?

Excerpted from *Religion and Public Education* by Edd Doerr and Albert J. Menendez, Centerline Press, 1991. Reprinted with permission.

No religious issue in education has so inflamed passions and prejudices as the question of school prayer, especially the kind of daily devotional exercise commonly held in about half of U.S. public schools when school recessed for the summer in 1962. And no Supreme Court decision in this area has been more misunderstood or misinterpreted than *Engel v. Vitale,* which the Supreme Court handed down that summer.

The Court was asked to rule on the constitutionality of the New York State Board of Regents prayer, a bland, 22-word "nondenominational" exercise composed by the Board and prescribed for daily use in New York State public schools. By a solid majority, the Court invalidated any kind of government-mandated religious exercise. Writing for the majority, Justice Hugo Black said, "It is no part of the business of government to compose official prayers for any group of the American people to recite as part of a religious program carried on by government." . . .

One year after *Engel,* the Supreme Court considered Pennsylvania and Maryland statutes which required Bible reading and the recitation of the Lord's Prayer each day in all public schools.

Once again the pattern varied. Some states required school prayer—mostly in the South and East. Some states were permissive. They allowed local school authorities to determine the extent of Bible readings or devotions. Some states forbade the practice. In some states the constitutions had been amended to mandate or forbid it, while in other states statutes provided guidance to local jurisdictions.

The 1963 case came from Abington Township, Pennsylvania, a pleasant, rather affluent suburb of Philadelphia. There, a Unitarian family, the Schempps, challenged the Pennsylvania law which required that "at least ten verses from the Holy Bible shall be read, without comment, at the opening of each public school on each school day."

During two trials the Schempp children testified that they were compelled to read passages embodying doctrines that they and their religious faith explicitly rejected. Fear of offending teachers and impairing relationships with other students made it impossible for them to absent themselves voluntarily from the daily worship. They therefore challenged the constitutionality of such compulsory practices in a public school system which operates under compulsory attendance laws.

Abington vs. Schempp

A three-judge District Court for the Eastern District of Pennsylvania agreed with the Schempps, finding the practice unconstitutional. The school district appealed, and the Supreme

Court accepted jurisdiction. . . .

The Court rejected the school district's claim that the Bible was being used merely as an instrument of nonreligious moral inspiration and a reference for the teaching of secular subjects.

While emphasizing that a genuine academic study of the Bible was acceptable, the Court majority nevertheless concluded that a public school may never require religious activities of a devotional or nonacademic nature.

Ed Gamble. Reprinted with permission.

The majority concluded, "The place of religion in our society is an exalted one, achieved through a long tradition of reliance on the home, the church and the inviolable citadel of the individual heart and mind. We have come to recognize through bitter experience that it is not within the power of government to invade that citadel, whether its purpose or effect be to aid or oppose, to advance or retard. In the relationship between man and religion, the State is firmly committed to a position of neutrality."

Failed Efforts

Repeated efforts to overrule *Engel* have failed. Dozens of proposed constitutional amendments have failed in Congress since the Becker Amendment failed to pass in 1964. Major efforts were mounted in 1966, 1971 and 1984. President Ronald Reagan even made the "restoration" of formal, government sponsored school prayer a centerpiece in his two successful campaigns for the White House.

Reagan proposed a so-called "voluntary" school prayer amendment to the Constitution in 1982. In March 1984 the Senate voted for it 56 to 44, eleven votes short of the required two-thirds necessary for constitutional amendments. It is unlikely that either house of Congress will give the requisite vote necessary before such proposals are sent on to the state legislatures. But attempts are still made from time to time. Rep. William Dannemeyer (R-CA) is the leading advocate in the House and his proposals have won a high level of support, largely the result of fear on the part of politicians that an "anti-prayer" vote could cost them an election.

It is significant that whenever congressional hearings have been held on proposed school prayer amendments, clergy and other representatives of Christian, Jewish, and other religious bodies have testified against such amendments, generally on the grounds that government intrusion into religious matters is undesirable and that children have all the protection they need for their right to pray. In the 1971 House of Representatives struggle over a prayer amendment, the anti-amendment forces were led by the one Catholic priest who served in Congress, Rep. Robert Drinan, who persuaded most Catholic members that the amendment was not a good idea.

Reagan's Amendment

In 1984, when Reagan's proposed amendment came before the Senate, Episcopal Bishop John Walker called government sponsored prayer "blasphemous." At a press conference on the proposal an Episcopal minister and a Church of Christ minister declared that their respective traditions regarding prayer, one favoring liturgical prayer and the other non-liturgical, vividly made the point that no government sponsored prayer could satisfy even all Christians.

Before the 1984 vote on the Reagan prayer amendment, fourteen religious leaders addressed a rally on the U.S. Capitol steps against the proposal. These leaders included representatives of the National Council of Churches, the National Council of Jewish Women, the United Methodist Church, the National Association of Catholic Laity, the Unitarian Universalist Association, the Seventh-day Adventist Church, the Presbyterian Church, the Friends Committee on National Legislation, and the Church of Christ.

The first speaker at the rally, Americans for Religious Liberty executive director Edd Doerr, declared that, "If the proposed amendment is approved, then prayer will no longer be the exclusive province of the individual conscience and the church and family, but a collective activity engaged in when and how the state decides. Those who are promoting school prayer amendments are showing not how much they think of religion, but how little they think of it . . . . They would tell our children that the state, a powerful plurality, or a transient majority knows best the time, place, and manner of their prayers. They would replace our magnificent religious diversity with a deadening spiritual conformity."

Moment of Silence

Alternative schemes have been tried to circumvent *Engel* and *Schempp*. The most common is the "moment of silence." Since *Engel* 27 states have passed statutes requiring or permitting a specified moment of silence, which may be used for prayer or meditation by public school students.

Federal courts in New Jersey, Tennessee, and New Mexico have found moment of silence laws unconstitutional, and the Supreme Court invalidated Alabama's law in 1985 in *Wallace v. Jaffree*. In that case the Court held that the non-secular and therefore unconstitutional purpose of the contested law was, in the words of the law's sponsor, "to return voluntary prayer to our public schools." In her concurring opinion, however, Justice Sandra Day O'Connor noted that a "pure" moment of silence law without a religious purpose would probably pass constitutional muster.

Prayer Laws Unnecessary

Laws mandating "voluntary" prayer in the public schools are unnecessary. Moreover, were the state to mandate such prayer, it would be no longer genuinely voluntary. Devotional exercises to cultivate and nurture the religious faith of young people do not belong in the schools, but in the home and the church.

American Lutheran Church, *The Great Quotations on Religious Freedom*, 1991.

Although the Supreme Court's school prayer rulings have been widely misunderstood, they clearly are correct applications of the First Amendment's establishment clause, which is made applicable to state and local governments and school boards by the Fourteenth Amendment. Moreover, they mark the only reasonable course for our schools to follow. Consider:

Our country and virtually all of our communities and school districts are religiously pluralistic. We are a nation of the most varied kinds of Christians and Jews, plus Humanists, Muslims, Buddhists, Hindus, Confucianists, Bahais, and many other groups. There is no way that any level of government could sponsor a school prayer satisfactory and inoffensive to all.

Undisturbed Rights

The prayer rulings have in no way disturbed the right of every student in every public school to engage in personal, voluntary prayer during the many opportunities for such activity during the school day. Each student can then pray according to his or her own inclination or the way taught in the home, church, or synagogue. The rulings protect the student and his or her family from government intrusion into their religious lives.

Many Christians find government sponsored prayers incompatible with the biblical injunction in Matthew 6:5-7: "And when thou prayest, thou shalt not be as the hypocrites are: for they love to pray standing in the synagogues and in the corners of the streets, that they may be seen of men. . . . But thou, when thou prayest, enter into thy closet, and when thou hast shut thy door, pray to thy Father which is in secret; and thy Father which seeth in secret shall reward thee openly. But when ye pray, use not vain repetitions, as the heathen do: for they think that they shall be heard for their much speaking."

Even "moments of silence" for prayer, meditation, or reflection may be objectionable, for they imply that government knows best when students should engage in silent prayer or meditation and prefers that students involve themselves in that activity at the same time. The legislatively mandated "moments" also seem to favor certain types of activity, such as prayer or meditation (which has religious connotations to many), over others, such as doing good deeds, fasting, making a pilgrimage, or attending a religious service.

Finally, government sponsorship of vocal or silent prayer suggests that families and religious bodies need help from the state in carrying out religious functions.

"Rights and privileges accorded to other clubs must be accorded to religious clubs without discrimination."

Student Religious Clubs Should Be Allowed in Public Schools

Robert K. Skolrood

Public school students must have the right to form religious clubs in their schools, Robert K. Skolrood argues in the following viewpoint. Skolrood maintains that such clubs are classified as speech and may not be censored by schools merely because they are religious. He believes this type of censorship is unconstitutional and is a violation of the U.S. Supreme Court decision upholding religious students' right to gather in public high schools. Skolrood is the executive director and general counsel of the National Legal Foundation, a civil rights law organization in Virginia Beach, Virginia.

As you read, consider the following questions:

1. According to Skolrood, why should students with unpopular views be permitted to form school groups?
2. Why does the author believe that religious clubs should have the same rights and privileges as other student clubs?
3. What is the distinction between curriculum-related and noncurriculum-related student groups, according to Skolrood?

Reprinted, with permission, from the National Legal Foundation pamphlet *Bible Clubs and Student Religious Meetings in Public Schools* by Robert K. Skolrood. Specially adapted by the author for inclusion in *Education: Opposing Viewpoints.*

On June 4, 1990, the U.S. Supreme Court upheld the right of public high school students to form voluntary, after-school Bible Clubs. The landmark decision was the first time in recent memory that the Supreme Court approved any form of religious expression in or near our public schools. *Time* called the case a "spectacular win" for conservatives. *People Magazine* said the students' "desire for a Bible Club redrew the line between church and state." It is no exaggeration to label *Mergens v. Westside* the most significant victory for religious liberty in 25 years.

The Supreme Court's 8-to-1 ruling sent a clear message to liberal legal activists: Public schools must respect the religious liberties of their students, including the freedom to express and act upon the convictions of their faith. Schools may not censor students' religious speech and conduct. As Justice Anthony Kennedy put it, "membership in a religious club is one of many permissible ways for a student to further his or her own personal enrichment."

Equal Access Act

Congress passed the Equal Access Act primarily to protect religious speech and association in public high schools. Wittingly or unwittingly some public school administrators had prohibited religious groups from meeting on the public high school campus. The Act was an attempt to eliminate widespread religious discrimination. Despite the Act's passage by overwhelming majorities, there were administrators and judges who continued to prohibit meetings of Bible Clubs and other religious groups.

In 1990, the United States Supreme Court rendered its decision in *Westside Board of Education v. Mergens*. The ruling accomplished two tasks. First, the decision squarely upheld the constitutionality of the Equal Access Act. Second, the court's opinion clarified some of the key language in the Act.

At the heart of the Supreme Court's decision in *Mergens* is the fact that students themselves simply cannot violate the Constitution's prohibition against the "establishment of religion." The Establishment Clause only applies to school authorities or other government agents. As Justice Sandra Day O'Connor wrote in the majority opinion:

> There is a crucial difference between government speech endorsing religion, which the Establishment Clause forbids, the private speech endorsing religion, which the Free Speech and Free Exercise Clauses protect.

Schools may not censor student speech simply because it is religious. Students have a constitutionally-protected right to freely talk about their faith at school. The United States Supreme Court has held that students who engage in worship, prayer,

217

and religious discussion are exercising their private right to forms of speech protected by the First Amendment.

Granting Equal Access

For the Equal Access Act to apply to a particular school, three conditions must be met:

1. The school must be a public secondary school as defined by state law.
2. The school must receive federal financial assistance. (As is true of most public schools.)
3. The school must have a "limited open forum" as defined by the Act.

If these three criteria are met, the Equal Access Act applies to that school. The school is then prohibited from denying equal access to student religious groups based on the content of their speech.

Chuck Asay, by permission of the *Colorado Springs Gazette-Telegraph*.

A high school has created a "limited open forum" when at least one *noncurriculum related student group* is allowed the opportunity to meet on school premises during noninstructional time. The term *limited* refers to students at that particular school rather than outsiders. Another way of phrasing it would be a forum that is open and available to students at the public high school but not to outsiders.

According to the Supreme Court, school clubs are curriculum related if:

1. Subject matter of the group is or soon will be taught in a regularly offered course. [Example: French class relates to French club.]
2. Subject matter of the group concerns the body of courses as a whole. [Example: student government formulates proposals affecting the whole school.]
3. Participation with the group is required for a particular course. [Example: Band class requires participation in Band club.]
4. Participation in the group results in academic credit.

If the club does not meet one of these four criteria, it is a noncurriculum related student group and triggers the application of the Equal Access Act to the school. The actual practice, NOT STATED POLICY, of the school controls the evaluation of the four criteria.

Noncurriculum Groups

Examples of noncurriculum related student groups would include a *Chess Club* where there is no Chess class. The fact that the Chess Club supplements math and science courses does not make it a curriculum related club. Participation in community service clubs such as *Interact* or *Zonta* may promote effective citizenship, but do not qualify as curriculum related to social studies. The court specifically rejected the notion that "curriculum related" means anything remotely related to abstract educational goals. The school administration must not strategically describe existing student groups so as to evade the Act and its purpose.

All such clubs are entitled to official recognition by the school administration. Official recognition entitles all clubs "equal access" to the school's limited open forum. This includes:

1. Access to the school newspaper [and obviously to the school yearbook if other clubs are entitled to access].
2. Announcements on the school bulletin boards.
3. Announcements on the school public address system.
4. Participation in the annual club fair.

The Equal Access Act does not create new, preferred or extra privileges for student religious groups. The Act only ensures that rights and privileges accorded to other clubs must be accorded to religious clubs without discrimination. If clubs are allowed to have outside speakers, for example, then religious clubs must be allowed the same right.

School Authority

A school can place uniform time, place and manner conditions on student groups so long as they are neutral and applied equally to all groups. A school may assign a particular room for a meeting or may specify that all clubs meet on a particular day of the week. Such conditions must be reasonable and not designed to harass or disfavor religious clubs. A school could not, for instance, assign all religious club meetings to the janitor's closet while other groups were allowed to meet in empty classrooms. Time, place and manner restrictions are appropriate when they maintain order and ensure the safety of students and school personnel. They are invalid, however, when designed to suppress the rights of students. Equal access means equal treatment.

While the Equal Access Act was passed primarily to remedy discrimination against student religious groups, the Act also provides equal access to political, philosophical or other student speech when the Act applies to a school. Some people have feared that the Act might allow Neo-Nazi or Communist student groups to form on campus.

The Equal Access Act does not limit the school's authority to:
1. Maintain order and discipline on school premises.
2. Protect the well-being of students and faculty.
3. Assure that attendance of students at meetings is voluntary.
4. Prohibit meetings or actions that are illegal.
5. Prohibit any student meeting which "materially and substantially interferes with the orderly conduct of educational activities within the school."

However, any such disruption must be the product of the student group within the school itself and not other persons who wish to shut down the meeting by causing their own disturbance—the so-called "hecklers veto." Undifferentiated fear or apprehension of disturbance should not permit the administration to refuse to allow the club to meet.

Rights of Religious Students

In school we were taught that our Constitution prohibits the denial of rights and opportunities on the basis of religious belief. Yet the school banned our club simply because it was religious in nature. The Supreme Court sent a strong message to public schools: Religious students are not second class citizens. Kids don't give up their Constitutional rights at the schoolhouse gate.

Bridget Mergens Mayhew, *The National Legal Foundation Minuteman*, Summer 1990.

The school does not have to allow groups which are unlawful or which materially and substantially interfere with the orderly conduct of educational activities. Student groups cannot be denied access because their views may be unpopular or repugnant. Schools may, however, uniformly prohibit nonschool persons from being involved in student clubs and may prevent disruptive behavior consistent with the Equal Access Act. A school would not have to sanction or permit any unlawful activities associated with such meetings.

The First Amendment

As we have seen, the Equal Access Act provides for nondiscriminatory treatment of student religious groups when three criteria are met:

1. The school is a public secondary school,
2. Federal financial assistance is received, and
3. One or more noncurriculum related clubs are presented with an opportunity to meet.

Even if one of these elements is missing, either by design or inadvertence on the part of the school, it does not mean that religious groups may be banned. The First Amendment of the U.S. Constitution provides an independent basis for student groups to meet that may be broader than the Equal Access Act. While the Supreme Court did not have to address this issue in *Mergens* because the Equal Access applied, application of the First Amendment equal access principle to public secondary schools would be consistent with the Supreme Court's ruling in *Widmar v. Vincent,* 454 U.S. 263 (1981).

In *Widmar,* the High Court required religious groups to be granted equal opportunity to meet on the campuses of public colleges and universities. The decision was based entirely upon the equal access principle of the First Amendment.

The Equal Access Act was passed to extend the same opportunity to high school student groups. Congress and the courts have rejected the argument that high school students are more impressionable than college students and would therefore interpret an equal access policy as government endorsement of religion. As Justice O'Connor wrote in *Mergens,*

> We think that the logic of Widmar applies with equal force to the Equal Access Act. We think that secondary school students are mature enough and are likely to understand that a school does not endorse or support student speech that it merely permits on a nondiscriminatory basis.

In addition to *Widmar,* the First Amendment's guarantee of freedom of speech for high school students was underscored in *Tinker v. Des Moines* 393 U.S. 503 (1969). The court stated emphatically that students do not shed their constitutional rights at the schoolhouse gate.

Therefore, public high schools should establish equal access policies even if there is uncertainty over the applicability of the

Equal Access Act. Such policies would be the surest means of complying with both Federal Law and court precedent.

School officials may not hide behind high-sounding legal arguments to discriminate against the faith of students. Religious persons in the public schools may not be treated as "second-class citizens." As Justice O'Connor wrote in *Mergens*, quoting from *McDaniel v. Paty*:

> . . . (I)f a State refused to let religious groups use facilities open to others, then it would demonstrate not neutrality but hostility toward religion. "The Establishment Clause does not license government to treat religion and those who teach or practice it . . . as subversive of American ideals and therefore subject to unique disabilities."

As Congress and the Supreme Court have made clear, public schools may not discriminate against the religious faith of students. The equal access principle is consistent with the religious liberty clauses of our Constitution both as presently interpreted and as intended by our Founding Fathers. Equal access is the law. Any other practice would be the worst form of governmental bias and censorship.

"It is obviously a violation . . . for Congress to force secondary schools to . . . allow religious clubs onto their campuses. "

Student Religious Clubs Should Be Banned from Public Schools

Jon G. Murray

In 1984 Congress passed the Equal Access Act, a law which bars public high schools from discriminating against student groups because of their religious, political, or philosophical views. In the following viewpoint, Jon G. Murray disagrees with this law and argues that religion is a private affair that should not be permitted in a public school environment under any condition. Murray believes that high school students are very impressionable, and easily convinced by religious groups to start religious clubs on campus. The purpose of schools is education, he contends, not to expose students to religious propaganda. Murray is president of American Atheists, an Austin, Texas organization that advocates the separation of church and state.

As you read, consider the following questions:

1. According to Murray, why is it unconstitutional for public schools to grant official recognition to student religious clubs?
2. Why does the author believe that religion has no academic value?
3. In Murray's opinion, why are religious groups eager to influence the minds of children?

Jon G. Murray, "An Open Forum for Evangelizing," *American Atheist,* July 1990. Reprinted with permission from the *American Atheist.*

Bridget C. Mergens was a student at Westside High School in Omaha, Nebraska, in September 1984 when she and friends went to the principal of that institution to seek permission to form a "Christian club," which they desired to call the "Christian Bible Study Club," for the purposes of Bible reading, discussion, prayer, and fellowship. The policy of Westside High had been to permit students to join various clubs, which met after school on school premises. There were about thirty such clubs in 1984, from which students could choose on a voluntary basis. School board (city/county level) policy provided that each group must have a faculty sponsor and that it may not be sponsored by any political or religious organization. Westside High itself had no written policy on the formation of student clubs, but merely a tradition that any student or group of students wishing to start a club would present the idea for their club to a school official (principal, vice principal), who would then determine whether the club's goals were consistent, in an overall way, with school board policies and the school district's general written goals for secondary education. Ms. Mergens' request was denied by the principal because she did not have a faculty sponsor and because of school fears that allowing a religious club at the school would violate the Establishment Clause. The denial was appealed to the board of education, which backed up the principal. Mergens and her parents then filed suit in the federal district court alleging that the refusal had violated the Equal Access Act, which had been signed into law 11 August 1984, as well as their First (freedom of speech, free exercise of religion) and Fourteenth Amendment (due process, freedom of association) rights. Westside High alleged that the Equal Access Act did not apply to it, because its extracurricular club program did not constitute a "limited open forum," and if the act did, it was unconstitutional because it violated the Establishment Clause. . . .

Clear Violation

It is obviously a violation of the Establishment Clause for Congress to force secondary schools to not alone allow religious clubs onto their campuses but to grant them "official recognition." The violation of the Establishment Clause principle, as applied to the special situation of public schools, has not been properly addressed by this [U.S. Supreme] Court.

If one applies the *Lemon v. Kurtzman* test to the Equal Access Act, it cannot pass muster. What is the "secular legislative purpose" of the act? The Court has clearly admitted in its own analysis of the act's legislative purpose that it was initiated by Congress "to address perceived widespread discrimination against religious speech in public schools" and "in response to two federal appellate court decisions holding that student religious groups could not, consistent with the Establishment Clause, meet on school premises during noninstructional time." That is to say that Congress specifically drafted the act with the end in mind of getting more "religious speech" into public schools and to overturn legitimate appellate court law which had come to the conclusion, more than once, that allowing student religious groups on campuses *did* violate the Establishment Clause. I contend that an act of Congress that is drafted with the intent of injecting public secondary schools with religious speech and circumventing precedent Establishment Clause, on point, case law cannot have a "secular" purpose.

Treat Them Differently

Religious groups are not just like any other groups in the public school setting. The message of the Establishment Clause is that religious activities must be treated differently from other activities to ensure against governmental support for religion. The state's compulsory school attendance laws are responsible for the presence of students in school buildings and should not provide an opportunity for government-approved religious activity. Such activity can easily occur in schools where there is official encouragement of religious proselytizing, which can become coercive.

American Civil Liberties Union, *ACLU Briefing Paper*, 1989.

Does the Equal Access Act have a "principal or primary effect" that "neither advances nor inhibits religion"? I contend that its only effect is to advance religion in that the majority of the Congresspersons involved in drafting it labored under the conviction that religion was being discriminated against in public school fora, so they set out with the express purpose of writing a bill to force public schools to take on religious clubs. That is a primary effect that *advances* religion. To pass a law requiring school authorities to allow religious meetings and advertisements on their premises is hardly inhibiting religion. The fact that Congress threw into the act some verbiage about "political" or "philosophical" speech was a C.Y.A. [Cover Your Ass] of more concern to the lawyers who advised them than to the members themselves.

A Private Affair

Does the Equal Access Act foster "an excessive government entanglement with religion"? How can it not? Government, in the form of public, taxpayer-supported schools, must engage in monitoring various aspects of the speech content and activities of any religious student club applying for access under the act. Just a determination of "curriculum-relatedness" would require the entanglement of interrogating the religious club to determine if what they planned to do was related to any current course offerings, not to mention the continued monitoring to see its speech remained the same. We have, in addition, two justices (Thurgood Marshall and William Brennan) who have now urged the schools into the further entanglement of issuing of disclaimers.

Even Justice John Paul Stevens, in his dissent, goes not to the constitutional issues, but into a tussle of how to define "curriculum-relatedness." The entire Court has seen the forest instead of the trees on this one.

Religion, is religion, is religion. It matters not if it is clothed in another name (meditation, moment of silence), is done off campus (released time), is "related" to some other study, or is cloaked as "freedom of speech" or "student initiated." Religion is a private affair and does not belong in public school fora under any guise. It is a subjectively held, nonintellectual opinion and is not "academic" in any sense of the word, so it does not belong in an academic setting unless it truly wishes to encourage its own end. I can think of nothing more detrimental and self-defeating for religion than to voluntarily hand its dogma over to true, academic, classroom scrutiny.

Religious Propaganda

We are back to the same premise of the church, which is "give me a child until he is six and I've got him." There are only two avenues for the church to get to children. One is through the parents and the other is through the state institutions in which they are held captive for the greater part of each year. In a sociological climate where fewer adults are going to church and do not take the time to haul their children to places for religious instruction, the church is manic to get its propaganda into the public school. Organized religion has failed to get formal religious ceremonies into public schools, floundered on "released time" concepts, and can only pass out religious materials off school grounds in most areas. It is but strategically wise, on the part of the organized church, to try a new tactic in which the most zealous young proponents of religion are encouraged to establish these "Bible clubs" in schools across the nation. In these times of apathy and of students' being interested more in computer games, mutant animal friends, and drugs than in education, it stands to reason that only the most hysterically committed youngster for Christ would be at the forefront of those approaching school authorities for campus meeting space. This reality is reflected in the fact situations of most of the district and circuit court cases which led to the *Mergens* decision. These young evangelists, within the peer group forum of their schools, are certain to proselytize. The hallways, the lunchroom, the exercise field, and the classrooms when teacher is looking the other way, will be fertile fields to be harvested by this new cadres of evangelical youth. If that is what they choose to do, or are led to do, with their "extracurricular" time, then so be it, but why should the schools be forced to officially sanction this behavior that has nothing whatsoever to do with the advancement of the academic purpose that I for one was under the impression was still the reason behind compulsory education?

Religious Clubs Pose Problems

It is disingenuous to protest that barring bible clubs denies the students' right to "free speech." Students will continue to be free, as they always have been, to pray voluntarily in school, to read the bible during free time, to wear crosses, and to speak to others about their faith—as long as these actions are individual, unorganized, and nondisruptive. The problem arises when religious meetings become regular and organized. Not only does this give the appearance of school endorsement, but creates the danger of church backing.

Annie Laurie Gaylor, *Freethought Today*, March 1990.

Let me also say a word here about "student initiated" Bible clubs. It may, in fact, be the case that a student here or there comes up with the idea of forming a Bible or prayer club on his own, but I think it far more likely that such an idea is the implant of a religiously saturated upbringing, parental nudging, pastor, priest, or rabbi pressure, or a hearty church camp fireside chat. In short, I question the motivation of any student who steps into a principal's office and asks to form a religiously oriented club, as being an idea solely generated between his own two ears.

The Purpose of Schools

With a church on literally every corner in this country, there is ample opportunity for youth to make "a joyful noise unto the Lord." They need not be given a passkey to the public school system to try to make others listen.

Public schools are for education, a commodity this nation lacks more each day. They should not be thought of as a grove of minds ready for the plucking, as the oft pictured apple on teacher's desk, by whichever advocacy group can cry the loudest to Congress. The purpose of public schools, at least when I attended them, was to impart to the students the basic fundamentals of fact and problem-solving technique which they would use for the rest of their lives in pursuit of whatever career they chose. An open marketplace of ideas, inside of our schools, is one thing, but turning schools into a corral for advocacy group recruitment is another. It is a hard enough job for our schools to teach children how to think, and think for themselves, without that process being interrupted by a multifaceted sea of distractions from sports to spirituality. Every time I read the remarks of an educator, I see the repeated cry of "back to basics." How can instructors get students to concentrate on those basics when they are bombarded with sometimes more activities surrounding their classes than within them? Now Congress and the courts have seen fit to expand that pool of distraction with the addition of yet another, and highly controversial, element. . . .

Offensive Message

The final point here is that religion never gives up. Those with a religious message will do whatever it takes to get that message across. If it means disrupting the entire public education system, religionists don't care. It is the message that the religionists bear that is the problem, more than the lengths to which they go in shoving it down the nation's throat. Yet it is that message that is never examined or questioned, only the technique of its transportation to its ultimate victim, the human mind, young or old. That is what the Supreme Court has done here in the case at hand. Religion is psychologically harmful and deserves to be kept out of our schools, but the only thing on which the courts can concentrate is to make certain that whatever mechanism used to import that mental illness into the school system is "constitutional." Would it be all right to introduce smoking or drug clubs into the schools as long as that introduction was done under a fair and impartial plan? I think not.

I think it is time that we began examining the real issue about religion: its suitability for our culture—for those of any age. That is the question that the courts and the legislature will not face. Of what good is the maintenance of an "open forum" in schools, to give religious nuts a fair chance to roam the halls encouraging departure from reality, when those same institutions are turning out students who cannot read or comprehend the very Constitution under which that forum has been approved, find their hometown on a map, or address an envelope correctly?

Distinguishing Bias from Reason

When dealing with controversial subjects, many people allow their emotions to dominate their powers of reason. Thus, one of the most important critical thinking skills is the ability to distinguish between statements based upon emotion or bias and those based upon a rational consideration of the facts. For example, consider the following statement: "Religious clubs should be allowed in public schools because they instill moral values in students and help them lead decent, productive lives." This statement is biased. The author is basing this opinion on an emotional, unsubstantiated belief that religious clubs improve students' lives. In contrast, the statement, "Students have the right to participate in religious clubs just as other students participate in athletics or social clubs" is a reasonable statement. The law states that if a public secondary school permits noncurriculum-related student groups to meet, it must treat all such groups equally.

Another element the reader should take into account is whether an author has a personal or professional stake in advancing a particular opinion. For example, an attorney may defend a public school student's right to start a religious club. If the attorney's religious beliefs are identical to the student's, the reader should ask whether this religious interest influences the attorney's statements. Note also that it is possible to have a strong interest in a subject and still present an objective case. For example, this same attorney may be in a good position to discuss students' constitutional rights.

The following statements are adapted from opinions expressed in the viewpoints in this chapter. Consider each statement carefully. *Mark R for any statement you believe is based on reason or a rational consideration of the facts. Mark B for any statement you believe is based on bias, prejudice, or emotion. Mark I for any statement you think is impossible to judge.*

> R = *a statement based upon reason*
> B = *a statement based upon bias*
> I = *a statement impossible to judge*

229

If you are doing this activity as a member of a class or group, compare your answers with those of others. Be able to defend your answers. You may discover that others come to different conclusions than you do. Listening to the rationale others present for their answers may give you valuable insights into distinguishing between bias and reason.

1. After-school religious clubs are attempts by religious zealots to brainwash young students' fertile minds.

2. Unlike mathematics or chemistry, religion is based on belief, not fact. It is a non-academic subject that has no place in public schools.

3. Public schools must respect the religious freedom of all students to act upon their religious convictions.

4. Those who promote school prayer show how little respect they have for atheists or agnostics.

5. Banning school prayer and students' right to acknowledge their Creator is the sole cause of the moral decay in our schools.

6. School prayer is one possible way for any student to express his or her religious faith.

7. A curriculum that teaches about religion is really just a smokescreen. Its real purpose is to promote Christianity over other religions.

8. "Organizing religious clubs in public schools is a right that the U.S. Constitution protects."—Robert Skolrood, executive director of the National Legal Foundation.

9. The U.S. was built on Christian values. If religion is taught in public schools, that religion should only be Christianity.

10. "Americans have historically supported the separation of church and state."—Robert L. Maddox, executive director of Americans United for the Separation of Church and State.

11. Schools that ban religious clubs blatantly discriminate against religious students.

12. Allowing students to pray silently ensures that no one religion is favored over another. Silent prayer is a measure that respects the religious beliefs of all students.

13. The increase in religious diversity taking place in the U.S. will expand students' understanding of different world religions.

14. "Permitting some students to form religious clubs will encourage others to start Satanist or white supremacy clubs."—Jon Murray, director of American Atheists.

Periodical Bibliography

The following articles have been selected to supplement the diverse views presented in this chapter.

John Alexander	"School Prayer or School Breakfasts?" *The Other Side*, September/October 1991. Available from The Other Side, 300 W. Apsley St., Philadelphia, PA 19144.
James M. Banner Jr.	"Teaching About Religion," *The Education Digest*, December 1990.
Edd Doerr	"Teaching Religious Liberty—The Wrong Way," *The Humanist*, November/December 1989.
Annie Laurie Gaylor	"The Case Against Bible Clubs in Schools," *Freethought Today*, March 1990. Available from the Freedom from Religion Foundation, PO Box 750, Madison, WI 53701.
Thomas W. Goodhue	"Introducing Religion into the Classroom," *The Christian Century*, April 17, 1991.
Nat Hentoff	"Even in High School," *The Progressive*, August 1989.
Norman Lear	"Educating for the Human Spirit," *The Education Digest*, March 1991.
Joe Maxwell	"The Textbook Reformation," *Christianity Today*, September 16, 1991.
Jon G. Murray	"Equal Access," *American Atheist*, February 1990. Available from American Atheists, PO Box 140195, Austin, TX 78714-0195.
Sonia L. Nazario	"Religion Is Returning to Public Schools," *The Wall Street Journal*, May 1, 1991.
Charles E. Rice	"Equal Access for All Americans," *The New American*, November 5, 1990. Available from The Review of the News Inc., 770 Westhill Blvd., Appleton, WI 54915.
Alain L. Sanders	"Let Us Pray," *Time*, June 18, 1990.
Timothy L. Smith	"Why Johnny Doesn't Know About Mennonites," *Christianity Today*, February 5, 1990.
Lauren Tarshis	"From High School to the High Court," *Scholastic Update* (teachers' edition), January 26, 1990.
Kenneth L. Woodward	"The Return of the Fourth R," *Newsweek*, June 10, 1991.
Perry A. Zirkel	"Opening the Door to After-School Prayer," *Phi Delta Kappan*, September 1990.

What Is the State of Higher Education?

EDUCATION in America

Chapter Preface

Historically, many Americans, particularly minorities, could not attend colleges and universities. Most minorities seeking a college education either could not afford the tuition or were denied enrollment because of their race. As a remedy, in 1972 the U.S. enacted affirmative action laws. These laws stipulated that universities had to increase their percentage of minority students. As a result of these laws, the number of minority students attending college rose. While minorities comprised only 8.8 percent of all college students in 1970, by 1989 their numbers almost doubled to 15.3 percent.

Advocates of affirmative action argue that the program is absolutely necessary to remove unfair racial barriers against minorities. They contend that without affirmative action progress would not have occurred and minorities would continue to be denied the benefits of a college education.

Despite these well-intentioned goals, affirmative action remains highly controversial. While almost all Americans welcome the increase in racial diversity that has resulted from affirmative action, many argue that the program reduces the quality of higher education. To meet affirmative action goals, they contend, colleges lower their academic standards to admit minorities with low entrance scores, while rejecting qualified whites with higher grades. These detractors argue that affirmative action must be eliminated if the goals of higher student performance and standards are to be reached.

One goal of affirmative action—an increase of minority groups in colleges and universities—has been met. But this goal has not been achieved without intense scrutiny of the merits of the programs. As affirmative action continues to be debated in the courts and colleges across the nation, whether the program is fair is sure to remain an important issue.

"Tenure [is] the principal guarantor of
academic freedom, *ensuring the right to teach
what one believes"*

The Tenure System Should Be Preserved

Henry Rosovsky

A professor who achieves tenure is secure in the knowledge that
his or her position is permanent until retirement. In the following viewpoint, Henry Rosovsky argues that the purpose of
tenure is still valid. It guarantees professors' academic freedom
by allowing them to teach unpopular views or advocate unpopular causes without fear of retribution by university officials.
Rosovsky believes the tenure system must be retained to protect
professors and to maintain the quality of higher education.
Rosovsky, a specialist in Far Eastern economies, is an economics
professor at Harvard University in Cambridge, Massachusetts.

As you read, consider the following questions:

1. Why is academic freedom important, according to Rosovsky?
2. Why does the author believe that universities are cautious
   about granting tenure?
3. According to Rosovsky, why is it important for universities to
   maintain the highest quality faculty possible?

Reprinted from *The University: An Owner's Manual,* by Henry Rosovsky, with the permission
of W.W. Norton & Company, Inc. Copyright © 1990 by Henry Rosovsky.

I learned long ago that the overwhelming majority of non-academics view tenure with deep suspicion. *The Economist* described tenure as a promise to professors that "they can think (or idle) in ill-paid peace, accountable to nobody." Somehow we, in academia, are getting away with something; that is the general feeling. Lifetime tenure induces laziness, stifles incentives, and directly contributes to lack of performance on the job. It is a prescription for going to seed. There is a belief as well, that the custom is immoral—even un-American! To these dim views might be added the widely held undergraduate opinion that their favorite teachers are systematically denied tenure, as well as the conviction of some non-tenured younger faculty members that they are smarter and more qualified than the old bastards who deny them promotion. That is the bill of particulars. . . .

The Case for Tenure

Let me now try to state the affirmative case for tenure as one of the necessary virtues of academic life. The first habitual line of defense is *tenure as the principal guarantor of academic freedom*, ensuring the right to teach what one believes, to espouse unpopular academic and non-academic causes, to act upon knowledge and ideas as one perceives them without fear of retribution from anyone. Few professors will treat the need for this type of protection lightly since our country has a long history of professorial persecution for naked political reasons. In my own lifetime I have seen the ravages of McCarthyism and other kinds of witch-hunts.

As a group, university teachers are probably less conventional—less conformist—than the average population, thereby attracting suspicion as corrupters of youth. Conservatives seem especially fond of this view. Professors also tend to be verbal and visible and are trained in the advocacy of ideas. Passions easily reach a boiling point in universities and can attract a great deal of attention. Protection may be as much needed from inside as from outside assault.

Administrations, with or without external pressure, have been known to attempt to enforce their own versions of orthodoxy. I must admit that if I had been a university president during the turmoil of the late 1960s, the temptation to fire certain faculty members would have been almost irresistible. I am thinking not of unpopular ideas or speech, but of sit-ins, violent disruptions, and other forms of uncivilized behavior, especially on the part of those who should have been examples to students. Looking back, I am glad that tenure, and more importantly, the tradition of academic freedom provided a defense against those with my hot temper and base impulses.

Nothing can diminish the need for academic freedom; its absence has reduced universities to caricatures in many parts of the contemporary world. The difficulty lies in making a tight connection between academic freedom and tenure. Do not young non-tenured teachers need protection just as much or even more? It is sometimes suggested that a corps of senior (tenured) unafraid colleagues serves as guarantors of liberty for all. This is not convincing. To be at all effective, this mythical corps would have to be united precisely when freedom is threatened and controversy abounds, and that is a pipe dream. We need not theorize. During the early 1950s a number of Harvard instructors and assistant professors became victims of McCarthy-style political pressures. Some term appointments were prematurely rescinded; a few left "voluntarily" rather than facing investigation of their political opinions or affiliations. The same was true everywhere else, and I do not recall that their elders organized an effective defense anywhere. Of course, liberty for some is better than liberty for none: one has to recognize that tenure helps the maintenance of academic freedom.

Academic Freedom

Tenure is a means to certain ends; specifically: (1) Freedom of teaching and research and of extramural activities and (2) a sufficient degree of economic security to make the profession attractive to men and women of ability. Freedom and economic security, hence, tenure, are indispensable to the success of an institution in fulfilling its obligations to its students and to society.

1940 Statement of Principles on Academic Freedom and Tenure, *Academe*, May/June 1990.

And yet the United States is a considerably more tolerant country now than, say, twenty-five years ago. We are less provincial and more indulgent; some would say more (or too) permissive. The fact is that the range of socially accepted behavior and thought is exceedingly wide. Our courts are also more activist in defending individual rights. For all these reasons, academic freedom may not be especially threatened at this time, although a retrograde movement is always possible. It does not seem to me very likely in the near future, but who am I to make a forecast?

Internal Discipline

Another line of support for (working) life-time contracts is a group of reasons that I will call *tenure as a source of internal discipline.* Granting tenure is costly for institutions, departments, and colleagues. Once awarded, a university obliges itself to pay a relatively high salary for a long period of time—on average, I would think for at least twenty-five years. Academic departments grant membership for the same length of time, and they have to be concerned about the costliness of mistakes. Once in possession of tenure, stripping someone of a professorship becomes virtually impossible. And who wants a mistake for a colleague for twenty-five years! Of course, generations of students are also concerned: departmental errors of judgment have a direct effect on the quality of their education. An important and salutory consequence of high cost in many different senses is that the existence of tenure encourages departments and those who review their actions to make tough decisions that would otherwise be all too easily avoided. Thus tenure is a major factor in maintaining and raising standards; electing life-time colleagues becomes a matter of utmost seriousness.

But why go down this road in the first place? Because without long-term obligations, our sense of internal discipline would be much weaker. The temptation to extend an individual's employment many times for "one more year"—just to avoid inevitable unpleasantness—could become irresistible. It cannot be an accident that professions in which collegiality is important use systems that approximate academic tenure very closely. Law firms are the best example: partnerships resemble professorships, and the discipline of selection is improved by the implied length of commitment. Both law firms and universities avoid periodic and perpetual reviews of partners or tenured professors. These would be time-consuming, divisive, and destructive of the collegial ideal. Once is enough: at the time when partners are chosen or when tenure is offered. But that "once" has to be subject to extraordinarily rigorous standards.

Affirming Tenure

There are other traditional arguments in favor of tenure. The practice is said to contribute to institutional stability; those with the security of tenure are expected to judge others more fairly or professionally and not on the basis of personal competitive advantage; an "up or out" system—a corollary of tenure—prevents the long-term exploitation of teacher-scholars in junior ranks. All of these points are valid to some degree, though they seem equally reasonable in other forms of employment, ranging from the Japanese factory to an American hospital. For me, the essence of academic tenure lies in the consideration of one more reason.

I have in mind *tenure as social contract:* an appropriate and essential form of social contract in universities. It is appropriate because the advantages outweigh the disadvantages. It is essential because the absence of tenure would, in the long run, lower the quality of a faculty. And faculty quality is the keystone of

237

university life. The best faculty will attract the ablest students, produce the finest alumni, generate the most research support, and so on. Unlike most other sectors of the economy, the possibilities of technological (and organizational) progress are more limited in higher education. Substituting capital for labor does not appear especially promising, and nearly everything hinges on the quality of people.

Financial Rewards

Our professional lives, as I have already attempted to show, can be described as a "good deal." There are comparatively few unpleasant routines; for many of us, work approaches pleasure in pleasant settings. There is, however, another aspect that has to be considered. Our jobs—as senior professors at major universities—require high intelligence, special talents, and initiative. These attributes are in general demand: business, law, medicine, and other professions are looking for people with similar characteristics. And some of these careers promise, at considerable risk, far greater financial rewards. At the point of career selection all of us faced a variety of choices, and nearly all were potentially more lucrative than teaching. The current (1988-89) average annual salary of a full professor in Arts and Sciences at Harvard University is about $70,000. That is one of the highest averages in U.S. universities. Average age of tenured faculty is about fifty-five and the average professor is a recognized world authority in some subject or other. Assistant professors, all with Ph.D. degrees, start at about $32,000. Lawyers, fresh out of school, will be hired by New York firms with annual compensation of about $70,000. What Teddy Roosevelt said in 1905 is still valid:

> . . . I appreciate to the full the fact that the highest work of all will never be affected one way or the other by any question of compensation. . . . But it is also true that the effect upon ambitious minds can not but be bad if as a people we show our very slight regard for scholarly achievement by making no provision at all for its reward.

Choosing higher education still involves a trade-off. The cost is economic, and that burden is shared by the family. Benefits are not in the narrow sense material, and one of the most essential is tenure. In my view, tenure carries the implication of joining an extended family; that is the social contract. Each side can seek a divorce: the university only in the most extraordinary circumstances and the professor as easily as a male under Islamic law. It is not an uneven bargain because the university needs its share of talented people, and professors trade life-long security and familial relations for lesser economic rewards.

That was how I interpreted tenure as dean, and I had many occasions to put this social contract interpretation into practice.

My door was open at all times to colleagues, and I tried to place at their disposal Harvard's resources in personal as well as professional matters. Problems of alcoholism, divorce, long-term illness all came to my attention and were, I hope, approached in a family spirit. In Arts and Sciences we had no detailed sick-leave policy for professors; it was dealt with informally and with great generosity. One of my teachers had a stroke and was incapacitated for about six years. The faculty simply kept him on the payroll. Perhaps poor business practice—but excellent family practice.

Basis for Quality

In our leading universities, the granting of tenure is taken with utmost seriousness. It is not merely a question of time. Tenure is awarded only after a long period of probationary service (usually eight years), and extensive inside and outside peer review; it is a highly competitive selection process. At Harvard we ask a traditional question: who is the most qualified person in the world to fill a particular vacancy, and then we try to convince that scholar to join our ranks. We may reach the wrong conclusion, and we may not succeed in attracting our first or even second choice, but our goal is elevated.

Henry Rosovsky: *The University: An Owner's Manual*, 1990.

I do not wish to leave the impression that membership in the tenured faculty family is only another, slightly more generous form of health insurance. It is a much broader vision; in reality, a state of mind. For example, when special opportunities arose, rules were cheerfully broken or reinterpreted in favor of the individual. A tempting invitation from abroad might mean the need for travel funds or extra leave time; a new research idea could call for seed money; one was always able to approach faculty resources through the dean. Not everyone got what they wanted, but the dean would try to help, while loudly proclaiming that his actions in no ways constituted a precedent.

Am I, with excessive sentimentality, urging an inordinately paternalistic interpretation? Not if one thinks of professors as shareholders without bosses, and not as employees. The dean is *primus inter pares*, a colleague temporarily running the show before being replaced by another peer. His actions are not favors granted from above. Instead, they are investments in the general welfare, and therefore in the high quality of the family enterprise: in those with permanent membership who form one set of owners.

There is one other aspect of tenure that should be mentioned

239

when we emphasize "extended family" and "ownership." Having the assurance of a position until retirement obviously removes one of the main fears faced by many workers in our society. Far more significant, the tenure system seen as a social contract also means that aging does not bring overt loss of respect. The rights of the individuals are secure and do not change until retirement. Even after retirement, most universities continue to extend valuable privileges to *emeriti*: scientists retain (reduced) laboratory space, others are given offices, and the use of all common facilities—libraries, clubs, etc.—continues. These are expensive habits—some would label them bad management—and one has to admit that there are abuses. Nevertheless, the possibility of aging with dignity is enormously attractive and exceedingly rare in our country, and relatively insignificant abuses are a small cost. . . .

The notion that tenure fosters deadwood is false—especially at top rank universities. The combination of tenure and low quality is dangerous and admittedly may perpetuate mediocrity or worse. That is not an issue for the type of schools discussed here.

It is true that a large tenured faculty presents peculiar problems of management, especially if threats, fear, or direct orders are a preferred managerial tool. Instead, the emphasis has to be on consensus and persuasion—on a democratic and participatory style.

"Bad as the tenure system has been, there are indications that it is getting worse."

The Tenure System Needs to Be Eliminated

Page Smith

Tenure, or permanent teaching status, is often granted to professors who publish a sufficient number of research articles or books. In the following viewpoint, Page Smith argues that the tenure system causes professors to focus on publication rather than teaching. Smith states that this focus is the primary reason why many faculty members oppose tenure. He asserts that most professors prefer teaching to research and advocates that teacher effectiveness, not publication, should be the criterion for promotion. Smith is a former provost of the University of California at Santa Cruz and the author of *Killing the Spirit: Higher Education in America*, from which this viewpoint is excerpted.

As you read, consider the following questions:

1. How does the pressure to publish affect a professor's ability to teach, according to Smith?
2. In the author's opinion, why are younger faculty members apprehensive about tenure?
3. According to Smith, how has the hiring of minority professors caused controversy surrounding tenure?

When intelligent and decent people do foolish and cruel things, it seems safe to assume that they are the victims of institutions that encourage or demand such behavior. Such I believe to be the case with tenure. It is a major premise of this viewpoint that tenure . . . [has] inflicted what may turn out to be fatal wounds on higher education. The argument originally advanced for tenure was that professors needed to be protected in the expression of unpopular views by having an unusual degree—one might even say, an unprecedented degree—of security of employment. The fact is that, even after tenure had been accepted by all major universities, boards of trustees did not hesitate to fire professors who professed ideas that the trustees found objectionable. . . . Professors of Marxist persuasion, for example, were weeded out, often with the help or at least concurrence of their colleagues whenever the "threat" of communism in the United States was considered sufficiently dire, which was, in fact, whenever the trustees said the threat was dire. This was invariably done on the grounds that the Marxist professors couldn't be "objective" because they had given their allegiance to a particular dogma or doctrine, and a "foreign" one at that. Thus they were violating the academy's "hypocritical oath," to be completely objective in all things. All the other professors were assumed to be objective as long as *they* said nothing offensive. As it turned out in one of the greatest of the American universities, the faculty members didn't even have to profess anything to be canned; they just had to refuse to sign an oath declaring their loyalty to the government of the United States and the state of California, a requirement that the regents felt no reasonable professor would scruple to sign.

Job Security

The initial fight for tenure served a far more immediate and practical end. In the words of Laurence Veysey, author of *The Emergence of the American University*: "Demand for professorial tenure was in large measure a quest for security." Veysey quotes a candid Henry Seidel Canby: "Our strongest desire was to be made safe, to stay where we were on a living wage, to be secure while we worked. . . . We were dependent upon the college, which itself was always pressed for money, and could not be counted upon to be either judicious or just." In other words, the motives of the professors were no different from the motives of steelworkers or coal miners: they wished job security and proper procedures for protecting their right to due process. In actual fact, tenure seems to have been of more service in protecting professors accused of moral turpitude (or what the general public considered moral turpitude, which might be no more than getting a divorce) than in protecting professors' right

242

to speak out on controversial issues. For one thing, by the time a faculty member had made his careful, laborious way up the "ladder," he or she had demonstrated a dutiful compliance with the standards of the institution. Indeed, if the basic purpose of tenure was to protect the faculty member in the expression of unpopular or unorthodox opinions, it would clearly be most valuable to a faculty member at the beginning of his career.

Caste System

While piously pledging allegiance at the altar of "academic freedom," the tenured professors have set up a caste system in which they are accountable to no one, while they ruthlessly use thought control to liquidate original thinkers, dissenters and anyone who is a good teacher. They have made the academic culture actively hostile to teaching.

Phyllis Schlafly, *The Union Leader*, February 8, 1990.

The fight for tenure was thus far less a fight for the right to express unpopular opinions than against an imperious and autocratic administration. Whatever its motivation, tenure turned out to exercise a decidedly negative influence on higher education. What faculty needed and deserved to have was review procedures that protected them from arbitrary actions by administrators or trustees. What they got was much more: a degree of security unequaled by any other profession and difficult to justify in abstract terms.

Unfair Decisions

The campus of the University of California, Santa Cruz, has, like most University of California campuses, a number of faculty committees, among them a Committee on Educational Policy, on Privilege and Tenure, on Course Approval, on almost *ad infinitum*. In addition, they have innumerable *ad hoc* committees appointed to evaluate the scholarly progress of their colleagues, specifically their output or productivity in terms of research and publication. Since every faculty member must be evaluated every few years (advances in salary are usually in two-year increments—i.e., two years in first-step assistant professor, two years in step two, etc., on up to full professor), this debilitating process of constant review takes literally uncounted faculty hours, causes much grief, and often results in highly questionable or blatantly unfair decisions, leading, in that wonderfully revealing word, to "terminations," or, more happily, to tenure.

Since the assistant professor knows well that tenure depends almost exclusively on research/publication, you may imagine where his/her principal attention is directed. What is much more difficult to imagine is the strain that this barbarous system places on the psyches of the young men and women subjected to it. By the time they are considered ripe for tenure, they have spent some twelve to fifteen of the most important and formative years of their lives preparing for this moment (five or six, typically, in graduate school, six or seven in anticipation of tenure). What this does to their nerves, their families, their, as we like to say today, "self-esteem" should be evident. They live for seven years in a state of suspended animation, not knowing whether they are to be turned out in disgrace by their friends and colleagues or retained. The university, of course, comforts itself with the assurance that its decisions are entirely objective and unchallengeably fair.

These decisions, affecting people's lives in the most profound ways, are made by, one must assume, conscientious individuals, but they are nonetheless chancy in the extreme. Everyone who has spent any time in the academic world has a veritable anthology of horror stories revolving around the issue of tenure. Indeed, I have my own tale of tenure to tell. My academic advancement rested on precarious and (as it turned out) fortuitous circumstances. I had been invited to come to the UCLA department of history at the top step of the assistant professorship on the basis of the assurance of an editor of a university press that my Harvard dissertation, a rather pedestrian biography of James Wilson, one of the Founding Fathers, had, for all practical purposes, been accepted for publication. It was nice to have the modest amount of extra money that a second- or third-step (or whatever it was) assistant professor received, but the catch was that in two years I would be up for evaluation for promotion to associate professor, which brought with it TENURE. If, for any reason, the publication of my biography was delayed, or the press changed its editorial mind, I might find my stay at UCLA a brief one.

A Tenure Verdict

A year or so after my arrival in southern California, I received a letter from the editor of the press. One of their readers or referees, who had dallied so long over reading my manuscript that the press, having had two affirmative readings, had decided to go ahead with plans for publication, finally checked in with his criticism. His recommendation: the subject was not an appropriate one for a conventional biography, because relatively little was known of the subject's life. However, since he was unquestionably an important and original thinker, I should be asked to rewrite the manuscript as a critical study of James Wilson, political theorist. Since the TENURE decision was bearing down on me with alarming speed, I was frantic. I couldn't possibly drop a heavy teaching load, rewrite the manuscript from top to bottom, and then go through, once more, the long, uncertain review process. I said, in effect, This is it. Take it or leave it. No rewriting, no study of Wilson as a political theorist (that was, in fact, already in the biography). Fortunately for my career as an academic historian, the press decided to go ahead with publication. Even so, the book was not "off the press" in time to be considered by my TENURE committee; the members had to be (and were) satisfied to read the book in page proof. They considered it acceptable and I got TENURE. I have since written nineteen other books and immodesty requires that I note that eight of them were Book-of-the-Month Club Main Selections (and one was an alternate), which is not, of course, to suggest that they are monuments of scholarship. My point is that, if the press had been sticky and my book had not been published or had been substantially delayed, I doubtless would not have received TENURE, in which case I would have had to go away in disgrace and would probably have ended up a faro dealer in Las Vegas or a secondhand-car salesman in Santa Monica. . . .

Moral Tenure

That the most brilliant teaching will not save a young assistant professor if he/she fails to achieve the minimum standard of research/publication (many institutions like to point to an occasional exception, but the occasional exception has had to endure the humiliation of being just that, an exception, and he/she is never allowed to forget it) is well known. One form of humiliation in the University of California system is what is called "moral tenure." If a faculty member is retained for an eighth year, he or she is considered to have "moral tenure." Such rare survivors are generally stripped of their professorial title and taken off "the ladder." The ladder is the means by which junior professors climb up to the various benefits, including frequent "sabbaticals"—a sabbatical being, traditionally, every seventh year off for research uninterrupted by even the modest and constantly diminishing amount of teaching required when not on sabbatical. The sabbatical has been improved on in many institutions by an ingenious invention called a "semi-sabbatical." The semi-sabbatical comes at the end of three years. It is a half-year off, which, combined with the regular three months off in the summer, gives the professors three-quarters of a year off for research, a popular option with many faculty. Lately the university has employed another arrangement: an increasing dependence on "lecturers," heavily concentrated in the areas of language instruction and remedial English. They are denied the lofty title of professor, paid less, required to teach many more hours since they are not expected to publish books and articles; they are the peons of the academic world, secondclass citizens in a supposedly democratic community of scholars.

Bad to Worse

Bad as the tenure system has been, there are indications that it is getting worse. Howard Bowen and Jack Schuster's study of tenure suggests that many faculty are highly, if privately, critical of the system. "At many campuses," Bowen and Schuster report, "that until recently had only infrequently denied tenure, the lives of countless assistant professors were filled with dread or resignation, as the result of a confluence of factors. First, vacancies were scarce; many departments—especially in the humanities—were already heavily tenured-in, and those departments that still had one or two professors were understandably ambivalent about becoming 100 percent tenured." One problem with departments that are "heavily tenured" is that student preferences are highly volatile. If student enrollments shift, for example, from English to psychology, and the English department is filled with tenured faculty members and a diminishing pool of students, bad feeling may arise between colleagues in literature and psychology. The authors point out that the declining percentage of junior faculty members in recent years who receive tenure has caused additional anxiety. "Coupled with low salaries and high living costs in urban areas, the probationary period for young faculty members was often a grueling and lonely ordeal." The researchers found that even tenured faculty, especially in the associate-professor rank, "felt threatened by the new emphasis on research. At the research universities, where promotion to full professor has long depended on a respectable promotions record," nothing much had changed. "But at those institutions where the criteria for promotion are shifting, where effective teaching or even mere longevity were no longer sufficient for promotion to full professor, mid-career faculty were feeling the pinch." Bowen and Schuster found that such campuses were "legion." Faculty insecurity was increased by the consciousness that there was a "new breed of well-trained young faculty fixated on scholarship and performing— albeit out of dire necessity—at levels heretofore rarely seen on campus." At many campuses that in the past had placed a strong emphasis on teaching, the pressures to publish had increased greatly. In consequence, the "non-tenured faculty on the tenure track were under great stress." This was evident from their own testimony "but also from the comments of many senior faculty and administrators who observed their plight." Under such pressures, many junior faculty members "had ceased to function as fully participating members of their campus communities . . . as they 'burrowed toward tenure.'"

246

One assistant professor of English told Bowen and Schuster, "I like the University. . . . I feel that I'm doing all the right things—but it may not help. . . . I am a stone realist. I see my predicament as a function of larger social forces. I understand that I was born too late. If I had been born ten years earlier . . . I'd probably be an associate or full professor at a more prestigious institution."

A study conducted by Dwight R. Ladd in 1979 reported that three-fourths of the faculty surveyed agreed "that their interests lean toward teaching (as contrasted with research) and agree that *teaching effectiveness, not publications, should be the primary criterion for promotion of faculty*" (italics mine).

Questioning Tenure

Some universities and politicians are questioning the whole notion of tenure, which at some schools can mean permanent employment after as little as three years on the job. A 1987 survey by the Department of Education found that during the preceding three years, 93% of U.S. colleges and universities had taken some action that "may have had the effect of reducing the proportion of faculty members on tenure."

Priscilla Painton, *Time*, February 26, 1990.

In recent years some of the most excruciating decisions on tenure have involved "minority" faculty, specifically women and blacks and, more recently, Hispanics. Universities have been under great pressure in the last decade or two to appoint minorities to "ladder" faculty positions. Some administrations, prodded by threats of withheld government funding, have imposed a quota system on departments—you must hire X number of women, blacks, minorities in general. All well and good, but female and especially black academics are in short supply. It is a seller's market. Not infrequently, representatives of minorities are hired whose qualifications (at least as the university specifies them) are uncertain. Even if they appear highly qualified, there is always an element of uncertainty, just as there is with white males: can the appointee turn out the required amount of what passes for research in time to meet the dreaded tenure deadline? Sometimes, of course, the answer is "no." Something close to panic ensues. Minorities are so scarce that the thought of discarding one is alarming. Moreover, the minority faculty member has a minority following who are often devoutly attached to him or her and who can be counted on to make a considerable fuss. Often the charge is the familiar one of racism or sexism. The faculty and administration usually feel that they have bent over backward to try to begin to rectify the racial and sexual imbalance in the faculty, an imbalance that is the result of generations of indifference, if not actual discrimination. Finally, there is the fact that minorities are often very vocal in charging "institutional racism," a rather comprehensive term that covers not only the racial imbalance in the faculty and in the student body but the perhaps more basic fact that the underlying concepts and principles in the various established academic disciplines outside the hard sciences are seen by minorities as white male distortions of much more complex realities, realities that include them and their cultures. It is small wonder, for example, that a Mexican American from a culture steeped in Hispanic Roman Catholicism finds the aggressively secular tone of the American university campus cold and uncongenial; the same for blacks and Arabs and Cambodians. In making a more or less respectable effort to include as many representatives of as many minorities as possible, the university, its curricular practices, and even the assumptions underlying its various disciplines often come under fire. This relatively recent development has added to the already considerable disarray of the academic noncommunity.

Disenchantment with Tenure

To me, the tenure ritual is comparable to ancient rites of human sacrifice. If a certain number of nontenured faculty are not terminated each year at University X, the general impression gets around that University X is not upholding proper academic standards, and University X suffers in the eyes of the academic world. Conversely, University Y is admired for its hard-nosed policy. Fortunately, one consequence of a growing disenchantment with the whole tenure process is the number of court cases brought by faculty members who think they have been treated unfairly. Twenty years ago such cases were virtually unheard of; now they are commonplace, and in a number of instances courts have ordered universities to reverse negative decisions on tenure or have granted litigants substantial sums of money on the grounds that they have been unjustly terminated.

"Affirmative-action admissions are . . . a way of enriching the student culture."

Universities Should Strive for a Culturally Diverse Student Body

Troy Duster

Demographic changes and affirmative action programs have resulted in increasing numbers of minority students attending America's universities. Differing views among these ethnic groups can sometimes cause conflicts for students of all races. In the following viewpoint, Troy Duster argues that both students and universities benefit from this clash of views because such conflict occurs in later life. Duster believes that students who can resolve conflict in racially diverse universities will be better prepared to succeed than students at universities that are more homogeneous. Duster is a sociology professor at the University of California at Berkeley.

As you read, consider the following questions:

1. Why does Duster believe that Berkeley's student population should reflect the diversity of races and cultures in California?
2. In the author's opinion, why is affirmative action necessary?
3. According to Duster, why is it important to make students aware of the historical treatment of minorities?

Adapted from "They're Taking Over!" by Troy Duster, *Mother Jones*, September/October 1991. Copyright © 1991, Foundation for National Progress. Reprinted with permission.

The University of California at Berkeley has been my permanent academic home since 1969, when I was appointed to the tenured faculty in the Department of Sociology. At the time, I was one of only 6 blacks on a faculty of 1,350, and the most junior. In those early years, it was not uncommon for students, white and black, to come to my office, look dead at me, and ask, "Is Professor Duster here?"

The question, which turned me into a living Invisible Man, reflected the depth of racial problems in U.S. higher education, even at its most progressive university. Years of fury and tumult followed. And for over two decades now, I've been thinking about race and higher education—both as my area of professional study, and because of the realities that have shaped my personal life here. I went to the retirement party of one of my original black colleagues, who caught me off guard by saying that I was now the senior African American on the faculty. From this vantage point, I have a story to tell about the remarkable transformation of Berkeley's undergraduate student population. Because Berkeley, once again, is at the center of a raging national controversy—this time over the issue of "multiculturalism" and what its enemies call "political correctness"—a storm that I believe to be, at bottom, about the shifting sands of racial privilege. It is also about the future of American education: what happens in Berkeley, one of the nation's largest public universities and the bellwether of social change and innovation in academia, will affect all of us.

Campus Multiculturalism

In January 1989, Berkeley's chancellor commissioned me and the Institute for the Study of Social Change to prepare a report on multiculturalism on campus. Our research team intensively interviewed hundreds of students over an eighteen-month period—first in single-ethnic groups with an interviewer of the same background, then in mixed groups. We asked them what kind of environment they'd hoped to find upon arriving on campus, and what they actually encountered. Who were their friends, where and how powerfully were racial tensions felt, what did they think of other ethnic groups, of affirmative action? We asked them about their frustrations and their positive experiences around racial and ethnic issues, and what they would do to change things. We developed a rich and complicated portrait of campus culture at Berkeley, drawn directly from the students who make it up. It isn't an easy picture to draw, nor to compress into a headline. And it certainly isn't the side of the story that ideologues like Dinesh D'Souza and his imitators have focused on. What the study, and my own experience, tell me, is that multiculturalism's critics are selling students short by propagating key myths.

Multiculturalism is tearing the campus apart.

Self-segregation. Balkanization. School days claustrophobically lived out in ethnic enclaves. That's how Berkeley's and other campuses are often portrayed these days, as intellectual and cultural disaster zones racked by racial conflict.

Very rarely is there any mention of the forces that push students into familiar groups. Long before there were African-American theme houses, even before World War II, on-campus Catholic and Jewish societies helped those "minority" students survive; the Hillel and Newman Foundations supported students navigating through hostile WASP territory. Today, I almost never read that this phenomenon might also benefit African-American or Latino students. As many students told us, those who otherwise would feel alienated on a supercompetitive campus are getting together and finding support, creating a common comfort zone, making it easier to succeed.

In 1968, the Berkeley campus was primarily white. The student body was 2.8 percent black, 1.3 percent Chicano/Latino, and the massive Asian immigration of the 1970s had yet to occur. Only twenty-three years later, half the Berkeley student body is made up of people of color. Inevitably, with such a dramatic social transformation, there is tension and sometimes even open conflict over resources, turf, and "ownership" of the place.

Back in the 1950s, students either turned the campus radio station on or off. In the late 1980s, different ethnic groups fought over what kind of music it should play during prime time: salsa, rap, country, or heavy metal? (This same issue surfaced during the gulf war, when Latino troops demanded more salsa on Armed Forces Radio.)

Conflict is expected, perhaps even healthy, in a social situation where people have different interests and compete for scarce resources. Few of California's "feeder" high schools are racially integrated, so it's not surprising that students experience shock and tension when they arrive at their first experience of multiculturalism. But it may be a more realistic preparation for life's later turns.

Berkeley, of course, is no more a racial utopia than any other place in this divided and racially wounded country. Nonetheless, what strikes this sociologist as remarkable is how well and relatively peaceably it works.

The Competence Myth

Multiculturalism is diluting our standards.

Nowadays we hear that the academy is in deep trouble because multicultural admissions policies let in students who are less capable. Actually, by the measures the critics themselves tend to use, SAT scores and grade point averages, the typical

Berkeley student is now far more competent, far more eligible, far more prepared than when this was an all-white university in 1950. Of the more than 21,300 students who applied in 1989, over 5,800 had straight-A averages—and all were competing for only 3,500 spots in the freshman class.

As recently as 1980, only 8,000 students *total* applied to Berkeley. In 1988, about 7,500 Asians alone applied. Such demographic facts can't help but heighten racial awareness on campus. Many more thousands of students wanting the relatively scarce Berkeley diploma create increasingly ferocious competition at the same-sized admissions gate.

Diversity Fosters Excellence

Our commitment to affirmative action is grounded in our actual experience with the benefits of diversity. In the last two decades, the [Georgetown University] Law Center's national reputation has grown significantly. This is exactly the period in which we have achieved much greater diversity in our faculty, student body and administration. The real story at Georgetown is that not only has there been no conflict between diversity and academic excellence, but that diversity has fostered excellence.

Judith Areen, dean of Georgetown University Law Center, *The Washington Post,* May 26, 1991.

Back in the 1960s, when the campus was mainly white, almost every eligible student who applied to Berkeley was admitted. So in a framework of plenty, people could afford to be gracious, and say that civil rights, even affirmative action, were good ideas. When the United States changed its immigration laws in the 1970s, well-qualified candidates with families from China, Hong Kong, and Korea swelled the pool of applicants. Suddenly, not everyone who was eligible could get in. Today, Berkeley is 30 percent Asian, and that means that white students who are not getting in are feeling the crunch from the "top" (students with higher GPAs and SATs) and from the "bottom" (students admitted through music, athletic ability, affirmative action, and other eligibility allowances). The media, so far, has chosen to emphasize the beleaguered white student who has to adjust to affirmative action. Isn't it a shame, stories imply, that these students are feeling uncomfortable in an environment that used to be *their* university?

It isn't theirs anymore. Since the demographics of this state are changing at a rapidly accelerating rate—by 2000, whites will account for only 52 percent of California's population—shouldn't the university population and curriculum reflect more of this new reality? Meanwhile, the quality of student at Berkeley is only getting better.

Getting rid of affirmative action and other special admissions programs would improve the university.

In the 1960s, there was so little diversity on campus that white students experienced other cultures voluntarily, on their own terms, like choosing ethnic cuisine on the night you're in the mood for it. Now there's no way to avoid it, and that leads to the big question on campus: *Why are you here?* Some white students have told us in their interviews how unfair they think a policy is that permits students with lower GPAs and SATs to be here.

Black and Chicano students know the rap. What they never hear, even from university officials, is strong morally, historically, and politically informed language that justifies affirmative action. Most of the black and Chicano students we interviewed were themselves unclear on why affirmative action exists.

It exists because, over the past two hundred years, blacks and Latinos have had a difficult time entering higher education, and that legacy hasn't gone away. The median family income of white Berkeley students is approximately $70,000 a year, and for blacks it is $38,000 a year. The gap isn't closing; the economic barriers that restrict minority access to college aren't disappearing.

Cultural Enrichment

But Americans' cultural memory lasts about five years, so the idea that affirmative action exists to redress past grievances doesn't resonate with today's students—of all colors. The notion that black people have a past of slavery and discrimination, that this is a fact of American history, is buried so deep in the consciousness of most students that it doesn't surface. The right wing says that if you bring that fact to the fore and teach it, that's called Oppression Studies, or "political correctness," and by telling people of color they should feel good about themselves, you're making white people feel bad about themselves.

There is a different way to argue for affirmative action, which hits home with even historical amnesiacs. That is to remind students that the future will reward those who master the art of coming together across ethnic, cultural, and racial lines. Suddenly, affirmative-action admissions are not a debt payment that lets in students who "don't deserve to be here," but rather a way of enriching the student culture—and career hopes. Just as Xerox or other corporations that promote executives who have proven their ability to "manage diversity."

A lot of white students are already intuitively on board. When we asked graduating students what they regretted about their time on campus, many told us, in effect, "I wish I had spent more time availing myself of the potential of Berkeley's diversity." The smartest among them also see that in a globalized economy, Berkeley's multiculturalism can make them better leaders. . . .

Beyond the Myths

Berkeley students have a chance that students at the far more white University of California at Santa Barbara don't have—they're rubbing up against difference all the time. Many of them told us they came here specifically for that reason, though some graduated with stereotypes intact, or disappointed that they weren't leaving with a better sense of other cultures. How can we make diversity a constructive experience? We asked Berkeley's students and they told us.

First they gave us the Don'ts. Don't, they said, try to fix things by putting us through three-hour sensitivity sessions designed to raise our consciousness about gender or racial issues or homophobia. Those are too contrived and short-lived to make much of a difference.

Positive Race Relations

Students attending colleges and universities today—white and black, majority and minority—are part of a transitional generation, the members of which are learning to relate to one another in ways not yet entirely familiar and comfortable. But they are doing so with an earnestness and good faith that in the end will create a far better climate for the achievement of true equality than this country has yet known.

James O. Freedman, *Los Angeles Times*, August 28, 1991.

And don't force matters by asking different cultures to party together. Black students told us whites are too busy drinking to want to dance up a storm. White students said Chicanos and blacks would rather be raucous than sociable. The perfectly integrated, all-university "We Are the World" dance party is a bad idea, all sides told us, mainly because we don't all like the same music.

What then, did Berkeley's diversity-seekers remember as their most positive experiences when they reflected on their four years here? Again and again, they would describe the time when an instructor had the class break into groups and work on joint projects. Engaged in a collective enterprise, they learned about other students' ways of thinking and problem solving, and sometimes they found friendships forming across the ethnic divide.

A more cooperative approach to learning, then, would breathe some fresh air into the sometimes tense ethnic atmosphere on Berkeley's campus. And a clear explanation and endorsement of the merits of affirmative action by the school administration, something on paper that every student would receive, read, and perhaps debate, would counteract the tension that grows in the present silence. These are two concrete recommendations our report makes.

Sharp Differences

But Berkeley is not a sealed laboratory, and students don't arrive here as tabulae rasae. They bring their own experiences and expectations; some are angry about injustices they've felt firsthand, while some are blithely unaware of their implications.

What our hundreds of interviews showed is that there is a sharp difference between the ways black and white students feel about racial politics; Asians and Chicanos fall somewhere in between. White students tend to arrive with an almost naive good will, as if they are saying, "I think I'll just go and have some diversity," while music from *Peter and the Wolf* plays in the background. They expect to experience the "other" without conflict, without tension, without anything resembling bitterness or hostility. Meanwhile, many blacks arrive after being told in high school that Berkeley is a tough place, an alien environment, and that in order to survive, they should stick with other black people.

Imagine then what happens in the first few weeks of the first semester. White students looking for diversity run into black students already sure that race is political, so pick your friends carefully. White students seeking easy access to a black group can quickly find their hands slapped. They might say something offensive without knowing it and get called "racist," a word they use to mean prejudging a person because he or she is black. *Why do you call me racist? Hey, I'm willing to talk to you like an ordinary person.*

But when black students use the term, they tend to aim it at a person they see participating in a larger institution that works against black people. *If you're not in favor of affirmative action, that means you're racist.*

The white student retorts: *I'm willing to have dinner with you, talk with you about ideas. I'm not prejudiced.* But the two are talking past each other, the white student describing a style of interaction and friendship, the black student talking about the set of views the white student appears to hold.

Resolving Conflict

It is misunderstandings such as these, arising in an atmosphere of fierce competition, in a setting of remarkable ethnic and racial diversity, that lead some critics to jump gleefully to the conclusion that diversity is not working. But there is another, more hopeful interpretation. Berkeley's students are grappling with one of the most difficult situations in the world: ethnic and racial turf. They are doing this, however modestly, over relatively safe issues such as what kind of music gets played or who sits where in the lunchroom. Perhaps they will learn how to handle conflict, how to divvy up scarce resources, how to adjust, fight, retreat, compromise, and ultimately get along in a future that will no longer be dominated by a single group spouting its own values as the ideal homogenized reality for everyone else. If our students learn even a small bit of this, they will be far better prepared than students tucked safely away in anachronistic single-culture enclaves. And what they learn may make a difference not just for their personal futures, but for a world struggling with issues of nationalism, race, and ethnicity.

VIEWPOINT

*"The university's quest for racial equality
produces a conspicuous academic inequality."*

Cultural Diversity Does Not Produce Quality Education

Dinesh D'Souza

Dinesh D'Souza is a research fellow at the American Enterprise Institute, a Washington, D.C. think tank. He is the author of *Illiberal Education*, a best-selling critique of higher education, from which the following viewpoint is excerpted. D'Souza argues that the goal of increasing racial diversity on U.S. campuses has led to a decrease in the quality of education. D'Souza believes that affirmative action favors minorities whose average academic performance is unacceptably below university standards. D'Souza maintains that those minority students who cannot compete academically with others tend to seek solace within their own minority group, thereby preventing integration and promoting further racism.

As you read, consider the following questions:

1. Why do university administrators feel the need to recruit more minority students, according to D'Souza?
2. In the author's opinion, why is it difficult for disadvantaged minorities to adjust to a university environment?
3. According to D'Souza, why do minorities unjustly blame white racism for their academic problems?

Although university leaders speak of the self-evident virtues of diversity, it is not at all obvious why it is necessary to a first-rate education. Universities such as Brandeis, Notre Dame, and Mount Holyoke, which were founded on principles of religious or gender homogeneity, still manage to provide an excellent education. Similarly, foreign institutions such as Oxford, Cambridge, Bologna, Salamanca, Paris, and Tokyo display considerable cultural singularity, yet they are regarded as among the best in the world.

Diversity of Mind

The question is not whether universities should seek diversity, but what kind of diversity. It seems that the primary form of diversity which universities should try to foster is diversity of mind. Such diversity would enrich academic discourse, widen its parameters, multiply its objects of inquiry, and increase the probability of obscure and unlikely terrain being investigated. Abroad one typically encounters such diversity of opinion even on basic questions such as how society should be organized. In my high school in Bombay, for example, I could identify students who considered themselves monarchists, Fabian socialists, Christian democrats, Hindu advocates of a caste-based society, agrarians, centralized planners, theocrats, liberals, and Communists. In European universities, one finds a similar smorgasbord of philosophical convictions.

By contrast, most American students seem to display striking agreement on all the basic questions of life. Indeed, they appear to regard a true difference of opinion, based upon convictions that are firmly and intensely held, as dangerously dogmatic and an offense against the social etiquette of tolerance. Far from challenging these conventional prejudices, college leaders tend to encourage their uncritical continuation. "Universities show no interest whatsoever in fostering intellectual diversity," John Bunzel, former president of San Jose State University, says bluntly. Evidence suggests that the philosophical composition of the American faculty is remarkably homogenous, yet Bunzel says that universities are not concerned. "When I raise the problem with leaders in academe, their usual response is that [the imbalance] is irrelevant, or that there cannot be litmus tests for recruitment."

But universities do take very seriously the issue of *racial* underrepresentation. Here they are quite willing to consider goals, quotas, litmus tests, whatever will rectify the tabulated disproportion. "What we're hoping," said Malcolm Gillis, a senior official at Duke, "is that racial diversity will ultimately lead to intellectual diversity."

The problem begins with a deep sense of embarrassment over

the small number of minorities—blacks in particular—on campuses. University officials speak of themselves as more enlightened and progressive than the general population, so they feel guilty if the proportion of minorities at their institutions is smaller than in surrounding society. Moreover, they are often pressured by politicians who control appropriations at state schools, and by student and faculty activists on campus. As a consequence, universities agree to make herculean efforts to attract as many blacks, Hispanics, and other certified minorities as possible to their institutions.

The number of minority applicants who would normally qualify for acceptance at selective universities is very small; therefore, in order to meet ambitious recruitment targets, affirmative action must entail fairly drastic compromises in admissions requirements. University leaders are willing to use unjust means to achieve their goal of equal representation. In one of the more radical steps in this direction, the California legislature is considering measures to *require* all state colleges to accept black, Hispanic, white, and Asian students in proportion with their level in the population, regardless of the disparity in academic preparation or qualifications among such groups.

Racial Polarization

I'm beginning to see a disturbing pattern of identification among the [Berkeley] student population. Each group stays within its own boundaries, within its own territory. The black students sit together on the left side of Sproul Plaza, the Latinos occupy another corner, the Asian students assemble somewhere else and the whites mostly disappear to their sororities and fraternities.

What happened to socializing among the "diverse student population" of UC Berkeley? What happened to the goal of diversity: a mixed campus population conducive to promoting understanding of other customs and peoples?

Rather than gaining understanding and forming friendships, students seem less tolerant. Polarization along the lines of skin color is increasing at Berkeley.

Lorenza Muñoz, *Los Angeles Times*, May 19, 1991.

The first consequence of such misguided policies is a general misplacement of minority students throughout higher education. Thus a student whose grades and qualifications are good enough to get him into Rutgers or Penn State finds himself at Williams or Bowdoin, and the student who meets Williams' and Bowdoin's more demanding requirements finds himself at Yale or Berkeley. Many selective universities are so famished for minority students that they will accept virtually anyone of the right color who applies. In order to fulfill affirmative action objectives, university admissions officers cannot afford to pay too much attention to the probability of a student succeeding at the university.

Academic Problems

For many black, Hispanic, and American Indian students who may have struggled hard to get through high school, the courtship of selective universities comes as a welcome surprise. They receive expenses-paid trips to various colleges, where they are chaperoned around campus, introduced to deans and senior faculty, and most of all assured that their presence is avidly desired, indeed that the university would be a poorer place if they chose to go somewhere else. These blandishments naturally enhance the expectations of minority students. These expectations are reinforced by such focused events as the minority freshmen orientation, where black, Hispanic, American Indian, and foreign students are given to understand that they are walking embodiments of the university's commitment to multiculturalism and diversity. Universities emphasize that they are making no accommodations or compromises to enroll affirmative action students; on the contrary, they insist that these students will make a special contribution that the university could not obtain elsewhere.

Their lofty hopes, however, are not realized for most affirmative action students. During the first few weeks of class, many recognize the degree to which they are academically unprepared, relative to other students. At Berkeley, for instance, admissions office data show that the average black freshman's GPA and test scores fall in the 6th percentile of scores for whites and Asian; anthropology professor Vincent Sarich remarks, "As we get more and more selective among Asians and whites, the competitive gap necessarily increases." Yet once these students get to class, professors at demanding schools such as Berkeley take for granted that they know who wrote *Paradise Lost*, that they are capable of understanding Shakespearean English, that they have heard of Max Weber and the Protestant ethic, that they can solve algebraic equations, that they know something about the cell and the amoeba. Students are expected to read several hundred pages of literature, history, biology, and other subjects every week, and produce analytical papers, appropriately footnoted, on short notice.

Unfortunately the basic ingredients of what E.D. Hirsch terms "cultural literacy" are by no means uniformly transmitted in American high schools, nor are regular intellectual habits of concentration and discipline. Thus in the first part of freshman year, affirmative action students with relatively weak preparation often encounter a bewildering array of unfamiliar terms and works. Coping with them, says William Banks, professor of Afro-American Studies at Berkeley, "can be very confusing and frustrating." While they wrestle with the work load, affirmative action students also notice that their peers seem much more comfortable in this academic environment, quicker in absorbing the reading, more confident and fluent in their speech and writing. Even if affirmative action students work that much harder, they discover that it is not easy to keep pace, since the better prepared students also work very hard.

Remedial Programs

For many minority students, especially those from disadvantaged backgrounds, these problems are often complicated by a difficult personal adjustment to a new environment. It is not easy going from an inner-city high school to a college town with entirely new social routines, or settling into a dormitory where roommates have a great deal more money to spend, or cultivating the general university lifestyle that is familiar to prep schoolers and sons and daughters of alumni but alien to many minority and foreign students.

University leaders have discovered how displaced and unsettled minority freshmen can be, and typically respond by setting up counseling services and remedial education programs intended to assure blacks and Hispanics that they do belong, and that they can "catch up" with other students. Neither of these university resources is well used, however. Students who are struggling to keep up with course work hardly have time to attend additional classes in reading comprehension and algebra. If they do enroll in these programs, they run the risk of falling further behind in class. Relatively few minority students attend counseling because they correctly reject the idea that there is something wrong with them. Nor would the therapeutic assurances of freshman counselors do much to solve their academic difficulties. For many minority undergraduates, therefore, the university's quest for racial equality produces a conspicuous academic inequality.

Separate and Unequal

As at Berkeley, Michigan, and elsewhere, many minority students seek comfort and security among their peers who are in a similar situation. Thus many sign up for their campus Afro-American Society or Hispanic Students Association or ethnic theme house or fraternity, where they can share their hopes and frustrations in a relaxed and candid atmosphere, and get guidance from older students who have traveled these strange paths. The impulse to retreat into exclusive enclaves is a familiar one for minority groups who have suffered a history of persecution; they feel there is strength and safety in numbers, and tend to develop group consciousness and collective orientation partly as a protective strategy.

Minority Separatism

Bewildered at the realities of college life, many minority students seek support and solace from others like them, especially older students who have traveled the unfamiliar paths. Thus begins the process of minority separatism and self-segregation on campus, which is now fairly advanced and which has come as such a surprise to universities whose catalogs celebrate integration and the close interaction of diverse ethnic groups.

Dinesh D'Souza, *The New Republic*, February 18, 1991.

But when minority students demand that the college recognize and subsidize separatist institutions, the administration is placed in a dilemma. The deans know that to accede to these demands is problematic, given their public commitment to integration of students from different backgrounds—indeed the promise of such interaction is one of the main justifications for the goal of diversity sought through affirmative action. At the same time, university leaders realize how dislocated many minority students feel, and how little the university itself can do to help them. Further, the administration does not know how it could possibly say no to these students, and harbors vague and horrific fears of the consequences.

Virtually every administration ends by putting aside its qualms and permitting minority institutions to flourish. The logical extreme may be witnessed at California State University at Sacramento, which has announced a new plan to establish an entirely separate "college within a college" for blacks. To justify this separatist subsidy, university leaders have developed a model of "pluralism," which they insist is not the same thing as integration. Since integration implies the merging of various ethnic groups into a common whole, it does not really contribute to diversity. By contrast, pluralism implies the enhancement of distinct ethnic subcultures—a black culture, Hispanic culture, American Indian culture, and a (residual) white culture—which it is hoped will interact in a harmonious and mutually enriching manner.

There is a good deal of camaraderie and social activity at the distinctive minority organizations. Most of them, especially ethnic residence halls and fraternities, help to give newly arrived minority students a sense of belonging. They do not, however, offer any solution to the dilemma facing those students who are inadequately prepared for the challenges of the curriculum. Virtually none of the minority organizations offers study programs or tutorials for affirmative action students. Indeed, some separatist institutions encourage anti-intellectualism, viewing it as an authentic black cultural trait. As researchers Signithia Fordham of Rutgers and John Ogbu of Berkeley describe it, "What appears to have emerged in some segments of the black community is a kind of cultural orientation which defines academic learning as 'acting white,' and academic success as the prerogative of white Americans." Thus many minority freshmen who are struggling academically find no practical remedy in the separate culture of minority institutions.

What they do often find is a novel explanation for their difficulties. Older students tell the newcomers that they should be aware of the pervasive atmosphere of bigotry on campus. Although such racism may not be obvious at first, minority freshmen should not be deceived by appearances. Racism is vastly more subtle than in the past, and operates in various guises, some of them as elusive as baleful looks, uncorrected mental stereotypes, and the various forms of deceptively "polite" behavior. In addition to looking out for such nuances, minority freshmen and sophomores are further warned not to expect much support from the university, where "overt racism" has given way to "institutional racism," evident in the disproportionately small numbers of minorities reflected on the faculty and among the deans and trustees. Everywhere, forces of bigotry are said to conspire against permitting minority students the "racism-free environment" they need to succeed.

Preferences and White Racism

Typically, minority beneficiaries are strong supporters of preferential treatment, although their natural pride requires that its nature be disguised. They may speak more freely about it among themselves, but among white students and in the mainstream campus discussion, they understandably refrain from admitting that academic standards were adjusted to make their enrollment possible. Instead, these students assert, often under the banner of their minority organization, that the view that blacks, Hispanics, and American Indians benefit at the expense of overrepresented students is itself evidence of pervasive bigotry. Consequently, in the minds of minority students, affirmative action is not a cause of their academic difficulties, but an excuse for white racism which is the real source of their problems.

263

"Sensitivity to issues of race, class, ethnicity, and gender would . . . rid us of the ignorance in which we have basked."

Universities Should Teach Multiculturalism

Beverly Guy-Sheftall

Many minorities and others argue that university humanities courses are biased against minority cultures because they are based on white Western culture. In the following viewpoint, Beverly Guy-Sheftall contends that this bias reinforces the view that Western culture is superior and more influential than other world cultures. She believes that in order to correct this bias, universities must include courses across the curriculum that incorporate international perspectives. Guy-Sheftall is director of the Women's Research and Resource Center at Spelman College in Atlanta, Georgia.

As you read, consider the following questions:

1. Why does a focus on Western culture alienate minority students, according to Guy-Sheftall?
2. How did the arrival of Columbus affect the New World, in the author's opinion?
3. According to Guy-Sheftall, how can college students best understand race and gender issues?

In a compelling essay describing her own revolutionary pedagogy, black feminist theorist and professor Bell Hooks invokes
Miss Annie Mae Moore, her favorite high school teacher who
embodies the idea of the teacher as subversive and whom
Hooks reverentially calls her "pedagogical guardian." Miss
Moore was "passionate in her teaching, confident that her work
in life was a pedagogy of liberation . . . one that would address
and confront our realities as black children growing up . . .
within a white supremacist culture. Miss Moore knew that if
we were to be fully self-realized, then her work, and the work
of all our progressive teachers, was not to teach us solely the
knowledge in books, but to teach us an oppositional world
view—different from that of our exploiters and oppressors, a
world view that would enable us to see ourselves not through
the lens of racism or racist stereotypes but one that would enable us to focus clearly and succinctly, to look at ourselves, at
the world around us, critically—analytically. . . ."

In his introduction to Paulo Freire's *Pedagogy of the Oppressed*,
which delineates the concept of "education as 'the practice of
freedom,'" Richard Shaull, Hooks reminds us, offers a concise
definition of revolutionary pedagogy to which Miss Moore
might have exclaimed "amen": "Education either functions as an
instrument . . . to facilitate the integration of the younger generation into the logic of the present system and bring about conformity to it, or it becomes the practice of freedom, the means
by which men and women deal critically and creatively with reality and discover how to participate in the transformation of
their world."

Identity and Alienation

My own teaching over the past twenty-one years has struggled
against two major problems in the academy. First, much of what
goes on reinforces the problematic and erroneous notion that the
normative human experience is white, Western, male, Christian,
middle-class, and heterosexual. A deep sense of alienation is
likely to plague students whose own identities are different from
what they've been led to believe is the norm by the texts they
read and the Eurocentric values they are encouraged to embrace.
Students who represent this dominant majority—and they're fast
becoming a minority in many educational settings—have difficulty seeing the world and their place in it differently.

Second, because students have not been encouraged to feel
connected to what they learn, it is no surprise that students feel
unattached to the world of real human beings and therefore dis-
inclined to want to change the conditions under which too many
people live. As I consider the academy and my own professional
career as a professor/activist, these questions intrude:

- Can the university be a site for radical political work?
- Can one be truly radical or subversive as a university professor within one of society's most hierarchical institutions?
- Can we teach in ways that don't reinforce structures of domination, racism, sexism, class exploitation?
- How can we use our power as teachers in ways that are not coercive, punitive, controlling?
- Can we undo the "miseducation" that most students have been subjected to by the time we get them in our college classes?
- Can we undo our own "miseducation," since most of us are also victims of patriarchal, racist, sexist ways of knowing and teaching?

In Defense of Multiculturalism

We have to defend multiculturalism, and I urge everybody to defend multiculturalism against the racist right wing in this country, and in the face of what is a still dominant monoculturalism throughout the academy. But let's remember always that at its intellectual and moral core, the left isn't multi-anything. Yes, the left should be diverse in its representation and its constituencies, but the left always has to be primarily an attempt to find in all the rich diversity of the human world, some point of moral unity that brings us all together.

Barbara Ehrenreich, *Democratic Left*, July/August 1991.

Are we willing to endure the anger and frustration—even hostility—of students when we challenge their most cherished ways of seeing the world and themselves? Christopher Columbus, for example, did not "discover" this country in 1492; he invaded indigenous peoples' territory, exploited the people, and began a process of decimation and even genocide, from a native American's perspective. I continue to be haunted by discussions following a video in which a black male was mistakenly perceived by the audience to be a thief when in fact it was a white male who had stolen. How radical it would be for us to teach in a way that all children would know who the real thieves have been throughout history! One gets a hint by visiting museums here and in Europe and seeing artifacts belonging to someone else. How refreshing it would be to know who the real victims have been throughout history and what has been stolen by whom! How radical it would be simply to tell the truth, which would begin with admissions about the annihilation of native peoples here in our own country! It now would be impossible for me to teach an American literature course as I experienced it as an undergraduate English major.

In my own classrooms on the first day of class, I am explicit about what I am attempting to do. I don't present myself as politically neutral, void of a value system and biases. I indicate that much of what I think and believe and value is not consistent with the dominant culture's belief system. I acknowledge that I don't know everything, that I am always in the process of growth and self-evaluation, that I'm not the same teacher that I was ten or fifteen years ago, and that I am not the ultimate authority in the class. . . .

Students Become Experts

Where one begins is very important. In my literature classes I begin where human civilization began—not with the *Iliad* and *Odyssey*, but with texts from ancient Africa. In our "Introduction to Women's Studies" class, I begin with the experiences not of middle-class Western white women but of many so-called Third World women who are still agricultural workers, food producers who work very hard and whose very survival depends on, for example, their ability to locate water and find firewood.

Learning by Doing

A second major pedagogical strategy is making central to my students' learning the idea that knowledge is also experiential. We learn not just by reading books and doing library research, but by getting outside the parameters of conventional classroom instruction. A major assignment in "Introduction to Women's Studies" requires students to choose a site where gender/race/class issues are played out; students visit their chosen sites not just as objective, unconnected participant observers, but as workers (volunteers, if you will). Then they must do a paper and oral report that synthesize their reading (about domestic violence, for example, if their site is a battered women's shelter), the insights they have gained on the site, and analyses of the concepts and theories they have learned from class and assigned readings about race/class/culture/gender.

I am convinced by our students and our observations that teaching in these new ways—being very conscious of what we teach and why we teach what we teach—which Bell Hooks has described as adopting a revolutionary feminist pedagogy, has the potential for real change in our students. The class I co-taught in 1990 with Johnnetta Cole was an unusual one for Spelman. The lone white student from Agnes Scott College (a white women's college in Atlanta) admitted on the first day that she was very nervous and had never experienced being a minority in a classroom; two students from Morehouse College (a historically black, all-male college in Atlanta) also were nervous and huddled close to Johnnetta and me on the first day.

Within three weeks one of the men (who died tragically in a fraternity hazing incident during the semester of the class) was talking openly about his new ideas about being a good father, especially in terms of raising a daughter, which he admitted he preferred to a son. His friend talked honestly about violent behavior in his relations with his sister and why it was necessary to reconceptualize notions of masculinity. He chose as his site Men Against Violence, a self-help group for men attempting to understand domestic violence. The Agnes Scott student spent a semester interning in Washington, D.C., at a nonprofit minority organization and wrote to us after the governor's election in Georgia that her grandfather had voted for Andy Young; this astounded her, she explained, because he had been the person who, in his role as jailer, locked up Martin Luther King, Jr., during his early jail experience in Georgia.

I am convinced that what happened in that class is suitable—even critical—for students everywhere. They left this Afrocentric, women-centered class knowing more about themselves and the world in which they live but also feeling connected to the people about whom they studied and among whom they worked.

Power to Change

We have tremendous power, as teachers, to influence the direction in which this country will move as we approach the twenty-first century. White students need an inclusive curriculum and "oppositional" pedagogy as much as "ethnic" students do. We must not lose sight of the ultimate purpose of "revolutionary" pedagogies: educating students who will work to make this planet a better place for all humans to live. We must prepare students for a world in which non-Western women of color are the world's majority. We must not teach only "the canon," which consistently has excluded or devalued the experiences of people of color and women. We must discontinue the harmful practice of educating many students away from themselves. We must disrupt the practice of "miseducating" the majority of our students. Sensitivity to issues of race, class, ethnicity, and gender would begin the process of cultural literacy and rid us of the ignorance in which we have basked so blissfully and arrogantly for decades. Our collective human survival—and the freedom and dignity in which some of us can live—will depend, in large part, on our commitment as educators to helping eradicate racism, sexism, and other forms of domination.

"It is condescending and deeply anti-democratic when intellectuals consign blacks, or women, or ethnics . . . to confining categories."

Multiculturalism Harms Higher Education

George F. Will

Some educators blame Western, white civilization for the historic oppression of women and minorities. To remedy this oppression, they propose establishing multicultural courses to expose students to a variety of cultures, primarily through the works of writers and artists from different ethnic backgrounds. In the following viewpoint, George Will opposes such courses. He maintains that stressing the importance of different ethnic groups threatens America's national unity. Will defends the contributions of Western civilization and believes that Western culture should not be blamed for the oppression and exploitation of minorities and women. Will, the author of *Political Essays*, is a well-known syndicated columnist and news commentator.

As you read, consider the following questions:

1. According to Will, why is it wrong to study artistic works as part of social science?
2. Why does the author discount the idea that a minority student can be taught only by members of his or her own group?
3. Why does Will argue against becoming too sensitive to the feelings of other groups?

George F. Will, "Commencement at Duke." Reprinted, with permission, from *The American Scholar*, vol. 60, no. 4, Autumn 1991. Copyright © 1991 by George F. Will.

Abraham Lincoln said: "A house divided against itself cannot stand." It is equally true that a society unaware of itself—with no consensus about its premises and purposes—cannot endure. In Lincoln's day, a collision of two clear and diametrically opposed premises nearly proved fatal to America. Today there is a potentially fatal idea in circulation. It is the idea that there should not be in this pluralistic society any core culture passed on from generation to generation.

To those who say we are threatened by a suffocating "hegemony" of Western civilization's classic works, I say: If only that were the problem! The real danger is not cultural hegemony but cultural amnesia, and the concomitant Balkanization of the life of the mind.

I just used a verb derived from a proper noun, the verb "to Balkanize." That verb was born of the sorrows of the Balkan nations in that unhappy European region where, it was said, more history was produced than could be consumed locally. The First World War, and hence most of this century's horrors, began in the Balkans, where fragmentation was contagious.

Intellectual Fragmentation

Today there is ample evidence of the Balkanization of America's intellectual life. This Balkanization begins with the assertion that any syllabus composed of traditional classics of Western civilization will "underrepresent" certain groups— racial, sexual, ethnic, or class-based groups.

Well, are the great works of Western civilization primarily products of social elites? Yes, of course—for many reasons, including the fact that these works come to us from centuries where literacy itself was an elite attainment. But it is fallacious to argue that therefore these works perpetuate an oppressiveness that allegedly is the essence of Western civilization.

Some people who fancy themselves intellectually emancipated—who think themselves liberated from what they call a stultifying cultural inheritance—are, in fact, far from free. They actually reside in "the clean, well-lit prison of one idea." Today's imprisoning idea is philosophically primitive and empirically insupportable. It is that any humanities text merely "reflects" its social context and thus should be read as a political document.

Too often the meaning of the crucial word *reflects* disappears in a mist of imprecision. Usually the assertion that a text "reflects" its context is either trivially true or flagrantly false. It is trivially true if it means only that the text, like its author, stands in some relation to the setting in which the author wrote. But it is false if it means that any text should be construed politically, with politics understood crudely as mere power relations of domination and subordination in the era in which the author wrote.

Such thinking causes the study of literature to become a subdivision of political history and to be studied as sociology. This reduction of the arts to social sciences is reverse alchemy—turning gold into lead.

Signe Wilkinson. Reprinted with permission.

This is the result of the imprisoning idea that the nature of everything, from intellectual works to political acts, is determined by race, gender, and class. Alas, any single idea purporting to be a universal explanation, a comprehensive simplifier of social complexities, requires its adherents to be simple, and makes them so. Today's dubious idea also makes its adherents condescending—and worse.

Confining Categories

It is condescending and deeply anti-democratic when intellectuals consign blacks, or women, or ethnics, or the working class, or whomever, to confining categories, asserting that they can be fully understood as mere "reflections" of their race, sex, or class, and that members of those groups have the limited "consciousness" supposedly characteristic of those groups.

The root of this mischief is the assertion—the semantic fiat—that everything is political. If the word *political* is promiscuously used to describe any choice or judgment involving values, then *political* becomes a classification that does not classify. One cannot say it too emphatically: Not all value judgments are political judgments.

It is not a political judgment that certain works have contributed mightily to the making of our civilization and hence must be known if we are to know ourselves. It is not a political judgment that certain books have demonstrated the power, down the generations, to instruct us in history, irony, wit, tragedy, pathos, and delight. Education is an apprenticeship in those civilized—and civilizing—passions and understandings, and not all texts are equal as teachers.

We must husband our highest praise, as Karl Marx did. Marx celebrated the art of Greek antiquity, not because it had a proletarian origin—it did not—but because it met—indeed, set—standards that transcend any particular class or culture.

Valuing Other Cultures

The legacy of Western thought is a mind capable of comprehending and valuing other cultures while avoiding the nihilism that says all cultures are incommensurable and hence all of equal merit.

Sensible people rejoice at any chance to study another culture's Rousseau or Cervantes or Dickens. But education is too serious a matter to become a game of let's pretend, a ritual of pretending that enduring works of the humanities are evenly distributed throughout the world's cultures.

We want to be able imaginatively to enter, and to empathize with, other cultures. But we must live in our own. And our own is being injured by some academic developments that impede understanding.

We see on campuses the baneful habit of joining what Robert Frost would have considered too many gangs—and the wrong sorts of gangs. We see the spread of intellectual gerrymandering, carving up curricula into protected enclaves for racial, sexual, and ethnic groups. Often this is done on the condescending premise that members of these groups have only a watery individuality—that they have only derivative identities, derived from membership in victim groups.

The premise of this analysis is that Western civilization has a disreputable record consisting primarily of oppression and exploitation—that Western civilization has been prolific only at producing victims.

Victim Groups

That idea leads, in turn, to the patronizing notion that members of a victim group are disadvantaged unless taught by members of their own group and unless they study works by group members. Otherwise (or so the theory goes) members of the group will lack self-esteem, an attribute which is presumed to be a precondition for, not a result of, achievement. This sort of thinking promotes envy, resentment, suspicion, aggression, self-absorption, and, ultimately, separatism.

It is a crashing non sequitur to say that because America is becoming more diverse, university curricula must be Balkanized. Actually, America's increasing diversity increases the importance of universities as transmitters of the cultural legacy that defines and preserves national unity.

Some policies advanced today in the name of "diversity" might better be associated with a less agreeable word—"fragmentation."

Some policies instituted in the name of "multiculturalism" are not celebrations of the pluralism from which American unity is woven. Some of these policies are capitulations: they involve withdrawal from the challenge of finding, and teaching, common ground on which Americans can stand together—not the little patches of fenced-off turf for irritable groups, but the common ground of citizenship in the nation, which is one of the good gangs of which Robert Frost spoke.

Many of today's Balkanizing policies are products of a desire to show sensitivity to the feelings of particular groups. Sensitivity is a good thing. But, remember: the four most important words in political discourse are "up to a point." Armies, police, taxation, even freedom and equality are good only "up to a point."

In the context of today's campus disputes, sensitivity, too, is good—up to a point. What is not good is the notion that sensitivity about one's own opinions generates for oneself an entitlement not to be disagreed with or otherwise offended. Or that the only way to prove one's sensitivity is by subscribing to a particular political agenda.

True Radicalism

Some critics complain that a traditional curriculum built around the canon of great works of the Western mind necessarily reinforces authority and docile acceptance of existing arrangements. But these critics, some of whom fancy themselves radicals, could take lessons in real radicalism from many of the writers of those classic works.

Virtually every subsequent radicalism was anticipated in Plato's inquiries. No person more radical than Machiavelli ever put pen to paper—Machiavelli, whose *The Prince* became the handbook for modern masterless men and women who are obedient only to rules they write for themselves.

Four years after *The Prince* was written, Martin Luther nailed his 95 theses to a church door, asserting the primacy of private judgment—conscience. There is a golden thread of magnificent radicalism connecting that white German theologian to his namesake, the black American minister—a thread connecting Luther's 95 theses and Dr. King's "Letter from Birmingham Jail.". . .

273

There is today a warmhearted idea that every academic activity must contribute to the reforming of society by assuaging this or that group's grievances. This idea leads to fracturing the community into antagonistic groups; to the drowning of individuality in group thinking; to the competitive cultivation of group grievances; to the subordination of education to political indoctrination. In short, some good intentions produce bad educations. . . .

On March 4, 1861, with the fabric of America unraveling around him, Lincoln delivered his First Inaugural Address. In one of the most felicitous phrases in American rhetoric, he held out the hope that Americans would be summoned back to friendship by "the mystic chords of memory."

Prudent Pessimism

It is always thus: America is always dependent on its collective memory. And universities are keepers of that flame. Arguments about university curricula are not narrowly, crudely political, but they are, in an important sense, constitutional arguments: they concern how the American mind shall be constituted. And in a democracy, mind is all that ultimately matters, because everything rests on the shiftable sands of opinion.

That is why democracies are in permanent danger; and why it is prudent to be pessimistic—not fatalistic, not resigned to the worst, but pessimistic, alert to the dangers.

I subscribe to the "Ohio in 1895 Theory of History," so named, by me, for the obscure but illuminating fact that in 1895, in Ohio, there were just two automobiles—and they collided. The moral of the human story is that things go wrong more often than they go right because there are so many more ways to go wrong. Truths increase arithmetically; but errors increase exponentially. Most new ideas are false; hence most "improvements" make matters worse. That is why wise people are wary of intellectual fads and are respectful of the received greatness which, in academic context, is called the canon.

a critical thinking activity

Understanding Words in Context

Readers occasionally come across words they do not recognize. And frequently, because they do not know a word or words, they will not fully understand the passage being read. Obviously, the reader can look up an unfamiliar word in a dictionary. By carefully examining the word in the context in which it is used, however, the word's meaning can often be determined. A careful reader may find clues to the meaning of the word in surrounding words, ideas, and attitudes.

Below are excerpts from the viewpoints in this chapter. In each excerpt, one of the words is printed in italics. Try to determine the meaning of each word by reading the excerpt. Under each excerpt you will find four definitions for the italicized word. Choose the one that is closest to your understanding of the word.

Finally, use a dictionary to see how well you have understood the words in context. It will be helpful to discuss with others the clues that helped you decide on each word's meaning.

1. For years campus radicals have been attacking Western culture. Their greatest success came when Stanford University *EXPUNGED* from its curriculum its traditional course in Western civilization.

   EXPUNGED means:

   a) derived   c) adapted
   b) brought   d) deleted

2. Christopher Columbus did not "discover" this country in 1492. He was a foreigner who invaded *INDIGENOUS* peoples' territory and began a process of decimation and genocide.

   INDIGENOUS means:

   a) wealthy   c) fierce
   b) native   d) various

3. There is a warmhearted idea that every academic activity must contribute to harmony on college campuses by *AS-SUAGING* this or that group's grievances.

ASSUAGING means:

a) suffering   c) delaying
b) ignoring   d) easing

4. For decades professors had to obey their superiors. Thus, the fight for tenure was less a fight for the right to express unpopular opinions than against an *IMPERIOUS* and autocratic administration.

IMPERIOUS means:

a) domineering   c) angry
b) sly   d) original

5. Racial, sexual, and ethnic groups tend to keep to themselves. They should not divide themselves up into their own protected *ENCLAVES*.

ENCLAVES means:

a) endangered species   c) separated units
b) prideful families   d) radical activists

6. Racism causes much unrest on college campuses. It is up to all students to find, expose, and *EXTIRPATE* it.

EXTIRPATE means:

a) praise   c) question
b) destroy   d) ignore

7. The goal of diversity is a mixed campus population *CON-DUCIVE* to promoting understanding of other customs and peoples.

CONDUCIVE means:

a) reduced   c) opposed
b) contributing   d) relative

8. Faced with the difficulties of college life, many minority students seek support and *SOLACE* from others like them.

SOLACE means:

a) money   c) service
b) ideas   d) comfort

Periodical Bibliography

The following articles have been selected to supplement the diverse views presented in this chapter.

William J. Bennett — "Why Western Civilization?" *National Forum: The Phi Kappa Phi Journal*, Summer 1989. Available from PO Box 16000, Louisiana State University, Baton Rouge, LA 70893.

John Bunzel — "Alienation and the Black College Dropout," *The Wall Street Journal*, April 3, 1991.

Helen Cordes — "Oh No! I'm PC!" *Utne Reader*, July/August 1991.

Dinesh D'Souza — "Sins of Admission," *The New Republic*, February 18, 1991.

Robert Drinan — "Should Hate Speech on Campus Be Punished?" *America*, September 21, 1991.

Barbara Ehrenreich — "The Challenge for the Left," *Democratic Left*, July/August 1991. Available from Democratic Socialists of America, 15 Dutch St., New York, NY 10038.

Henry Louis Gates Jr. and Donald Kagan — "Whose Culture Is It, Anyway?" *The New York Times*, May 4, 1991.

Harvey C. Mansfield Jr. — "Political Correctness and the Suicide of the Intellect," *The Heritage Lectures*, No. 337. Available from The Heritage Foundation, 214 Massachusetts Ave. NE, Washington, DC 20002-4999.

Elizabeth Martinez — "Willie Horton's Gonna Get Your Alma Mater," *Z Magazine*, July/August 1991.

The New Republic — Special issue on race on campus, February 18, 1991.

Newsweek — "Taking Offense," Special section on political correctness, December 24, 1990.

E. San Juan Jr. — "Theorizing Anti-Racist Struggle," *Against the Current*, September/October 1991.

Catharine R. Stimpson — "Big Man on Campus," *The Nation*, September 30, 1991.

John Taylor — "Thought Police on Campus," *Reader's Digest*, May 1991.

Jon Wiener — "Free Speech for Campus Bigots?" *The Nation*, February 26, 1990.

Organizations to Contact

The editors have compiled the following list of organizations that are concerned with the issues debated in this book. All have publications or information available for interested readers. The descriptions are derived from materials provided by the organizations. This list was compiled upon the date of publication. Names and phone numbers of organizations are subject to change.

American Association of University Professors (AAUP)
1012 Fourteenth St., Suite 500
Washington, DC 20005
(202) 737-5900

The AAUP is an organization of university teachers and research scholars that works to promote higher education and research. It supports the tenure system and advocates affirmative action and other measures that combat discrimination in universities. AAUP publishes the bimonthly *Academe: Bulletin of the AAUP.*

American Federation of Teachers (AFT)
555 New Jersey Ave. NW
Washington, DC 20001
(202) 879-4400

The federation is one of the nation's largest teachers' unions. AFT supports a national system of teacher certification and opposes merit pay plans. It also advocates parental school choice for public schools. AFT publishes the quarterly magazine *American Educator.*

Americans for Religious Liberty (ARL)
PO Box 6656
Silver Spring, MD 20916
(301) 598-2447

ARL is a public interest organization that defends the separation of church and state. It opposes formal prayer and religious clubs in public schools. ARL publishes the quarterly *Voice of Reason* newsletter and the book *Religion and Public Education: Common Sense and the Law.*

Association for Supervision and Curriculum Development (ASCD)
1250 N. Pitt St.
Alexandria, VA 22314
(703) 549-9110

ASCD is an organization of school supervisors, curriculum coordinators, teachers, and parents who work to improve supervision and curriculum in public education. The association advocates parental school choice and a curriculum that teaches about religion. ASCD publishes the monthly magazines *Educational Leadership* and *ASCD Update,* and the pamphlets *Religion in the Public School Curriculum* and *The Equal Access Act and the Public Schools.*

The College Board
45 Columbus Ave.
New York, NY 10023
(212) 713-8000

The board, comprised of public and private secondary schools and universities, provides research and services for prospective college students. It designs and administers several standardized tests, such as the SAT, to determine the placement levels of incoming and continuing college students. Publications include the *College Board News* and *College Board Review* quarterlies.

Eagle Forum

PO Box 618
Alton, Il 62002
(618) 462-5415

Eagle Forum is dedicated to preserving traditional family values. It opposes centralized government control of public education, including measures such as national teacher certification. The forum publishes the monthly *Education Reporter* and *The Phyllis Schlafly Report*.

The Heritage Foundation

214 Massachusetts Ave. NE
Washington, DC 20002
(202) 546-4400

The foundation is a conservative public policy research institute that advocates parental school choice as a means of improving public education. It publishes the quarterly *Policy Review* and other papers and monographs on such issues as political correctness and discrimination in universities.

Home School Legal Defense Association

PO Box 159
Paeonian Springs, VA 22129
(703) 882-3838

The association believes that every family has the right to educate their children at home, rather than enrolling them in public or private schools. It provides legal assistance to home-schooling families challenged by state government or local school boards. It publishes *The Home School Court Report* quarterly newsletter and brochures on home education.

National Association for Bilingual Education (NABE)

Union Center Plaza
810 First St. NE
Washington, DC 20002

NABE consists of educators, administrators, and laypeople who advocate bilingual education programs. It works to increase public understanding of the importance of learning different languages and learning about cultures. NABE publishes the triannual *Journal* and a newsletter eight times per year.

National Association for Year-Round Education

PO Box 711386
San Diego, CA 92171-1386
(619) 276-5296

The association consists of parents and school representatives opposed to the traditional school calendar. It believes that year-round education, with both a reorganized and an extended school year, will benefit students and schools. The association publishes the quarterly *Year-Rounder* newsletter.

National Association of Scholars (NAS)
575 Ewing St.
Princeton, NJ 08540
(609) 683-7878

NAS is an organization of professors, college administrators, and graduate students committed to academic freedom and the free exchange of ideas in universities. It believes in a curriculum that stresses the achievements of Western civilization and it opposes restrictive speech codes, preferences for faculty and students based on race or gender, and an overemphasis on multiculturalism. NAS publishes the quarterly *Academic Questions.*

National Center for Fair and Open Testing (FairTest)
342 Broadway
Cambridge, MA 02139-1802
(617) 497-2224

FairTest is an advocacy group that opposes the use of standardized tests. It works to end the abuses, misuses, and flaws of standardized testing and to ensure that student evaluations are accurate, relevant, and educationally sound. FairTest publishes the quarterly *FairTest Examiner.*

National Committee for Citizens in Education (NCCE)
900 Second St. NE, Suite 8
Washington, DC 20002
(202) 408-0447

NCCE is dedicated to improving the quality of public schools through increased public involvement. The committee believes that public schools are the best way to educate children, and it works to make parents and the general public more involved in education. NCCE publishes the *Network* periodical five times per year, handbooks, and other resources on educational issues.

National Council for Black Studies (NCBS)
Ohio State University
1800 Cannon Dr., 1130 Lincoln Tower
Columbus, OH 43210
(614) 292-1035
The council consists of faculty members, students, and institutions united to promote and strengthen academic programs in black studies. It strongly supports an Afrocentric curriculum for black students. NCBS publishes the quarterly *Voice of Black Studies.*

National Legal Foundation (NLF)
PO Box 64845
Virginia Beach, VA 23464
(804) 424-4242

The NLF is a legal advocacy firm dedicated to preserving religious freedoms and constitutional rights. The foundation defends the rights of students to form religious clubs in public schools. It also supports invocations and benedictions at public school graduation ceremonies. NLF publishes *The National Legal Foundation Minuteman* quarterly newsletter.

Bibliography of Books

Douglas A. Archbald — *Beyond Standardized Testing: Assessing Authentic Academic Achievement in the Secondary School*. Reston, VA: National Association of Secondary School Principals, 1988.

Molefi Kete Asante — *Afrocentricity*. Trenton, NJ: Africa World Press, 1988.

Josie G. Bain and Joan L. Herman — *Making Schools Work for Underachieving Minority Students*. New York: Greenwood Press, 1990.

Jacques Barzun — *Begin Here: The Forgotten Conditions of Teaching and Learning*. Chicago: University of Chicago Press, 1991.

William J. Bennett — *Our Children and Our Country: Improving America's Schools and Affirming the Common Culture*. New York: Simon & Schuster, 1988.

David Boaz, ed. — *Liberating Schools: Education in the Inner City*. Washington, DC: Cato Institute, 1991.

Deborah P. Britzman — *Practice Makes Perfect: A Critical Study of Learning to Teach*. Albany, NY: State University of New York Press, 1991.

Marvin Cetron and Margaret Gayle — *Educational Renaissance: Our Schools at the Turn of the Twenty-First Century*. New York: St. Martin's Press, 1991.

John E. Chubb and Terry M. Moe — *Politics, Markets, and America's Schools*. Washington, DC: The Brookings Institution, 1990.

Joseph L. DeVitis and Peter A. Sola, eds. — *Building Bridges for Educational Reform: New Approaches to Teacher Education*. Ames: Iowa State University Press, 1989.

Susan Dichter — *Teachers: Straight Talk from the Trenches*. Los Angeles: Lowell House, 1989.

Edd Doerr and Albert J. Menendez — *Religion and Public Education: Common Sense and the Law*. Long Beach, CA: Centerline Press, 1991.

Dinesh D'Souza — *Illiberal Education: The Politics of Race and Sex on Campus*. New York: The Free Press, 1991.

Ruth B. Eckstrom, Margaret E. Goertz, and Donald A. Rock — *Education and American Youth: The Impact of the High School Experience*. New York: Falmer Press, 1988.

Edwin William Farrell — *Hanging In and Dropping Out: Voices of At-Risk High School Students*. New York: Teachers College Press, 1990.

Paula S. Fass — *Outside In: Minorities and the Transformation of American Education*. New York: Oxford University Press, 1989.

Lynda Beck Fenwick — *Should the Children Pray?* Waco, TX: Baylor University Press, 1989.

Chester E. Finn Jr. — *We Must Take Charge: Our Schools and Our Future*. New York: The Free Press, 1991.

Edward B. Fiske — *Smart Schools, Smart Kids: Why Do Some Schools Work?* New York: Simon & Schuster, 1991.

Samuel G. Freedman — *Small Victories: The Real World of a Teacher, Her Students, and Their High School*. New York: Harper & Row, 1990.

John I. Goodlad	*Teachers for Our Nation's Schools.* San Francisco: Jossey-Bass, 1990.
Roger Kimball	*Tenured Radicals: How Politics Has Corrupted Our Higher Education.* New York: Harper & Row, 1990.
David W. Kirkpatrick	*Choice in Schooling: A Case for Tuition Vouchers.* Chicago: Loyola University Press, 1990.
Jonathan Kozol	*Savage Inequalities: Children in America's Schools.* New York: Crown Publishers, 1991.
Myron Lieberman	*Privatization and Educational Choice.* New York: St. Martin's Press, 1989.
Daniel Patrick Liston and Kenneth M. Zeichner	*Teacher Education and the Social Conditions of Schooling.* New York: Routledge, 1991.
Kofi Lomotey, ed.	*Going to School: The African-American Experience.* Albany, NY: State University of New York Press, 1990.
Karen Seashore Louis and Matthew B. Miles	*Improving the Urban High School: What Works and Why.* New York: Teachers College Press, 1990.
Amado M. Padilla, Halford H. Fairchild, and Concepcion M. Valadez, eds.	*Bilingual Education: Issues and Strategies.* Newbury Park, CA: Sage Publications, 1990.
Carol S. Pearson, Donna L. Shavlik, and Judith G. Touchton, eds.	*Educating the Majority: Women Challenge Tradition in Higher Education.* New York: American Council on Education, 1989.
Joseph G. Ponterotto, Diane E. Lewis, and Robin Bullington, eds.	*Affirmative Action on Campus.* San Francisco: Jossey-Bass, 1990.
Rosalie Pedalino Porter	*Forked Tongue: The Politics of Bilingual Education.* New York: Basic Books, 1990.
Quality Education for Minorities Project	*Education That Works: An Action Plan for the Education of Minorities.* Cambridge, MA: Massachusetts Institute of Technology, 1990.
Diane Ravitch, ed.	*The American Reader.* New York: HarperCollins, 1990.
Sally D. Reed	*A Parent's Survival Guide to the Public Schools.* Alexandria, VA: National Council for Better Education, 1991.
Pedro Reyes, ed.	*Teachers and Their Workplace: Commitment, Performance, and Productivity.* Newbury Park, CA: Sage Publications, 1990.
Henry Rosovsky	*The University: An Owner's Manual.* New York: W.W. Norton, 1990.
Christine E. Sleeter, ed.	*Empowerment Through Multicultural Education.* Albany, NY: State University Press of New York, 1991.
Page Smith	*Killing the Spirit: Higher Education in America.* New York: Viking Penguin Books, 1990.
Charles J. Sykes	*The Hollow Men: Politics and Corruption in Higher Education.* Washington, DC: Regnery Gateway, 1990.
Jane van Galen and Mary Anne Pitman	*Home Schooling: Political, Historical, and Pedagogical Perspectives.* Norwood, NJ: Ablex Publishing, 1991.
John W. Whitehead	*The Rights of Religious Persons in Public Education.* Wheaton, IL: Crossway Books, 1991.

Index

285

public schools
compulsory schooling, 18, 128, 130, 225
improved by
extensive reform, 17-24
con, 25-31
government voucher plan, 115-116, 128
con, 121-122, 124, 125, 126
longer school year, 32-37
con, 38-41
multiculturalism, 148-149
con, 154-155
parental choice, 103, 104, 105-106, 134, 137-138
con, 109, 111
standardized-test elimination, 42-49
con, 50-56
religion in, 130, 131
Bible reading, 128-130
should be allowed, 191
con, 200, 202, 211, 212, 215
prayer should be allowed, 204-209
con, 210-215
should be studied, 189-196
con, 197-203
student religious clubs
should be allowed, 216-222
con, 223-228

racial discrimination, 126
racial segregation, 103, 116, 168
racism, 165-166, 263, 266
Raspberry, William, 68
Reagan, Ronald
school prayer and, 212-213
school vouchers and, 103, 114, 115
school year and, 33
Reed, Sally D., 52, 74, 113
Reich, Robert, 40
religion
in public schools
Bible reading, 128-130
should be allowed, 191
con, 200, 202, 211, 212, 215
prayer should be allowed, 204-209
con, 210-215
should be studied, 189-196
con, 197-203
student religious clubs
should be allowed, 216-22
con, 223-228
religious schools
parental choice plan should
include, 103, 105, 116, 127-132
con, 111, 123, 126, 133-138
Roosevelt, Theodore, 238

Rosovsky, Henry, 234, 239

salaries
of public school teachers, 34, 40, 79, 91-92
of university professors, 238
Schlesinger, Arthur, Jr., 151
Scholastic Aptitude Test (SAT), 27, 28-29, 30, 84, 110, 206
school reform
is badly needed, 17-24
con, 25-31
school year, 31
should be longer, 32-37
con, 38-41
Schuster, Jack, 246-247
science, 27-28, 31, 110
segregation, 103, 116, 168
Selden, Ramsay, 50
Shanker, Albert, 49
Shaw, George Bernard, 202
Skolrood, Robert K., 216
slavery, 160-161, 162, 253
Smith, Page, 241
Sobol, Thomas, 148
social studies, 193
multiculturalism benefits, 145-146, 147, 148
con, 154, 165
Soviet Union, 31, 153
states
multicultural curriculum and, 150
parental choice programs and, 104-105, 107, 123, 125
standardized testing and, 47, 55-56
student religious clubs
should be allowed, 216-222
con, 223-228

taxes
educational tax credits, 128
voucher plans and, 136, 138
teachers, 18
Afrocentrism and, 159-160, 161, 162, 166
Bible-reading statutes and, 128
bilingual education and, 178, 179-180
improved by
extended education requirements, 82-88
con, 89-96
longer school year, 34
con, 39
merit pay, 72-77
con, 70, 78-81
national certification, 62-67
con, 68-71